Illuminate
Publishing

WJEC
AS Law

Study and
Revision Guide

Louisa Walters
Karen Phillips
Sara Davies

First published in 2011 by Illuminate Publishing Ltd, P.O. Box 1160,
Cheltenham, Gloucestershire GL50 9RW

Updated Edition first printed 2014

Orders: Please visit www.illuminatepublishing.com
or email sales@illuminatepublishing.com

British Library Cataloguing in Publication Data

A catalogue record for this book is available from the British Library

ISBN 978-1-908682-36-9

Printed by 4edge Ltd., Hockley, Essex

1.16

The publisher's policy is to use papers that are natural, renewable and recyclable
products made from wood grown in sustainable forests. The logging and manufacturing
processes are expected to conform to the environmental regulations of the country of
origin.

This material has been endorsed by WJEC and offers high quality support for the
delivery of WJEC qualifications. While this material has been through a WJEC quality
assurance process, all responsibility for the content remains with the publisher.

WJEC examination questions are reproduced by permission from WJEC

Editor: Geoff Tuttle

Design and layout: Nigel Harriss

Permissions

All images copyright Shutterstock: individual credits as follows; p9 Vivid Pixels;
p12 ER_09; p17 Robert2301; p25 Csdesign; p26 etc PILart; p33 Evlakhov Valeriy;
p41, Denis Cristo; p51 maigi; p57 Virginija Valatkiene; p63 phil Holmes;
p67 Patrick Hermans; p72 nubephoto; p76 zimmytws; p81 ungureanu;
p82 Daniel hughes; p85 Axel Wolf.

Acknowledgements

The authors and publisher would like to thank:

Dr Pauline O'Hara for her thorough review of the book and expert insights and
observations.

Contents

Knowledge and Understanding

Exam Practice and Technique

Foreword

The updated version of this revision book is both timely and also needed. It is written by experienced teaching practitioners who have had a wealth of experience in teaching A and AS Level Law. The authors have been involved in the creation of educational resources in Law involving a variety of media including DVD.

As subject specialists, the authors demonstrate a deep knowledge of the specification on both practical and expository levels, whilst demonstrating an appreciation of the wider policy context of the operation of Law and more generally the Legal 'System' of England and Wales. The book comes alive and speaks to the reader by engaging with actual student answers, which are then mapped against examiner commentaries.

The book presents the material in an attractive and accessible way. It does not avoid the challenges posed by the specifications. I have no doubt that the book will assist teachers and students and am pleased to see it go into a revised edition.

Professor Iwan Davies
Pro-Vice-Chancellor and Hodge Chair in Law

How to use this book

This Study and Revision Guide is designed to guide you through the WJEC AS level Law specification and lead you to success in the subject. It has been written by a team of practising teachers and examiners with considerable experience of the WJEC Law specification who have pinpointed exactly what is required of candidates in terms of content to achieve the highest marks. In addition, common errors have been identified and support and advice given in order that these can be avoided, which should lead to success in your AS level examination.

The Guide covers both AS examination papers:

LA1 – Understanding Legal Values, Structures and Processes

LA2 – Understanding Legal Reasoning, Personnel and Methods

The book is split into two sections.

Knowledge and Understanding

The **first section** of the book covers the knowledge content that is required for each topic within the AS specification. This is written in a concise way and extension work is signposted, in order that you can get the best out of your revision.

Key terminology

Definitions of Key Terms are provided in an at-a-glance margin feature. All of these terms are key to the specification and should be learned.

Important features

Throughout the book, important cases are highlighted and underlined and important legal terms are emboldened for ease of reference at a glance.

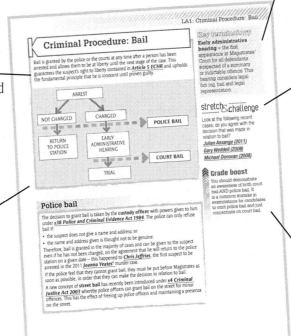

Stretch and challenge

This feature gives you the opportunity to research the topic further and gives you advice on wider reading. These are usually current affairs or areas under reform; knowledge of which will really impress the examiner.

Easy to use diagrams are used throughout to summarise information and make revision easier.

Grade boost

This feature gives you an insight into the examiners' minds and provides advice on things you should include to achieve the higher marks.

Exam Practice and Technique

This is the **second section** of the book and provides you with an opportunity for your own examination practice and an insight into the quality of answer that is expected to achieve a high grade.

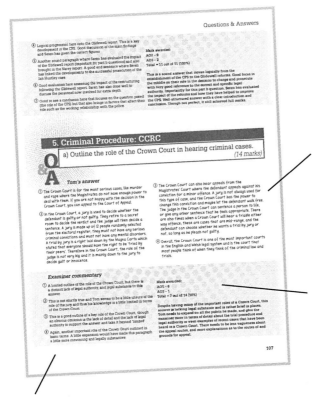

Answer

This section will outline higher and lower scoring answers. The most common examination questions are covered.

Marks

The marks that would have been given to this candidate are split into the Assessment Objectives, so you can see how the exam answer has been marked.

Examiner commentary

This is a useful section to get an insight into how exams are marked – detailed information is given as to how the candidate has achieved their marks and key tips on how these answers can be improved.

Knowledge and Understanding

LA1: Understanding Legal Values, Structures and Processes

LA1 focuses on developing students' understanding of Legal Structures and Processes. The unit explores the historical development of the English and Welsh Legal System along with understanding how equity came to supplement the common law to provide a wider range of remedies. It examines some of the key principles underpinning the legal system such as AV, Dicey's Rule of Law, and the conflict between law and morality. It looks at the importance of the EU on the legal system of England and Wales focusing on the key institutions that govern and run the European Union. LA1 also covers civil and criminal procedure, looking at court hierarchy, CPS, bail and appeal procedures along with exploring important reforms such as the Woolf reforms. Finally, the importance of providing legal funding to allow individuals a fair defence or to take their civil claim to court is considered. Throughout the whole AS level, the importance of human rights and the impact of the Human Rights Act 1998 are emphasised.

Revision checklist

Tick column 1 when you have completed brief revision notes.
Tick column 2 when you think you have a good grasp of the topic.
Tick column 3 during final revision when you feel you have mastery of the topic.

			1	2	3
Law and Morality	p9	Difference between law and morality			
	p9	Role of morality in the law			
	p10	Hart Devlin debate			
The Rule of Law	p11	Principles of the Rule of Law			
	p12	Arguments for and against a UK written constitution			
Juries	p13	Role of juries			
	p14	Qualification and selection of jurors			
	p15	Advantages of juries			
	p15	Disadvantages of juries			
	p16	Are juries representative of society?			
Common Law and Equity	p18	History of common law and equity			
	p19	Equitable maxims			
	p20	Equitable remedies			
Criminal Procedure	p21	Summary offences			
	p22	Triable either way offences			
	p22	Indictable offences			
Criminal Procedure: Bail	p23	Police bail			
	p24	Court bail			
	p24	Conditional bail			
	p25	Restrictions on bail			
	p26	Advantages and disadvantages of bail			

Law and Morality

Difference between law and morality

Laws and morals are normative, they state what ought to be done. Many types of behaviour offend both legal and moral rules, e.g. murder. Many areas of law raise moral issues – in Parliament MPs are allowed to vote according to their conscience, rather than their party, e.g. abortion, embryo research.

Some areas of law have obvious moral implications:

- Tort law – **Donoghue v Stevenson (1932)** Lord Aitken, 'do no harm to your neighbour' (Bible, 'love thy neighbour').
- Contract law – based on the principle that promises should be kept.

Some things may be considered immoral but they are not illegal, e.g. telling lies. Do moral values change over time, e.g. attitudes to homosexuality? Laws often lag behind moral changes, e.g. **R v R (1991)** – it took until 1991 to change the laws on rape within marriage.

Law and morality are closely linked, but there are differences: in **Re A (Children) (Conjoined Twins: Surgical Separation) (2001)** – separation of Siamese twins, the Court of Appeal said it was: 'Not a court of morals but a court of law and our decisions have to be taken from a solid base of legal principle'.

Role of morality in the law

Natural law theorists

Natural law theorists state there is a higher law and laws should be based on this moral code and those which are not cannot really be called laws at all. Professor Fuller in *The Morality of the Law* – said a legal system should have eight key requirements, in the absence of any of these, then it is not a legal system:

1. Generality – rules, not *ad hoc* decisions
2. Promulgation – rules should be made known to all
3. Non-retroactivity – rules should not work backwards in time
4. Clarity – laws should be clear
5. Consistency – laws should not conflict with one another
6. Realism – laws should not be impossible to comply with
7. Constancy – laws should not change frequently so as to cause confusion
8. Congruence – the administration of the rules should coincide with the information known to the public about the rules.

Utilitarianism – John Stuart Mill (1859)

Individuals should be free to choose their own conduct (as long as no harm to others) and not have morality forced upon them by society. Evaluation: just because someone's actions do not cause direct harm does not mean no harm at all, e.g. pornography. Who is another? E.g. abortion, embryo research – harming an unborn child – is this harming another person?

Grade boost

In this topic you'll be able to improve your marks if you can demonstrate a good knowledge of relevant cases. Answers to exam questions with little or no legal authority generally result in lower marks.

Some recent examples that question the relationship between law and morality include:

- *Appointment of female bishops* – in what other 'business' would the Chief Executive or Managing Director be prevented from being a woman?
- *Termination of pregnancy based on gender* – is this lawful, immoral or both?
- *Wearing of niqab in court* – is it in the interests of justice that a judge and jury can see the defendant's full face?

stretch & challenge

'It would not be correct to say that every moral obligation involves a legal duty; but every legal duty is founded on a moral obligation.'

LCJ Coleridge in **R v Instan (1893)**. Discuss the role of morality within the law of England and Wales.

Grade boost

Any answer on law and morality requires a thorough discussion of the Hart Devlin debate with supporting authority for each theorist.

This topic can be examined with the Rule of Law, so ensure you have a thorough understanding of both topics.

Hart Devlin debate

Wolfenden Report 1957

This recommended legalisation of homosexuality and prostitution.

- **Devlin** – opposed the report – common morality necessary to keep society together. The Law has a duty to uphold the common morality. Immoral behaviour is judged by the standard of the right-minded person.
- **Hart** – approved of the report – the use of the law to enforce morals was unnecessary, undesirable and morally unacceptable.

Criticisms

- The standard of the right-minded person is a difficult one.
- Individuals should have free choice.

Judicial support for Devlin's view can be seen in the following cases:

Shaw v DPP (1961), **Knuller Ltd v DPP (1972)**, **R v Gibson (1990)**, **R v Brown (1992)**

The Warnock Committee

The Committee considered issues relating to conception (IVF) and pregnancy. Recommendations from the 1984 Warnock Committee Report included:

- Setting up an independent statutory body to monitor, regulate and license infertility services and embryo experiments – **Human Fertilisation and Embryology Authority set up in 1990.**
- Experiments on embryos up to 14 days should be legal.
- Surrogacy arrangements should be illegal.
- Many of the Report's recommendations became law in the **Human Fertilisation and Embryology Act 1990.**

Controversial cases involving infertility treatment and 'designer babies' include:

- **R v Human Fertilisation and Embryology Authority, ex parte Blood (1997)**
- **R (on the application of Quintavalle) v Human Fertilisation and Embryology Authority (2005) (designer babies)**
- **Evans v UK (2007)**

Reform

2008 – **Human Fertilisation and Embryology Act** – replaces the 1990 Act, it provides for:

- The establishment of a Regulatory Authority for Tissues and Embryos.
- Extending the statutory storage period for embryos from 5 to 10 years.
- Hybrid embryos (both human and animal DNA) may be created for research purposes and kept for 14 days.
- Provision for allowing 'saviour siblings'.
- Sex election of embryos for non-medical reasons is prohibited.
- 'Right to know' biological parentage for those born as a result of infertility treatments.

The Rule of Law

The Rule of Law is a fundamental principle of our constitution. The Rule of Law simply means that the state should govern its citizens in accordance with rules that have been agreed upon.

Britain is different to other Western democracies in that Britain has an unwritten constitution – our constitution is not found in a specific document – but we do have a constitution from rules about who governs, and the powers they have and how that power is passed or transferred.

Sources of our constitution include:

- Acts of Parliament.
- Judicial decisions.
- Conventions – are not laws but are traditions that have been followed over time.

Principles of the Rule of Law

There are three main principles underpinning the Rule of Law which you must understand. These are the separation of powers, the supremacy of Parliament and the Rule of Law.

The separation of powers

State power can be divided into three types (Montesquieu, French Philosopher 18th century):

1. Executive – Government.
2. Legislative – Parliament.
3. Judiciary – Judges.

Each power should be carried out by different bodies – avoid abuse of power and conflict of interest.

Does our system operate according to the principle of separation of powers?

The supremacy of Parliament

- Parliamentary sovereignty – Parliament is the highest source of law.
- No one Parliament binds another.
- Britain – no Bill of Rights to override Parliament. Britain has no law which is entrenched.

Dicey – 'Parliament has under the English Constitution, the right to make or unmake any law whatever, and, further, that no person or body is recognised by the law of England as having a right to override or set aside the legislation of Parliament.'

However, the supremacy of Parliament has been eroded:

- The effect of EU membership on parliamentary sovereignty.
- Changes to the constitution – Scottish Parliament, Northern Ireland Assembly, Welsh Assembly.
- *Human Rights Act 1998* – European Convention not superior to Parliament, but the effects of *Sections 3 and 4 Human Rights Act 1998* on parliamentary sovereignty.

Grade boost

It would be impressive to show the examiner you are aware of some high profile alleged breaches of the Rule of Law. Research the following to include in an answer on Rule of Law:

- John Hemming MP who disclosed the famous footballer subject to an injunction by using parliamentary privilege.
- The proposal by Conservative MPs to ignore a ruling from the ECHR which gives UK prisoners the right to vote.
- The case of **Binyam Mohamed**
- Deportation of **Abu Qatada**.

stretch&challenge

The pressure group JUSTICE published a manifesto in 2007 for the Rule of Law. Research and summarise their recommendations.

Grade boost

When answering a question on the Rule of Law it is important to fully discuss the three key principles of our constitution, including Dicey, with current examples of breaches of the Rule of Law.

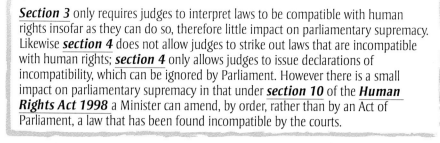

Section 3 only requires judges to interpret laws to be compatible with human rights insofar as they can do so, therefore little impact on parliamentary supremacy. Likewise **section 4** does not allow judges to strike out laws that are incompatible with human rights; **section 4** only allows judges to issue declarations of incompatibility, which can be ignored by Parliament. However there is a small impact on parliamentary supremacy in that under **section 10** of the **Human Rights Act 1998** a Minister can amend, by order, rather than by an Act of Parliament, a law that has been found incompatible by the courts.

The Rule of Law

Dicey – 19th century: *Three elements to the Rule of Law:*

1. No sanction without breach – no one should be punished unless they have broken a law.
2. One law should govern everyone.
3. Rights of individuals secured by decisions of judges.

Breaches of rule of law

You should be aware of one of the most significant breaches of the rule of law, which is extraordinary rendition - the abduction and detention of people by the state.

Constitutional Reform Act 2005

- *S 1 – 'the Act does not affect…the existing constitutional principle of the rule of law.'*

Arguments for and against a UK written constitution

Arguments for:

- Make things clearer
- Accessible for citizens
- Greater protection of rights and liberties.

Arguments against:

- Difficult to change
- Unwritten constitution part of our heritage
- Unwritten constitution allows flexibility.

Juries

Role of juries

- Try issues of fact in court weighing up the evidence presented to them in court.
- The judge will try issues of law and direct the jury on the relevant law.
- Juries are independent and free from influence as held in **Bushell's Case (1670)**.
- If summoned, all eligible members of the public are required to perform their jury duty.

Key terminology
Standard of proof = the standard to which a case has to be established. In criminal law, it is: *beyond reasonable doubt*. In a civil case it is: *on the balance of probabilities*.

Criminal cases

Juries only decide cases in the Crown Court. Of all criminal cases 95% are tried in the Magistrates' Courts and, of the 5% that are heard in the Crown Court, a large proportion of defendants will plead guilty, meaning there is no need for a jury trial. Consequently, only around 1% of criminal cases are tried by a jury. Despite this, they are still seen as symbolically important and a fundamental part of the English legal system. As Lord Devlin wrote in 1956, they are 'the lamp that shows that freedom lives'.

Their role in a criminal trial is to decide whether the defendant is guilty or not guilty of the crime with which they have been charged, based on the evidence presented in court. They have to be satisfied of the defendant's guilt *beyond reasonable doubt*. There are normally 12 jurors who should first try to reach a unanimous verdict. Under the **Juries Act 1974**, the judge can direct the jury to reach a majority verdict of either 10:2 or 11:1 if they have failed to reach a unanimous decision after a 'reasonable period of time'.

stretch&challenge

Think about why only a majority verdict of 10:2 or 11:1 is satisfactory. It supports the principle that guilt should be proved beyond reasonable doubt. If a jury cannot reach an acceptable minority verdict it is known as a hung jury.

Civil cases

Less than 1% of civil cases are tried by a jury. The **Supreme Courts Act 1981** gives a right to jury trial in the following civil cases:

- Libel and slander
- Malicious prosecution
- False imprisonment
- Fraud.

Coroner's Court

In an inquest in the Coroner's Court, the jury is not asked to return a verdict of guilty or not guilty. The role of the jury is to decide two factual things: firstly – the identity of the person that has died, and secondly – how, when and where the person died.

stretch&challenge

Prior to the Criminal Justice Act 2003 five categories of people were ineligible for jury service: the judiciary, those involved in administration of justice such as police officers and solicitors, the clergy, people with mental ill health and people on bail. Following the CJA 2003, only the mentally ill are ineligible. Have juries become more representative following the eligibility amendments of the Criminal Justice Act 2003?

Remember to consider law before the CJA 2003. Why were the changes made? Is the jury now more representative?

Grade boost

Disqualified

A person will have a life disqualification from jury service if:

- they have been in prison for 5 years or more or ever received an extended sentence.

A person will have a 10 year disqualification if:

- they have served a prison sentence in the last 10 years
- they have had a suspended sentence or community sentence placed on them in the last 10 years.

In addition, those on bail are disqualified.

Qualification and selection of jurors

The law is contained in the ***Criminal Justice Act 2003***, which amended the ***Juries Act 1974***, as a result of recommendations set out by ***Auld***.

Eligibility

- Aged 18–70
- Registered on the electoral register
- Resident in the UK, Channel Islands, Isle of Man for at least 5 years since the age of 13
- Not **disqualified**

Disqualification

- Persons on bail
- Those with serious criminal convictions
- Mentally disordered persons

Deferral

- Anyone can apply to defer their jury duty. Reasons for deferral include examinations, having a holiday booked, wedding, surgery, etc. Jury duty can be deferred once and must be retaken within a 12 month period of the deferral.

Excusal

Discretionary excusal can be applied for by:

- Those aged over 65
- Those who have served on a jury in the past 2 years
- MPs
- MEPs
- Certain members of the medical profession
- Those with religious beliefs that are incompatible with jury service
- Full-time members of the armed forces

Summoning the jury

The Central Juror Summoning Bureau summons jurors. Computers randomly select jurors from the electoral register and summons are sent out. Jurors arrive at court on the date requested and go to the jury assembly area where their identity is confirmed. The jury for a case is chosen by random ballot in open court where the Clerk calls out 12 names. These 12 will then be sworn in unless there are any challenges. There are normally 12 jurors in a criminal case and can never be fewer than 9. In a civil case in the County Court there are 8 jurors.

Challenges

A juror can be challenged in one of two ways:
- Challenge for the cause
- Stand by the Crown.

Challenge for the cause

A request that a juror be dismissed because there is a reason to believe that they cannot be fair, unbiased or capable. For example:

- Knowing someone in the case.
- Prior experience in a similar case.
- An obvious prejudice.
- Ineligibility or disqualification.

Stand by the Crown

This is rarely used and should only be invoked in cases of national security or terrorism. Where it is used, the permission of the Attorney General is needed.

Advantages of juries

- Ordinary people, who are supposed to be representative of society, get the opportunity to participate in the criminal justice system, which means there is the sense of being judged by society rather than the legal system. This upholds the *Magna Carta* principle of the *'right to be tried by one's peers'*.
- The jury is ancient and democratic:
  Professor Blackstone – *'it is the bulwark of our liberties'*.
  Lord Devlin – *'the lamp that shows freedom lives'*.
  Michael Mansfield QC – *'the most democratic element of our judicial system'*.
- **Jury** equity means that juries make decisions based on **fact**, which does not require any legal training. In ***Ponting (1985)***, the jury refused to convict even though the judge ruled there was no defence.
- Twelve opinions are better than one, and because of ***s8 Contempt of Court Act 1981***, juries' deliberations are conducted in secret, which means they are free from influence and pressure by the media and the public.
- Juries will often come to a decision that is fair and just rather than one which is legally correct. In ***R v Owen (1992)***, the jury sympathised with the defendant because he acted in a way which was perceived as getting justice for his dead son, even though legally, he had committed a crime.
- Juries are not prosecution biased or case hardened in the same way that a judge may be perceived to be. For many people, it will be the first and only time they have served on a jury and they therefore would be keen to do a good job and obtain the fairest result.

Disadvantages of juries

- People are often resentful of serving on a jury and are keen to finish in order that they can return to work and their families.
- Media Influence can often inadvertently affect the outcome of a case as seen in the case of ***R v Taylor and Taylor (1993)*** where a newspaper had published stills from CCTV footage giving a false impression of what had happened. This could interfere with the defendants' right to a fair trial under ***Article 6 ECHR***.
- Juries often have to sit through distressing and disturbing evidence and exhibits as seen in the horrific case of ***R v West (1996)***.
- It has been discovered that jurors often misunderstand the case presented to them. Research by Middlesex University show that only 43% of jurors understood everything that was happening in the trial. This has further been confirmed by Robert Howe QC who sat on a jury and was surprised at how little preparation jurors receive. The case of ***R v Pryce (2013)*** illustrates the danger of juries misunderstanding the case and their role. The trial of Vicky Pryce collapsed when the judge realised that the jury were struggling to understand the basics and asked

Key terminology

Perverse verdict = a jury's decision is unexpected based on the evidence presented or the verdict defies the direction of the judge.

Hung jury = where a jury cannot come to a unanimous or a majority verdict after deliberation. In these cases, a retrial will be ordered with a new jury.

Contempt of court = a criminal offence, punishable by imprisonment, where a person does something which substantially interferes with the course of justice or with the procedure of the court.

stretch&challenge

According to the 2010 research by Prof Cheryl Thomas, *'Are Juries Fair?'* are juries effective?

Grade boost

For every advantage or disadvantage you state, remember to support it with a relevant piece of legal authority.

Grade boost

Remember that Article 6 European Convention on Human Rights = a right to a fair trial.

Key case

R v Abdroikov (2007) – This case questioned whether police officers and a CPS solicitor sitting on juries affected the defendant's right to a fair trial. There was no clear conclusion in the case, but it was decided that on a case-by-case basis, it would be examined whether a juror's employment may jeopardise their ability to decide a case impartially. In **R v Khan (2008)** the Court of Appeal used **Abdroikov** as the basis for their decision but did not find it easy to apply. They declined to give guidelines but said that anyone whose employment would conflict with impartiality should be identified and if felt they would be biased, asked to stand down from the jury.

Another more recent key case is **Hanif and Khan v UK (2011)** where the European Court of Human Rights held that the presence of police officers on the jury could breach **Article 6 ECHR – right to a fair trial**. In this case, the police officer knows a police witness in the case in a professional capacity. Research it at www.gcnchambers.co.uk/gcn/news/police_officer_on_jury_made_trial_unfair.

ten questions which revealed 'fundamental deficits' in understanding.

- Statistics show that 43% of defendants are acquitted in the Crown Court as opposed to just 26% in the Magistrates' Court. This leads us to believe that juries can be unpredictable and often return 'perverse' verdicts. An example is **R v Young (1995)** where a retrial was ordered when it was discovered the jury had used a Ouija board to contact the dead victim.
- Juries are very difficult to research because of the secrecy element and the risk of **s8 Contempt of Court Act 1981** preventing jurors discussing the reasons behind their decisions. The cases of **R v Mirza (2004)** and **R v Connor and Rollock (2004)** confirmed that this practice was compatible with **Article 6 ECHR**.
- The jury may be easily influenced by one or two members of the jury, or strong-minded personalities. This is especially true if there is a legal professional serving on the jury – they may be perceived as knowing more, so will be allowed to make the decision on behalf of the other members.
- With increased technological advances and information being more accessible than ever before, we may see it become more difficult to control the secrecy of the jury room. An example came in **R v Karakaya (2005)** where it became apparent that a juror had conducted internet research and brought their results into the jury room.
- Juries may be influenced by factors other than the evidence and witness statements in the court room. An example came in **R v Alexander and Steen (2004)** where a juror had romantically propositioned the prosecution barrister.

Are juries representative of society?

Yes

- Eligibility reforms in the **Criminal Justice Act 2003** following **Auld's Review in 2001** – wider cross-section of society now able to serve as a juror; however, whilst this has made juries more representative of society, this has in turn created new problems, for example bias, particularly where a jury member is a police officer – see **R v Abdroikov (2007) and R v Khan (2008)**.
- However, bias is not just a problem with those who work within the criminal justice system, an ordinary jury member could be biased, if, for example, they had been a victim of a crime.
- Central Summoning Bureau – ensures random selection of jury members.
- Research by **Prof Cheryl Thomas (2010)** shows that participation has risen since the introduction of the reforms showing that the 'middle class' opt out has been removed.
- Use of discretionary excusal means that jury service is harder to get out of.
- **Diversity and Fairness in the Jury System (2007)** by Cheryl Thomas and Nigel Balmer showed that ethnic minority jurors are proportionate to the ethnic minority population. The report also found that jurors are representative of the population in terms of gender and age.

No

- Eligibility – not everyone is on the electoral register.
- Limits on random selection imposed by rules of eligibility and disqualification.

- Jury vetting impacts upon the random selection of jury members – vetting involves checking that a potential juror does not hold extremist views which would render them unsuitable to hear a case. For examples of this see: *R v Sheffield Crown Court, ex parte Brownlow; R v Mason (1980); R v Obellim (1996).*
- Legislation reducing the role of the jury – *Criminal Justice Act 2003* provides for trial by judge alone where the case involves complex or lengthy financial or commercial arrangements **(section 43)**; or where a serious risk of jury tampering exists **(section 44)**; for an example of this see *R v Twomey (2009)*.
- Representation of ethnic minorities – no need for a racially balanced jury – for an example of this **see *R v Ford (1989)*** and *Sander v UK.*
- Limits on random selection imposed jury challenging – Challenge for cause and Stand by.
- There have been criticisms that discretionary excusals are administered too freely.

Reforms of jury trial

- **Auld Review 2001** – recommended both prosecution and defence should prepare a written summary of their case to aid the jury in the jury room, this has not been implemented.
- Legislation to ensure that perverse verdicts cannot happen.
- Videoing of jury room deliberations.
- Allowing a 13th qualified person to retire with the jury to assist with the verdict.
- Written verdicts to assist in determining how the jury reached their verdict.
- Problems with the use of juries in serious fraud trials – see *R v Rayment and others (2005)*, has led to much debate concerning the abolition of juries in serious fraud cases. Alternatives to the use of juries in serious fraud cases include the use of a single judge or a panel of three or five judges, or a judge with lay experts/assessors with expertise in commercial and financial matters.

Contempt of Court

With the rise in the use of technology and social networking, the courts are becoming really strict on the use of the Internet, social networking and discussion of the case outside the jury deliberation room.

Recent cases include:

R v Fraill (2011)

R v Banks (2011)

Attorney General v Davey and Beard (2013)

Grade boost

- When discussing whether juries are representative of society, remember to support your arguments with a relevant piece of legal authority.
- It is good exam practice to mention all factors that could affect whether a jury is representative or not, including vetting, challenging and eligibility.

stretch&challenge

Research the recent 2013 case involving a Muslim defendant who wanted to deliver her evidence to the jury wearing the full niqab. What was the outcome of the case? What are the Human Rights implications of this?

Key terminology

Custom = tradition or behaviour that happens in a community which is not formalised into law, but is accepted practice, because it is 'customary' and is the way it has always been done in that community.

Common law = (1) judge-made law or case law; (2) historical concept which makes the law 'common' throughout the country; a distinct area of law from equity.

Equity = principles of law and decisions made based on '**fairness**' rather than following the rigidity of the common law.

⚜ Grade boost

Be mindful that this topic can be examined with other topics on the specification, even as diverse as the European Institutions.

Common Law and Equity

History of common law and equity

There are many sources of law in the United Kingdom, of which **common law** and **equity** are two. Common law is one of the oldest sources of law in our legal system, and developed from customs.

1066 **William the Conqueror** created the **Curia Regis**, or the King's Court where people could apply to the King for him to resolve their dispute.

1154 –1189 **Henry II** – the country was divided into **circuits** and the judges would use the local customs to resolve disputes, but eventually decided that the 'best' customs should be taken from each circuit to make a law that was common to all – this was the first indication that there would be a **common law**.

1258 **Provisions of Oxford** – this case stopped new **writs** being created. Prior to this case, if you wanted a case resolved you had to have a writ drawn up, but this case stopped new writs being created, so if you wanted your case resolved, you had to make your case fit into an existing writ.

Further, the only remedy available in the common law was **damages** and damages were not always a suitable remedy, for example if the case involved trespass.

BIRTH OF EQUITY

Due to the problems in the common law, people got fed up of petitioning the King with their disputes, so took their complaints to the Chancellor, who was regarded as the *'keeper of the King's conscience'*. The Chancellor made his decision based on **fairness**, rather than on precedent or on what had gone before.

1345 **Court of Chancery** began operating, which was controlled by the Chancellor and was a court of **equity**; that is, a court based on fairness which adopted the rules of equity.

Therefore, for many years the common law courts and the equity courts were separate, and would often come to different decisions on certain matters. **Lord Justice Coke** commented that *'equity varied with the length of the Chancellor's foot'* which often resulted in a conflict.

1615 **Earl of Oxford's Case** decides that where common law and equity conflict, **equity will always prevail**.

1873 *s25 Judicature Act* confirmed the strength of equity, formalising that equity should prevail where there is conflict.

MODERN EQUITY

1975 *Mareva Compania Naviera SA v International Bulkcarriers SA* established the **Mareva Injunction**, now known as a **freezing order**.

1976 *Anton Piller KG v Manufacturing Processes Limited* established the **Anton Piller Order** now known as a **search order**.

Equitable maxims

In order to be eligible for an equitable remedy, the court has to be convinced that you have satisfied the **maxims**; these are a set of rules or principles which the court uses to decide the case. Equitable remedies are **discretionary** in nature; they therefore do not have to be granted, the decision rests on whether the parties have complied with the maxims.

There are nearly twenty maxims; here are just a few:

'He who comes to equity must come with clean hands'

This means that an equitable remedy will not be given to those that have not acted fairly.

D&C Builders v Rees (1965) – Mr and Mrs Rees had some building work done at a cost of £732. The couple had already paid £250 before the work had commenced, and so owed £482 on completion. Mr and Mrs Rees knew the builders were in financial difficulty, but complained about the quality of the work and said they were only prepared to pay £300 of the total owed. The builders needed the money so accepted the £300 *'in completion of the account'*, but later sued Mr and Mrs Rees for the balance.

Lord Denning in the Court of Appeal was not prepared to offer the equitable remedy of **equitable estoppel** because Mr and Mrs Rees had not acted fairly and had taken advantage of the builders' financial difficulties. If the remedy had been applied, the couple would not have had to pay the money because a genuine agreement had been made to accept the £300.

'Delay defeats equity'

This means that a claimant must not leave it an unreasonable length of time before claiming as this is unfair to the other party.

Leaf v International Galleries (1950) – The claimant had bought what they believed to be a painting by the famous artist Constable. After five years, the claimant realised that it was not genuine, but the court held that too much time had elapsed between the sale and the discovery.

'He who seeks equity must do equity'

In order for a claimant to have an equitable remedy, he must be prepared to satisfy his side of the bargain.

Chappel v Times Newspapers (1975) – Employees at a newspaper were on strike and wanted an injunction against their employers who told them they would be sacked unless they stopped the strike action. The court held that in order for the remedy to be applied, the employees had to satisfy their part of the agreement which was to stop the strike action.

Key terminology

Discretionary = this means that the court cannot be FORCED to give the remedy; awarding of the remedy is dependent on the claimant's satisfaction of the equitable maxims.

Maxim = a 'rule' that has to be satisfied before the court will consider awarding an equitable remedy.

Mandatory injunction = an order forcing a party **to do** something.

Prohibitory injunction = an order forcing a party **not to do** something.

Interlocutory injunction = an order preserving the status quo until the case has been decided.

Grade boost

When you are talking about equitable maxims, make sure you explain the **rule** and discuss a **supporting case**. You should aim to include at least three maxims to guarantee high marks.

Equitable remedies

Equitable remedies are discretionary and are therefore not automatically granted; the only remedy available as of right to a successful claimant is that of common law damages.

Remedy	Definition	Case
Specific performance	This is an order forcing the parties to perform their part of the agreement. This is available for: • Contracts to buy a unique item • Contracts to buy land.	***Sky Petroleum v VIP Petroleum (1974)*** where petrol was deemed to be a unique item because it was in short supply at the time. ***Wolverhampton Corporation v Emmons (1902)*** where a builder was made to comply with his contract to build houses on a demolition site.
Rescission	This is a court order which orders the parties to be restored to their pre-contractual position as if the contract had not happened. It is available for contracts where a **vitiating factor** such as misrepresentation or duress has made the contract voidable.	***Grist v Bailey (1967)*** where a contract was set aside because both parties had made the mistake that a property for sale was covered by ***The Rent Acts***.
Rectification	This is a remedy where a written contract is rectified because a mistake has been made and the terms are not what the parties wanted or intended.	***Craddock v Hunt (1923)*** – a contract for the sale of a house included an adjoining yard, even though neither party intended or expected it to be included.
Injunctions	Injunctions can be **mandatory**, **prohibitory** or **interlocutory**.	***Warner Brothers v Nelson (1937)*** – an injunction was granted against the actress Bette Davis, preventing her from making films with another company.
Mareva Injunction (freezing order)	This is a relatively new remedy, and has the effect of freezing someone's assets until the case has been resolved to prevent any interference by the defendant while the case is being decided.	***Mareva Compania Naviera SA v International Bulkcarriers SA*** – was the first recorded case to grant this order.
Anton Piller Order (search order)	This is also a relatively new remedy and is commonly used in cases involving intellectual property – it gives the court power to search premises and seize evidence relevant to the case.	***Anton Piller KG v Manufacturing Processes Limited*** – was the first recorded case to grant this order.
Promissory (Equitable) estoppel	If a promise has been made to another person, that promise cannot be withdrawn if that other person has relied on it to their detriment.	***Central London Property Trust Ltd v High Trees House Ltd (1947)*** – where a promise to let flats at a reduced rate during the war was upheld because the tenants relied on that promise before moving in.

stretch&challenge

Super Injunctions – A super injunction is a type of injunction whereby the press are prevented from knowing of the existence and details of the injunction, as well as being prevented from publishing any facts or allegations surrounding the case.

They have recently been used against British tabloid newspapers in relation to celebrities to 'gag' the press and prevent them from publishing details of their private life. Research super injunction cases concerning the following celebrities:

• Andrew Marr
• Ryan Giggs – *CTB v News Group Newspapers (2011)*
• Jeremy Clarkson – *AMM v HXW (2010)*
• Rio Ferdinand – *Ferdinand v Mirror Group Newspapers (2010)*

Discuss the following:

1. By their very nature, the press, and therefore the public, are not permitted to know about the existence of a super injunction, so how do the public and the press find out about their existence?

2. Do you think super injunctions are an effective remedy in terms of balancing the right to privacy with the public's need to know?

Criminal Procedure

The law consists of many criminal offences, to which a suspect can plead guilty or not guilty, but the procedure that follows arrest varies depending on the **classification of offence** that has been committed. It is important to remember that throughout the whole process, the suspect is **innocent until proven guilty** and at all times, his ***Article 6 ECHR right to a fair trial*** should be upheld, and the courts have a duty under the ***Human Rights Act 1998*** to make sure this happens.

In terms of criminal procedure, remember every case has an initial hearing in the Magistrates' Court, so all criminal cases will visit the Magistrates first, even if it is only for the official passing over to the Crown Court.

There are three categories of criminal offence:

1. **Summary**: the **least serious** category of offence, heard solely in the **Magistrates' Court**. They cover minor offences, such as driving offences and some cases of assault.
2. **Triable either way**: these are offences that can be heard in **EITHER** the **Magistrates' Court** or the **Crown Court**. Where the defendant pleads not guilty, there is often a choice whether they go to Magistrates' Court and have a summary trial or to the Crown Court for an indictable trial by jury. Examples of offences in this category include Theft and Actual Bodily Harm.
3. **Indictable**: these are the most serious offences and are heard in the **Crown Court**. Examples of offences in this category include murder, manslaughter, rape and robbery.

Summary offences

EARLY ADMINISTRATIVE HEARING
This hearing deals with administration such as: Whether defendant should be bailed or remanded in custody What legal funding provisions are in place **Pre-sentence reports**

PLEAD GUILTY	PLEAD NOT GUILTY
SENTENCING AT MAGISTRATES' COURT	**SUMMARY TRIAL** AT MAGISTRATES' COURT

Key terminology

Pre-sentence report = helps the court to decide whether there are any factors in the defendant's history which may affect the sentencing.

Examination in chief = questioning of a witness in court by their own counsel.

Cross examination = questioning of a witness in court by the opposing counsel.

Plea bargaining = where the defendant pleads guilty to a lesser offence in return for a lower sentence to save court time and make the trial more predictable.

Disclosure = the obligation on both sides to disclose all evidence that may be relevant to the case to the other side.

stretch&challenge

In triable either way offences, the defendant has the option to choose whether or not he wishes to have a trial by jury. Research the implications of choosing a trial by jury, and the arguments for and against abolishing the right to choose a trial by jury.

 Grade boost

Remember that Magistrates have limited sentencing powers; they can sentence up to six months' custodial sentence and up to £5,000 fine.

Triable either way offences

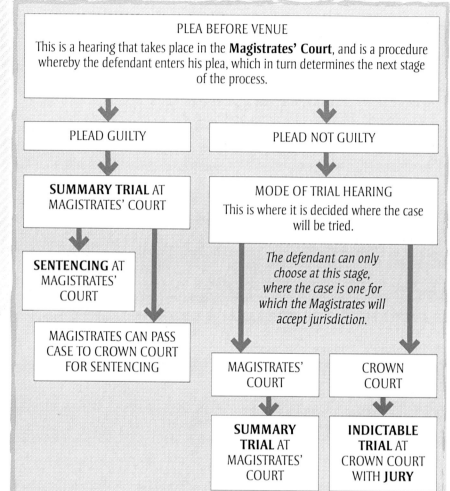

PLEA BEFORE VENUE
This is a hearing that takes place in the **Magistrates' Court**, and is a procedure whereby the defendant enters his plea, which in turn determines the next stage of the process.

PLEAD GUILTY → **SUMMARY TRIAL** AT MAGISTRATES' COURT → **SENTENCING** AT MAGISTRATES' COURT → MAGISTRATES CAN PASS CASE TO CROWN COURT FOR SENTENCING

PLEAD NOT GUILTY → MODE OF TRIAL HEARING This is where it is decided where the case will be tried.

The defendant can only choose at this stage, where the case is one for which the Magistrates will accept jurisdiction.

MAGISTRATES' COURT → **SUMMARY TRIAL** AT MAGISTRATES' COURT

CROWN COURT → **INDICTABLE TRIAL** AT CROWN COURT WITH **JURY**

Indictable offences

EARLY ADMINISTRATIVE HEARING

s51 Crime and Disorder Act 1998 stipulates that the Magistrates have to immediately send the case to Crown Court using **committal proceedings**.

PLEAD GUILTY → **SENTENCING** AT CROWN COURT

PLEAD NOT GUILTY → **JURY TRIAL** AT CROWN COURT

Criminal Procedure: Bail

Bail is granted by the police or the courts at any time after a person has been arrested and allows them to be at liberty until the next stage of the case. This guarantees the suspect's right to liberty contained in **Article 5 ECHR** and upholds the fundamental principle that he is innocent until proven guilty.

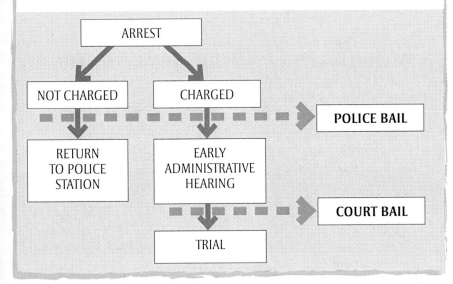

stretch&challenge

Look at the following recent cases; do you agree with the decision that was made in relation to bail?
Julian Assange (2011)
Gary Weddell (2008)
Michael Donovan (2008)

Grade boost

You should demonstrate an awareness of both court bail AND police bail. It is a common mistake in examinations for candidates to omit police bail and just concentrate on court bail.

Police bail

The decision to grant bail is taken by the **custody officer** with powers given to him under **s38 Police and Criminal Evidence Act 1984**. The police can only refuse bail if:

- there is doubt about the suspect's name or address; or
- detention is necessary to protect the suspect or somebody else; or
- it is reasonably believed that the suspect will fail to attend court or will interfere with witnesses or the administration of justice; or
- the suspect is charged with murder.

Therefore, bail is granted in the majority of cases and can be given to the suspect even if he has not been charged under **s37 Police and Criminal Evidence Act 1984**, on the agreement that he will return to the police station on a given date – this happened to **Chris Jeffries**, the first suspect to be arrested in the 2011 **Joanna Yeates** murder case.

If the police feel that they cannot grant bail, the suspect must be put before Magistrates as soon as possible, in order that they can make the decision in relation to bail.

A new concept of **street bail** has recently been introduced under **s4 Criminal Justice Act 2003** whereby police officers can grant bail on the street for minor offences. This has the effect of freeing up police officers and maintaining a presence on the street.

Surety = a sum of money offered to the court by a person known to the suspect which guarantees your attendance to court when required.

Bail hostel = a place of residence for people on bail who cannot give a fixed address; it is a kind of 'open prison' run by the probation service to give as many people as possible the chance of receiving bail.

stretch&challenge

Research and conduct an evaluation into the effectiveness of conditions being attached to bail, particularly in light of the case of **Weddell**.

Research the conditions that were attached to bail granted to Dave Lee Travis and Ryan Cleary.

Court bail

The court's powers to grant bail are governed by **The Bail Act 1976**, where **s4** contains a presumption in favour of bail, but there are other considerations which may prevent a suspect from being granted bail.

> **s4 Bail Act 1976** – presumption in favour of bail
> (remember: **Article 5 ECHR** right to liberty)

> Bail need not be granted, if there are **substantial grounds** for believing that the suspect would:
> - commit another offence whilst on bail
> - fail to surrender to bail
> - interfere with witnesses or otherwise obstruct the course of justice or
> - the suspect needs to be kept in custody for his own protection.
> - **The Legal Aid, Sentencing and Punishment Offenders Act 2012** adds a further exception where bail can be refused if the offender may commit an offence involving domestic violence.

> - **Schedule 1, para 9 Bail Act 1976** outlines factors that need to be taken into consideration when deciding whether or not to grant bail:
> - the nature and seriousness of the offence
> - the character, past record, associations and community ties of the defendant
> - the defendant's previous record of surrendering to bail
> - the strength of the evidence against him.
> - **S90 Legal Aid, Sentencing and Punishment of Offenders Act 2012** introduced the 'no real prospect test', where the courts' power to refuse bail is restricted where it appears that there is no real prospect that the defendant would receive a custodial sentence if convicted.

Conditional bail

The police **or** the courts can grant conditional bail under powers given to them by the **Criminal Justice and Public Order Act 1994**. These conditions are imposed to minimise the risk of the defendant committing another offence whilst on bail or otherwise interfering with the investigation and, in some circumstances, for his own protection.

Conditions that can be imposed include:
- curfew
- electronic tag
- surrendering passport
- reporting to police station at regular intervals
- residence at a **bail hostel**
- getting someone to stand **surety** for you.

Restrictions on bail

There have been many amendments over the years to *The Bail Act 1976*, over concerns that bail was being given too freely, and those that were granted bail were going on to commit further offences.

s14 Criminal Justice Act 2003

If defendant was on bail for another offence at the date of the offence, bail should be refused unless the court is satisfied that there is **no significant risk** that he will commit another offence.

s18 Criminal Justice Act 2003

The prosecution can appeal against the granting of bail for **any imprisonable offence**.

s19 Criminal Justice Act 2003

Bail will not be granted for an **imprisonable offence** where the defendant has tested positive for a **Class A drug** and where the offence is one connected with Class A drugs.

s25 Criminal Justice and Public Order Act 1994

s56 Crime and Disorder Act 1998

The courts are barred from granting bail in cases of murder, manslaughter and rape where the defendant had already served a custodial sentence for such an offence on a previous occasion.

This was held to be a breach of *Article 5 ECHR* in the case of *Caballero v UK (2000)*, so…

A defendant can only be granted bail in such cases if the court is satisfied that there are **exceptional circumstances**.

s24 Anti-Terrorism, Crime and Security Act 2001

All bail applications from suspected international terrorists should be made to the **Special Immigration Appeals Commission**.

s115 Coroners and Justice Act 2009 provides that where a person is charged with murder, bail can only be granted by a judge of the Crown Court. The power of the Magistrates' Court to consider bail in murder cases, whether at first hearing or after a breach of an existing bail condition, is now removed. The section goes on to stipulate that the defendant must be brought before the Crown Court judge within 48 hours beginning with the day after the defendant's appearance at Magistrates' Court.

Police (Detention and Bail) Act 2011 is an emergency piece of legislation that was passed through Parliament as a result of *R (ex p Chief Constable of Greater Manchester Police) and Salford Magistrates Court v Hookway (2011)*. The law amends the *Police and Criminal Evidence Act 1984* to stipulate that a suspect cannot be released on bail without charge for longer than 96 hours, which is the maximum detention limit.

Grade boost

Wherever possible, you need to show knowledge of the amendments to *The Bail Act 1976* as these are part of the factors that are taken into consideration when deciding a bail application.

stretch&challenge

Discuss the way in which the courts seek to address the balance between safeguarding a suspect's human rights and protecting the public from a potentially dangerous criminal.

Advantages and disadvantages of bail

It is very important that a balance is maintained in terms of upholding the defendant's Human Rights and protecting the public. This is especially important because at this point the suspect is still innocent until proven guilty, so should not be treated as a convicted criminal.

Advantages

The defendant can maintain employment and spend time with family during his bail period.

There is a reduction in the number of defendants on remand, which means less cost to the government.

The **Home Office** suggests that up to **20%** of those in our prisons are there awaiting trial and may go on to be found innocent, or be given non-custodial sentences.

The defendant can use the time to prepare for his trial by not being restricted in terms of being able to meet with his legal representatives.

Disadvantages

There is a risk that the defendant will interfere with witnesses or otherwise obstruct the course of justice – in the case of **Shannon Matthews**, had the suspects been granted bail, it would have been an opportunity for them to further conceal evidence and impede the investigation.

There seems to be disparity in the interpretation of the Bail Act 1976 in different courts.

There are startling statistics on the number of offences committed by people who are on bail; it is thought **a third of burglaries** are committed by people who are on bail for another offence.

Home Office statistics state that **12%** of bailed offenders fail to appear at their trial; so there is a risk of them absconding or not surrendering to bail.

Criminal Procedure: Crown Prosecution Service

History and role of the Crown Prosecution Service

The Crown Prosecution Service was set up in 1986 to take responsibility for making the decision whether or not to prosecute or charge a suspect. Prior to its establishment, this decision was taken by the police.

1970	**JUSTICE Report** – problems were identified with the police making the decision to prosecute; namely: • Prosecution bias. • Potential infringement of right to a fair trial after miscarriages of justice involving police tampering with evidence. • Conflict of interests – the same body investigating and prosecuting was seen as inappropriate.
1978	**Phillips Royal Commission** – recommended the establishment of an independent agency to take charge of prosecuting suspects.
1985	**Prosecution of Offences Act** – established the Crown Prosecution Service.

The CPS is headed by the **Director of Public Prosecutions** (DPP), who from 1 November 2013 is Alison Saunders, and she is answerable to the Attorney General. Generally speaking, the CPS takes control of the case as soon as the police have finished collecting evidence and conducting the investigation. It has five main roles:

1. **Advise** police on the charge that should be brought against the suspect, using the **CPS Charging Standards**.
2. **Review** cases that police present to them.
3. **Prepare** cases for court.
4. **Present** cases in court, as CPS lawyers now have rights of audience.

And their main role is:

5. **Decide** whether to bring a prosecution against the suspect.

There are 13 areas in the UK, each area headed by a **Chief Crown Prosecutor**. A 14th 'virtual' area is referred to as **CPS Direct**, which provides an out-of-hours service to the police on charging advice.

In 2011–2012, 87% of cases dealt with by the Magistrates' Court resulted in conviction and 81% in the Crown Court.

Key terminology

Charge = the decision that a suspect should **stand trial** for an alleged offence.

Convict = a judge or jury has come to the verdict that a person is **guilty** of the alleged offence.

Grade boost

This history and role of the CPS provides a very useful introduction to an essay on this topic.

stretch&challenge

What are the effects on diversity in the legal profession of having a female DPP?

Grade boost

The conviction rates cited here include guilty pleas, and there is an argument that this is masking the true performance of the CPS.

Research the report 'In the Public Interest: Reforming the CPS' by Karen Sosa and discuss potential shortcomings in the CPS. To what extent have these been resolved?

Admissible = useful evidence which cannot be excluded on the basis that it is immaterial, irrelevant or that it violates the rules of evidence.

Hearsay = second-hand evidence which is not what the witness knows personally, but is something that has been told to them.

Grade boost

When you are talking about the tests, you should make sure you give **examples:**

Evidential test – examples of reliable and unreliable evidence.

Public interest test – mention at least **three** or **four** questions and a brief explanation of the kinds of factors that influence that question.

You should mention the **Threshold test** whenever you can; showing knowledge of the two different tests and when they should be applied is crucial.

stretch&challenge

The DPP published guidelines on shaken baby cases in February 2011 because of the difference in opinion among medical experts – do you think it is always going to be in the public interest to prosecute in these cases because of the debate?

Code for Crown Prosecutors

This is the Code of Practice that Crown Prosecutors use to determine whether or not to charge a suspect with an offence. The Code is contained in ***s10 Prosecution of Offences Act 1985***.

The Full Code Test

It is based on two aspects:

Evidential test	**Public interest test**
Is there a realistic prospect of conviction?	*Is it in the public interest to prosecute?*

A case has to pass the evidential test before it moves onto the public interest test; if it fails the evidential test, then the case will proceed no further.

Evidential test

In order to pass the evidential test, the CPS must be satisfied that there is a realistic prospect of conviction. It is an **objective** test and it is not enough that there is lots of evidence; the evidence has to be **sufficient**, **reliable** and **admissible**.

Unreliable evidence	**Reliable evidence**
• Blurred CCTV • Confession obtained by oppression • Hearsay • Eyewitness testimony of a child • **Damilola Taylor** – unreliable witnesses and inadmissible evidence made the case the question of an investigation.	• DNA • Voluntary confession • Eyewitness from the scene of a crime.

Public interest test

The Code for Crown Prosecutors sets out questions which will identify and determine the relevant public interest factors tending for and against prosecution:

Para 4.12
    (a) How serious is the offence committed?
    (b) What is the level of culpability of the suspect?
    (c) What are the circumstances of and the harm caused to the victim?
    (d) Was the suspect under the age of 18 at the time of the offence?
    (e) What is the impact on the community?
    (f) Is prosecution a proportionate response?
    (g) Do sources of information require protecting?

Kier Starmer has made the statement that it will nearly always be in the public interest to prosecute in cases of assisted suicide. This was highlighted after the cases of **Kay Gilderdale** and **Francis Inglis**; two mothers who were both prosecuted for helping their offspring to die in very different circumstances. The DPP later published guidelines giving factors for and against prosecution in these cases.

Threshold Test

There are occasions when the CPS decides that the Full Code Test has failed, and there is not enough evidence to charge, but there is still the belief that the suspect is too much of a risk to be released. In these cases, the CPS will apply the Threshold Test.

Will a suspect be charged?

| Is there a reasonable suspicion that the person arrested has committed the offence in question? | Is there a realistic prospect of conviction? |

If both parts of this test are satisfied, then the CPS will then go on to apply the public interest test contained in the Full Code Test. This should be kept under review.

Reforms of the Crown Prosecution Service

The CPS has been the subject of much criticism and reform since its establishment and it has been suggested that it is not achieving what it set out to do.

1997 Narey Review –

Criticism	Reform
Lack of preparation and a delay in bringing the cases to court.	**Caseworkers** were trained to review files and present straightforward guilty pleas in court, which freed up CPS lawyers to deal with more complex cases.

1998 Glidewell Report –

Criticism	Reform
12% of cases were being **discontinued** by the CPS where the police have charged. Charges were **downgraded** in an alarming number of cases. Tense working relationships between the police and the CPS, with a hostile 'blame culture' leads to inefficiency and poor preparation. Long delays were reported between arrest and sentence, and a distinct lack of preparation. Witnesses were appearing in court that were unreliable, and in some cases not turning up at all.	The 13 areas were divided into 42 areas, to correspond with the police forces, each with a Chief Crown Prosecutor and each having the responsibility for making the decision to prosecute. The CPS is now based in police stations, and 'joined up working' is encouraged with an emphasis on the police and CPS to collaborate on shared issues.and cuts delays. The introduction of **Criminal Justice Units** has attempted to make the working relationships more amicable. A Revised Code for Crown Prosecutors was published with detailed guidance on the application of the evidential test.

Grade boost

Visit the CPS news pages at www.cps.gov.uk/news/ for information on recent reforms and press releases. All the current issues facing the CPS are recorded here and it is a useful place to keep abreast of new developments. For example, find out:

- The developments which have enabled witnesses to have pre-trial 'practice' interviews to improve their creditability and minimise the risk of not turning up to court because of intimidation or distress.

- Look at the CPS's stance on crime in sport. This is particularly useful as a link to the defence of consent which is used for many crimes. Are we seeing a more stringent approach to crime in sport?

Have a look on www.cps.gov.uk, at the News section and find out what the CPS have developed in relation to the following:

- Domestic violence
- Stalking and harassment
- Driving offences – 'nearest and dearest' cases and emergency vehicles
- Media and the CPS
- Role of CPS Direct.

stretch & challenge

In 2010, Gwent CPS received a visit from the CPS Inspectorate – do you think their findings are reflective of an improved service, or are we still seeing the problems identified by Glidewell?

It is not only the CPS that can charge a suspect; individuals are able to bring a **private prosecution**. Research the limitations on private prosecutions, paying particular attention to the case of *Whitehouse v Lemon (1976)*.

Grade boost

If you are asked to 'evaluate' or 'consider the effectiveness of' the CPS, make sure that you include as much as you can from the various reports and remember to create a **balanced** argument.

1999   **MacPherson Report** – written after the murder of Stephen Lawrence, the police were being investigated for potentially being racist.

Criticism	Reform
The police were **institutionally racist**, and there were serious criticisms of the investigation because the victim was black.	Every police force is now under a legal obligation to publish a Racial Equality Policy to protect victims and defendants. Regular inspections will be carried out to ensure that these rules are being followed.

2001   **Auld Review** – this review recommended the introduction of **statutory charging** – the CPS now determines the charge that should be brought in all but the minor cases. This ensures the correct charge is brought and that only those that are strong enough to stand trial get to court. This will reduce the number of cases that are discontinued, in line with the recommendations from **Glidewell**. This was later implemented in the *Criminal Justice Act 2003*.

2006   **Abu Hamza** – this case involved a Muslim cleric who was jailed for inciting murder and racial hatred. The police complained on several occasions that they had put evidence before the CPS and they had continually refused to prosecute. This suggests that working relationships between the police and the CPS are still hostile.

2009   **The Public Prosecution Service – Setting the Standard** – this is a report published by the former DPP Keir Starmer on his 'vision' for the CPS going into the 21st century. He spoke of an enhanced role for public prosecutors in engaging with their communities to inform their work and address their concerns.

Broadly speaking, he set out three main aims:

1. Protect the public
2. Support victims and witnesses
3. Deliver justice.

He sees the Crown Prosecution Service being able to achieve these aims by:

- Addressing offending and using out-of-court disposals where appropriate
- Deciding the charge in all but the most routine cases
- Taking the views of the victims into account
- Taking decisions independently of any improper influence
- Recovering assets from criminals
- Ensuring that witnesses are able to give their best evidence
- Presenting their own cases in court and
- Helping the court to pass an appropriate sentence.

This resulted in the CPS having to follow 'Core Quality Standards' that tell the public what they can expect the CPS to do when they prosecute people in court. However, in July 2013, an article in *the Guardian* commented that with a 25% cut in CPS lawyers this will be more difficult than ever to achieve.

Criminal Procedure: Appeals/CCRC

The Criminal justice system is in place to punish on behalf of the Crown those who commit crimes and to ultimately instill public confidence that law and order is being maintained and to act as a deterrent to those who may commit crimes.

When the case comes to court, the judge or jury has to be satisfied that the case has been proved **beyond reasonable doubt,** and the responsibility to convince a judge or jury of this, the **burden of proof**, lies with the prosecution in most cases. This is because, in criminal law, there is the **presumption of innocence**, and every suspect is innocent until proven guilty. Under *Article 6 ECHR*, every person has the **right to a fair trial** and it is important that all procedural rules are adhered to, else there could arise a **miscarriage of justice**.

Key terminology

Case stated = these are appeals on a **point of law**, and can be used by both the prosecution and defence.

Grade boost

You should make reference to the ECHR in EVERY question on criminal process. Relevant articles for criminal process are:

Article 5 ECHR – right to liberty.

Article 6 ECHR – right to a fair trial.

Criminal Court hierarchy

The diagram below shows the hierarchy of the Criminal Courts, including appeal routes. Criminal cases, in the first instance, are heard either in the **Magistrates' Court** or the **Crown Court**.

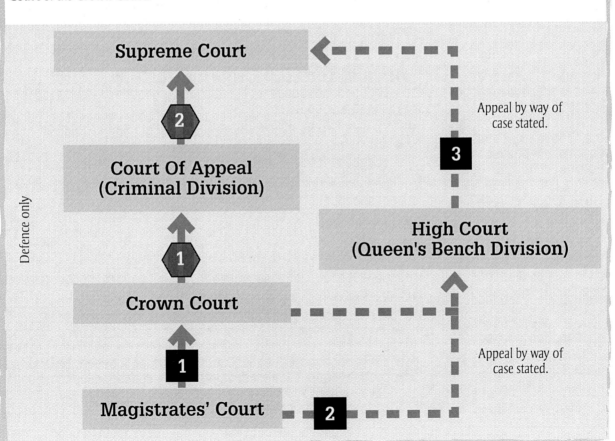

Supreme Court

Court Of Appeal (Criminal Division)

Crown Court

Magistrates' Court

High Court (Queen's Bench Division)

Defence only

Appeal by way of case stated.

Appeal by way of case stated.

Key terminology

Leave to Appeal = this is permission to appeal by a Court of Appeal judge; the rules for granting leave to appeal are contained in the **Criminal Appeal Act 1995** where it is stated that the Court of Appeal:

(a) Shall allow an appeal against conviction if they think that the conviction is unsafe; and

(b) Shall dismiss such an appeal in any other case.

stretch&challenge

Sometimes new evidence will come to light and that will prompt leave to be granted for appeal based on the fact that the conviction is *unsafe*. This is important on the grounds of *Article 6 ECHR*; however the courts sometimes take a different interpretation of *unsafe*. Look at the case of *Simon Hall* who has recently had his appeal against murder dismissed – do you think there has been a breach of his *Article 6 right to a fair trial* since he alleges that new evidence could prove his innocence?

Grade boost

When leave is granted, the Court of Appeal have the following powers available to them:

- allow the appeal, so the conviction will be quashed
- dismiss the appeal, so the conviction will stand
- decrease the sentence given
- lower the conviction to that of a lesser offence (such as murder to manslaughter)
- order a retrial in front of a new jury.

Appeals from the Magistrates' Court

Following a trial in the Magistrates' Court, there are two routes of appeal open to a defendant, depending on what basis they want to appeal.

1 If they wish to appeal against **conviction** or **sentence**, they must appeal to the **Crown Court**. This automatic right of appeal is open to the **defence** only.

2 If they wish to appeal by **case stated**, they must appeal to the **Divisional Court of the Queen's Bench Division in the High Court**. This method can be used by the **defence** against a conviction, **or** by the **prosecution** if the defendant has been acquitted. This appeal route is based on the fact that a mistake has been made in the application of the law. This route of appeal is not used very often.

3 A further appeal from the High Court is available to the **Supreme Court**; this will only happen if the matter is one of **public importance**.

This happened in the case of *C v DPP (1994)*, where the issue of children having criminal responsibility was considered. It was held in this case that it was not to be presumed that children aged between 10 and 14 knew the difference between right and wrong, and therefore criminal activity will not always result in prosecution. The Divisional Court of the Queen's Bench Division had wanted to change the law so that it was always presumed that a child aged 10-14 knew the difference between right and wrong, but the Supreme Court held that they were bound by precedent and were not at liberty to change the law.

Appeals from the Crown Court

By the defence

 Appeals from the **Crown Court** to the **Court of Appeal (Criminal Division)** are the most common route of appeal by the **defence** against conviction and/or sentence.

But, the defendant must have **leave to appeal**; and a request must be made within 28 days of the defendant being convicted.

By the prosecution

Appeals by the prosecution against an **acquittal** are rare, and can only be done with the permission of the **Attorney General**, who can:

a) refer a point of law to the Court of Appeal

b) apply for leave against an **unduly lenient** sentence

In 2009, 71 cases, out of 369 had their sentences increased after the Court of Appeal found the sentences to be unduly lenient.

 This route of appeal from the **Crown Court** to the **Supreme Court** is extremely rare and is available to the prosecution and defence. Leave to appeal is rarely granted and will only be granted on legal points of **'general public importance'**.

Criminal Cases Review Commission

The Runciman Commission reported in 1993 and recommended the establishment of an independent body to consider suspected miscarriages of justice as a result of a number of high profile miscarriages of justice, including the *Birmingham Six*, the *Guildford Four* and *Judith Ward*. The recommendations were implemented and the Criminal Cases Review Commission was set up under the *Criminal Appeal Act 1995*, and came into being in January 1997. There are 14 members of the Commission, all appointed by the Queen and consist of legally qualified professionals as well as others who have similar experience in the criminal justice system.

The Commission has the power to:

- investigate possible miscarriages of justice and to refer cases back to the courts
- the Court of Appeal may direct the Commission to investigate and report to the court on any matter if an investigation is likely to help the court resolve its appeal.

Case statistics

Figures to 30 June 2013

Total applications:	16458
Cases waiting:	608
Cases under review:	545
Completed:	15305 (including ineligible), 530 referrals
Heard by Court of Appeal:	498 (341 quashed, 145 upheld, 2 reserved)

Source: www.ccrc.gov.uk

One of the CCRC's earliest successes was that of *Derek Bentley*, who was hanged in 1953 for murder. The CCRC took over the case around 1998 and referred the case back to the Court of Appeal. The Court of Appeal held that the judge had unfairly summed up the trial and it quashed the conviction. This was a very famous case and illustrative of the effects of the CCRC.

Another famous case was that of *Ryan James*, who was convicted of the murder of his wife. When the case was investigated by the CCRC, it was decided to send the case back to the Court of Appeal on the basis that a suicide note had been found written by his wife. His conviction was quashed.

Advantages and disadvantages of the CCRC

In **June 2013**, statistics published by the CCRC showed they had instigated **341 quashed convictions**.

Advantages

The CCRC gives the defendant an 'extra' opportunity to challenge the criminal justice system.

The CCRC is very **accessible** – the defendant, their family and even the Court itself can all apply to the CCRC for the case to be considered.

The CCRC has been seen to highlight very high profile miscarriages of justice, such as ***Derek Bentley***.

The CCRC is not an appeal court, and therefore does not have the power to overturn an appeal, or quash a conviction.

Disadvantages

The CCRC will often send the case back to the police for investigation. This questions the independence of the Commission, since the police can often be the cause of the miscarriage of justice.

The CCRC can only consider cases which have been through, and failed the ordinary appeal routes.

The establishment of the CCRC has not eradicated the reasons why miscarriages of justice occur; there needs to be more control over the activities and evidence in the police station.

There has been evidence to suggest that the CCRC has a severe backlog of cases – indeed in June 2013, 608 cases were still waiting for consideration.
The case of ***Patrick Nolan***, which was a case of a confession obtained under duress, took the CCRC five years to deal with.

What the CCRC deems as a 'successful' case could include those whose sentences have been reduced, or those who have had their convictions substituted with lesser offences.

Civil Procedure

The Civil justice system is used to settle disputes between private individuals or organisations. The person bringing the action is called the **claimant** and the person defending the action is known as the **defendant.** The case has to be proved **on the balance of probabilities** (the standard of proof) and the burden to prove the case is on the claimant. The claimant is normally seeking some form of **remedy**, which could be the payment of compensation or an injunction.

Key terminology

Standard of proof = the standard to which a case has to be established. In civil law, it is on the balance of probabilities which is a lower standard than a criminal case which has to be proved beyond reasonable doubt.

The Civil Court hierarchy (including appeal routes)

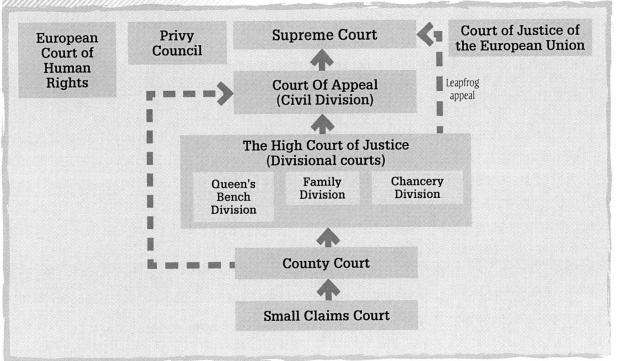

Civil procedure pre-1999 reforms

Before the Woolf reforms in April 1999, there were two separate sets of civil procedure depending on where the case commenced. For cases in the High Court and Court of Appeal there was the 'White Book' and for cases in the County Court there was the 'Green Book'. There were also different procedures for commencing a case. A case in the County Court was started with a **Summons**, but a case in the High Court was started with a **Writ.** The system had a tendency to be confusing for plaintiffs with differing rules of procedure and evidence.

Lord Woolf was tasked with reforming the civil justice system and undertook his review in 1996. This culminated in the report: **Access to Justice: Final Report** which was published in 1996. He concluded that the civil justice system of the time had some key flaws:

Adversarial = parties are opponents in a case (or adversaries) and present their position to the court so that an impartial judge (or jury) may reach a decision. This is opposed to the inquisitorial system where a judge or group of judges inquire into the case, making investigations in order to reach a conclusion.

Grade boost

Find out about the civil appeals process. This is another area that can be examined and it is important to have an understanding of the appeal routes and what can happen as a result of an appeal.

Grade boost

There may be a question that asks about the success/ failure of the Woolf reforms. Make sure you link your evaluation back to the main problems he found with the old system and the extent to which these have been overcome

stretch&challenge

Lord Jackson's suggestions following his **Review of Civil Litigation** were implemented by the *Legal Aid, Sentencing and Punishment of Offenders Act 2012* and came into force in April 2013. The overriding objective has been amended and now cases must be dealt with 'justly and at proportionate cost'.

- **Expensive** – his report found that costs often exceeded the amount in dispute.
- **Delays** – cases took an average of 3–5 years to reach the trial stage.
- **Complex** – with differing procedures for the County and High Courts, litigants found the system complex. As a result, lawyers would be hired, increasing costs for plaintiffs.
- **Adversarial** – there was an emphasis on exploiting the system rather than co-operation between parties.
- **Unjust** – there was also an imbalance of power between the wealthy represented party and the underrepresented party. This was a particular problem with out of court settlements with one party under pressure to settle more than the other.
- **Emphasis on oral evidence** – led to trials being slow and inefficient. Most evidence did not need to be presented orally and could have been pre-assessed by the judge. This also led to an increase in costs with expert witnesses having high fees.

As a result of the findings of the '**Woolf Report**', the main recommendations were put into effect in the **Civil Procedure Rules 1998**, which came into force in April 1999. They represent one of the biggest ever reforms of the civil justice system, with some questioning whether such wide reforms were needed.

r.1.1(2) states: Dealing with a case justly includes, so far as is practicable:

(a) ensuring that the parties are on an equal footing

(b) saving expense

(c) dealing with the case in ways which are proportionate: (i) to the amount of money involved; (ii) to the importance of the case; (iii) to the complexity of the issues; and (iv) to the financial position of each party

(d) ensuring that it is dealt with expeditiously and fairly and

(e) allotting to it an appropriate share of the court's resources, while taking into account the need to allot resources to other cases.

The Woolf reforms

The main changes made as a result of the **Civil Procedure Rules 1998** are as follows.

The Civil Procedure Rules – Simplified Procedure

The overriding aim of this reform is to provide a common procedural code for the County and High Court. Some terminology has also been changed to make it more accessible for claimants (previously plaintiffs).

Pre-Action Protocols

One of the biggest themes of the reforms is to encourage parties to co-operate with each other. Pre-Action Protocols are designed to encourage parties to exchange as much information as early as possible, be in contact with each other and co-operate over the exchange of information. Their overall aim is to get parties to settle out of court, thus reducing costs and delay.

Case Management

One of the most important reforms has been judges becoming the managers of cases, with proactive powers to set timetables and sanction parties that do not co-operate. The overall aim of this reform is to pass the management of the case to the court and not the parties. Again this should improve efficiency and reduce costs.

Alternative Dispute Resolution (ADR)

Parties can postpone proceedings for one month to attempt to settle the case using ADR. Courts should also actively promote its use. However, in **Halsey v Milton Keynes General NHS Trust (2004)**, the Court of Appeal said the courts cannot force parties to ADR as it might be against Article 6 of the European Convention on Human Rights – right to a fair trial.

The Three Tracks

1. **Small Claims Track** – cases with a value of less than £10 000 (or £1000 for personal injury) – heard in Small Claims Court.
2. **Fast Track** – cases with a value of between £5 000 and £25 000 – heard in County Court.
3. **Multi-Track** – cases with a value of over £25 000 – heard in either County or High Court.

Sanctions

The overriding aim of the reforms is to ensure that cases are as efficient and cost effective as possible. With judges taking on the role of case managers, they have been given powers to issue sanctions where parties do not follow the timetables they set or delay unnecessarily. Two main sanctions are:

- Adverse award of costs
- Order for a case to be struck out (in part or full).

In **Biguzzi v Rank Leisure plc (1999)** it was held that striking out a case would only happen if it was proportional and there are other options available to deal with delay.

In **UCB Halifax (SW) Ltd (1999)**, however, it was stressed that a lax approach should not be used for serious cases and courts should use the new powers available to them.

Criticisms of the reforms

Two key reports:

'Zander on Woolf' by Michael Zander, *New Law Journal 13 March 2009*

'A Few Home Truths' by Tony Allen, *New Law Journal 3 April 2009*

There has been a mixed response to the passing of the **Civil Procedure Rules 1998** – on the whole, they have not been met with much approval. Key commentators in this area include **Prof. Michael Zander** and **Tony Allen.**

Costs

- Early exchange of information means that there is front loading of costs.
- Many cases are settled before trial, therefore there are needless costs for clients.
- BUT Woolf says that an *earlier* appreciation of the facts means a *fuller* appreciation of them leading to a better result.
- The **Advisory Committee on Civil Costs** has been set up to monitor litigation costs.

Delay

- Delay has remained the same, despite the introduction of fixed date trials. Zander argues that the fixed trial dates mean that there is no time for legal professionals to undertake thorough preparation.

stretch&challenge

ADR has been promoted heavily since the Woolf reforms. Gather some statistics to demonstrate how this has led to an increase in cases being settled out of court. Consider the benefits of this for parties involved and for the courts. You may also want to look at the section on ADR.

Grade boost

Find out some features of each of the three tracks. How do they try to remedy the three main problems Woof found of cost, delay and complexity?

Find out about **Money Claim Online**.

Grade boost

Remember ADR is just a part of the **Civil Procedure Rules**; so when an examination question asks you about the Civil Procedure Rules remember to talk about ALL the Woolf reforms. It is a common mistake for students to only talk about ADR in a Civil Procedure question.

In preparation for the examination, it is worth mentioning any recent cases you have researched that have involved **ACAS**; it is always impressive to examiners to show knowledge of current affairs, and also make sure that you mention all relevant sections of the **Arbitration Act 1996**.

But...

- Allen believes that advance notice and exchange of information HAS to be a good thing – why encourage ambush?
- Allen believes waiting lists have dwindled and cases seem to reach trial quicker.

Judicial case management

This has not been successful, because Zander believes that the lawyers are not the only sources of delay, there is delay caused by parties and the difficulty in getting reports from experts and court administration. Zander believes that Woolf ignored this and just saw the lawyers as the villains.

Complexity

- Lord Woolf wanted the civil justice system to be simpler – **Peter Thompson QC** – under the old rules there were 391 pages of procedure, and under the new rules there are 2,301 pages with 49 updates.

Adversary culture

- Zander believes this area to have worked as more cases are settling out of court.
- However, he contends that Woolf's finding that the primary cause of delay was the adversarial process was misplaced.

Encouragement of ADR

- Allen argues that the requirement to try ADR is not being enforced at the allocation stage.
- Allen is a great supporter of mediation, and is questioning the sanctions given for UNREASONABLE LITIGATION BEHAVIOUR. What could be deemed to be unreasonable?

stretch&challenge

It is always impressive to the examiner if you can show a knowledge of the procedure in a civil case.

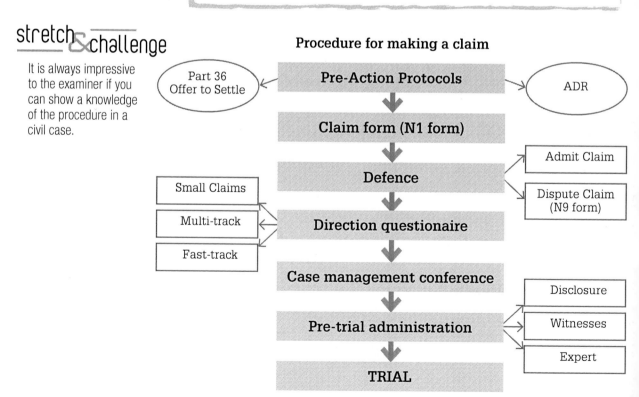

Procedure for making a claim

Alternative Dispute Resolution

Reasons for alternative dispute resolution

Court action is not always the most appropriate means of resolving a dispute because of the following reasons:

- Complexity of legal procedures.
- The delay in resolution.
- The cost of court action.
- Intimidating atmosphere of the courts.
- The public nature of court action.
- The adversarial nature of court action which will result in a deterioration of the relationship between the parties.

ADR is encouraged by **Part 1 Civil Procedure Rules 1998**, where it is part of judge's role in **active case management** to encourage ADR where appropriate. Remember ADR is only used in civil cases; this is because in criminal cases, there is too much at risk to justify an alternative to the criminal justice system. ADR has grown over the last 50 years, and is now increasingly being seen as a compulsory step in the process, rather than an alternative. Indeed, there have been examples where parties have been 'punished' with an **adverse costs order** for refusing to co-operate in a method of ADR.

Forms of alternative dispute resolution

Definition	Legal authority	Advantages	Disadvantages
Arbitration			
Commonly used in commercial and contract cases, and most notably high profile sports cases.			
The parties agree to let an independent arbitrator make a **binding** decision. Many contracts include a *Scott v Avery* clause to agree pre-contractually to arbitrate in the event of a dispute.	- *s1 Arbitration Act 1996* - *s5 Arbitration Act 1996* - *Institute of Arbitrators*	- The parties have discretion as to the choice of arbitrator with the existence of the *Institute of Arbitrators*. - The hearing procedure is left to the discretion of the parties; they can choose the venue, date, number of witnesses etc. - There is rarely any publicity. - The award is binding and can be enforced by the courts. - The arbitrator is an expert in the field.	- Public funding is not available, so one party may have an advantage from the outset. - Appeals are restricted in the arbitration process. - Parties may feel they do not get their 'day in court'. - If a legal point arises, there is not always a legal professional in the hearing.

continues over

Definition	Legal authority	Advantages	Disadvantages

Mediation

Commonly used in family disputes or any area where a relationship needs to be maintained.

The parties are encouraged to come to their own settlement with the help of a third party neutral mediator who acts as a 'go-between'.	• *Dunnett v Railtrack* • *Halsey v Milton Keynes NHS Trust* • *s13 Family Law Act 1996* • new government proposals.	• It is a private and confidential process. • The parties enter into mediation *voluntarily*. • It is quick, cost effective and accessible. • There is a good chance that the parties can maintain a relationship.	• The dispute may end up going to court anyway if mediation fails, resulting in greater costs. • Increasingly being seen as a compulsory step in the process. • Where parties are 'forced' into mediation, there is a half-hearted commitment; decreasing the chances of success.

Conciliation

Commonly used in industrial disputes.

The third party plays a more ACTIVE role in the proceedings in order to push them in the direction of a settlement.	• **ACAS** • **Examples of current issues where ACAS are involved – (see website)**	• It is a cheaper option than litigation. • It is a private and confidential process. • ACAS adopts a prevention rather than cure approach to dispute resolution. • It identifies and clarifies the main issues in the dispute.	• Heavily relies on the skills of the conciliator. • The dispute may end up going to court anyway if conciliation fails, resulting in greater costs.

Negotiation

Used in most cases at the outset of the dispute.

Resolving the dispute between the parties themselves; can involve solicitors. At its most basic, involves returning faulty goods to a shop: at its most complex involves solicitors, and settlement offers being exchanged.	N/A	• Completely private. • Quick resolution, maintaining relationships. • Relatively informal method of resolution.	• Involving solicitors can make the process costly. • Offers are often exchanged and are not agreed until the day of court; wasting time and money. • People see it as a 'halfway' house, and think that they are not receiving as much as if they had gone to court.

stretch&challenge

From April 2011, all divorcing couples, as part of their application, are expected to attend a **Family Mediation Information and Assessment Meeting** to consider with a mediator, whether the dispute may be capable of being resolved through mediation.
Do you think this will cause resentment for the system, or encourage people to be more amicable in their disputes, and will it eventually replace solicitors?

Tribunals

Tribunals are an important part of the legal system and act as 'specialist courts' for disputes in a specialised area, mainly concerning welfare and social rights. For example, employment disputes are very often resolved using a Tribunal, as are immigration and social security disputes.

There are three different types of tribunal:

Administrative: this type of tribunal deals with disputes between individuals and the State over rights contained in social welfare legislation, such as social security, immigration and land.

Domestic: these are internal tribunals used for disputes within private bodies, such as the Law Society and the General Medical Council.

Employment: these are the biggest use of tribunals, and deal with disputes between employees and employers over rights under employment legislation.

A Tribunal usually consists of three people; one neutral chairperson and one representative from each side, usually a union representative or a specialist in the area.

Tribunals date back to the birth of the welfare state and were established to give people a way of making sure their rights were enforced. When they were first introduced, there were more than 70 different tribunals; all with different procedures and administration. This led to over-complication and users felt intimidated and confused by the system.

Tribunals are frequently seen as another alternative to the courts, but the biggest difference is that if the case fails at the Tribunal stage, there is no redress to the courts, whereas if any other form of ADR fails, the parties still get the option of going to court to resolve their dispute.

Grade boost

When you are writing an essay on Tribunals, make sure you include a little about the **history** of the Tribunal system, but more importantly you need to show knowledge of the current system and be able to cite the ***Tribunals, Courts and Enforcement Act 2007*** and its provisions.

Example of an Employment Tribunal

A Tribunal usually consists of three people; one neutral chairperson and one representative from each side, usually a union representative or a specialist in the area.

Legally Qualified Chairperson

Employer's Representative

Trade Union Representative

History of tribunals

1957   **Franks Committee** recommended that tribunal procedures should be an example of **'openness, fairness** and **impartiality'**. The recommendations were implemented in the *Tribunals and Inquiries Act 1958*.

1958   **Council on Tribunals** was set up to supervise and review tribunal procedures. The Council was a body that would deal with complaints and submit recommendations for improvement. However, it was regarded as a *'watchdog with no teeth'* meaning it had very little power to make changes.

2000   **Sir Andrew Leggatt**: *'Tribunals for Users – One System, One Service'* – this report marked a radical reform of the Tribunal system, since Leggatt reported that Tribunals lacked independence, coherence and were not user friendly.

Recommendation	Details
A single tribunal service to be responsible for the administration of all tribunals	• This makes the tribunal service independent of its relevant government department. • The support that the service gives to tribunals is unified both in procedure and administration.
Tribunals should be organised into divisions, grouping together similar tribunals	• The Divisions that were created are: Education, Financial, Health and Social Services, Immigration, Land and Valuation, Social Security and Pensions, Transport, Regulatory and Employment. • Each Division is headed by a **Registrar** who takes on **case management duties** in line with the *Civil Procedure Rules*.
The system should be user friendly	• Users are encouraged to bring their own cases without legal representation. • Written judgments should be given in Plain English. • Information about procedures, venues, etc., should be made freely available. • There is a single route of appeal.
Single route of appeal	• There is a single route of appeal, with each Division having a corresponding appeal tribunal, and only then will there be a redress to the Court of Appeal.

2007   *Tribunals, Courts and Enforcement Act* – this was the Act that formalised and implemented most of **Leggatt's** reforms and contributed to the most radical shake up of the Tribunal system seen for many years.

Tribunals, Courts and Enforcement Act 2007

This Act implemented many of Leggatt's reforms, and of particular note is *Part 1*, which established a **Tribunal Service** that unified all the procedures and created a new structure that addressed many of Leggatt's concerns. There are now only two tribunals; the First-Tier Tribunal and the Upper Tribunal, within which are **chambers**, or groups of tribunals with similar jurisdictions. For the first time ever, the Upper Tribunal will have the power to conduct a **judicial review** of a case which has been heard in the First-Tier Tribunal, thus minimising the need for the courts to get involved in the case. All members or judges working in the new system will be appointed by the *Judicial Appointments Commission*, and are thus recognised as judges, which increases the status of Tribunals. Further appeal from the **Upper Tribunal** is available to the **Court of Appeal**, but this is very rarely used because of the well-structured system.

The whole system is headed by the **Senior President of Tribunals** who is responsible for assigning judges to the chambers and for looking after their general welfare and helping with any issues that may arise. The President has the power to issue **practice directions** in order to help Tribunal judges maintain a unified procedure across all the chambers.

The **Council on Tribunals** has been replaced by the **Administrative Justice and Tribunals Council**, and this body is much more powerful than the previous system in terms of reviewing the system, keeping it under control and advising the government on future reforms of the **Tribunal Service**.

Court Of Appeal

Upper Tribunal

Administrative Appeals Chamber			Tax and Chancery Chamber		Lands Chamber	Asylum and Immigration Chamber
Social Entitlement Chamber	Health, Education and Social Care Chamber	War Pensions and Armed Forces Compensation Chamber	General Regulatory Chamber	Taxation Chamber	Land, Property and Housing Chamber	Asylum and Immigration Chamber

First-Tier Tribunal

Employment tribunals

Employment tribunals are not included in the new structure because it was felt that the types of disputes dealt with by Employment tribunals were very different from the other tribunals, and so the **Employment Tribunal** and the **Employment Appeals Tribunal** remain distinct from the structure.

From 29 July 2013, all employment tribunal claims and appeals will be required to pay a fee. This is because employment tribunals are the biggest form of tribunal and cost around £74m per year to run.

Grade boost

Be prepared to talk about Tribunals both as a topic in its own right, and as a form of Alternative Dispute Resolution.

Advantages and disadvantages of tribunals

Cost

Parties are encouraged to take their own cases without the need for representation. This has been made even easier with the availability of application forms online and a more transparent **tribunal service** since the reforms.

Speed

There is a duty on the tribunal judges to take on case management duties, so they are able to impose strict timetables to ensure that most cases can be heard within one day.

Advantages

Expertise

At least one member of the Tribunal will be an expert in the relevant field, so this will save time explaining complex technicalities to a judge in court.

Informality

Tribunals are much less formal than a court hearing, though they are more formal than other methods of ADR. The parties benefit from a private hearing and have the chance to maintain a relationship after the case is over.

Independence

Because of the involvement of the **Judicial Appointments Commission** in appointing Tribunal Judges, the Tribunal system is much more transparent, independent and thus fair. Further, the unified set of procedures and rules minimises the risk of inconsistencies between tribunals.

Lack of funding

Legal funding is available for some disputes; for example, if you are a member of a union, you may get your case paid for by them, but it is not always available, which can be detrimental to a person taking on a big company that has the benefit of the most expensive representation.

Disadvantages

Delay

If the case is one of a complex nature, then there can be a delay in getting the case heard.

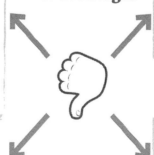

Intimidated parties

There is still the problem of parties feeling intimidated and daunted at the prospect of taking a case to 'court', particularly without the comfort of having a legal representative.

Lack of precedent

Tribunals do not operate a strict system of precedent, so there is sometimes an element of unpredictability to the outcomes of cases.

Legal Advice and Funding

What is meant by the unmet need for legal services?

There are many people who have an unmet need for legal services, this simply means that a person has a problem which could possibly be solved by going to law, but that person is not able to get help from the system.

People fail to get help for many reasons:

- People fail to see that their problem has legal implications.
- People choose not to pursue the case because of implications such as cost, or see solicitors as unapproachable.
- People do not know of the existence of a legal service or cannot find one that could help.

History of legal aid

- **1949** – first state-funded legal aid scheme
- **1980s** – system had developed into six different schemes
  1. Legal advice and assistance scheme (the 'green form' scheme)
  2. Assistance by way of representation (ABWOR)
  3. Civil legal aid
  4. Criminal legal aid
  5. Duty solicitor – police stations
  6. Duty solicitor – Magistrates' Courts.
- **Legal Aid Board** – administered the schemes
- **Cost** of the system escalating
- **1999 – *Access to Justice Act 1999*** – Legal Services Commission replaces Legal Aid Board
- **2012 – *Legal Aid, Sentencing and Punishment of Offenders Act 2012*** – major changes to the system. Legal Aid Agency replaces the Legal Services Commission.

Access to Justice Act 1999

- Legal Aid Board replaced with **Legal Services Commission (LSC)**
- Community Legal Services Partnerships developed
- Introduction of a quality mark
- Six schemes replaced with two new schemes:
  - **Community Legal Service**
  - Criminal Defence Service.

Grade boost

You must be able to fully explain the reasons why people have an unmet legal need and whether recent reforms have addressed this unmet legal need.

Research the following cases which will highlight why there is an unmet legal need, and why a legal aid system is needed:

- ***Bevan Ashford v Geoff Yeandle (1998)***
- ***Thai Trading Co v Taylor (1998)***.

Grade boost

Don't forget that you should also consider the other sources of advice available:

- Law centres
- Community Legal Advice Centres
- Citizens' Advice Bureaux
- Local Authorities
- Trade Unions
- Motoring organisations
- Pro Bono clinics
- Insurance

Advantages and disadvantages of the Access to Justice Act 1999 reforms

Advantages	Disadvantages
• Better control over costs – civil cases now fixed budget. Legal aid costs the government £2 billion; new Funding Code should help to reduce this. • Higher standards of work – only those firms with a contract can provide legal services. • Quality mark – reinforces high standards. • Resources better allocated. Fixed budget for civil cases allows better allocation of resources, also cases taken out of the civil legal aid budget as mentioned earlier.	• Limited access to justice – only those providers with a contract can offer state-funded legal services. • Cost cutting – fixed budget for civil cases may mean that these cases will suffer because of the priority in funding given to criminal cases. • No legal aid for defamation cases – **_McLibel Two (Steel v UK (2005))_**. • Cases removed from civil legal aid as highlighted earlier. • Problems with conditional fee agreements. • Concerns over public defenders. Are they truly independent? Do they offer as good a service as private defence solicitors? • Poorer standards of work – reliance on contracted firms only. • Huge costs of criminal cases – with criminal cases taking priority over civil cases in the budget.

stretch&challenge

Examine the reforms made to legal aid following LASPO. Make a table of the advantages and disadvantages similar to the one above for the AJA reforms.

Grade boost

The changes meant some types of case were no longer eligible for public funds – including divorce, child contact, welfare benefits, employment, clinical negligence, and housing law except in very limited circumstances. Evaluate the potential impact of this.

stretch&challenge

The cuts to legal aid following LASPO might have been more significant had it not been for the UK's membership of the ECHR. Why do you think this is? How might any further cuts have conflicted with the ECHR?

Legal Aid, Sentencing and Punishment of Offenders Act 2012 (LASPO)

Legal Services Commission

- Under LASPO the Legal Services Commission has been abolished and replaced by the **Legal Aid Agency**, which is an Executive Agency of the Ministry of Justice.
- **Community Legal Service** (CLS) will be referred to as **civil legal aid** from 1 April 2013 but will not have a new logo.
- **Criminal Defence Service** (CDS) will be referred to as **criminal legal aid** from 1 April 2013.
- **CDS Direct** will be renamed as **Criminal Defence Direct** (CDD) from 1 April 2013.

Significant changes to civil legal aid in England and Wales came into effect on 1 April 2013, as part of a plan to reform the legal aid system and save £350m a year. Further cuts are planned.

Legal aid and civil cases

It reverses the position where legal aid has been available for all civil cases except those specifically excluded by the **_Access to Justice Act 1999_**. LASPO removes some types of case from legal aid funding, and states that other cases will only qualify when they meet certain criteria.

The reforms apply across civil litigation, but have a particular impact in personal injury cases, where no win no fee conditional fee agreements are used significantly. This is now referred to as civil legal aid.

Which cases will no longer qualify?

LASPO has removed funding from entire areas of civil law. They include:

- Private family law, e.g. divorce and custody cases.
- Personal injury and some clinical negligence cases.
- Some employment and education law.
- Immigration where the person is not detained.
- Some debt, housing and benefit issues.

LASPO will continue to fund certain cases

These include:

- Family law cases involving domestic violence, forced marriage or child abduction.
- Mental health cases.
- All asylum cases.
- Debt and housing matters where someone's home is at immediate risk.

Exceptional Cases Funding Scheme

LASPO has introduced a new Exceptional Case Funding Scheme (ECF) which allows cases to be funded where there are exceptional circumstances, i.e. where failure to grant legal aid would result in breach of a client's rights under the **European Convention on Human Rights**.

Telephone gateway service

A new mandatory telephone gateway service operates for clients who want debt, education (special education needs) and discrimination advice.

Alternative funding

Civil legal aid may be refused in any individual case suitable for alternative funding, such as a conditional fee agreement (CFA) except in Family or Mental health tribunals.

Changes to eligibility for civil legal aid

- All applicants will be subject to a capital assessment regardless of whether they are in receipt of certain benefits.
- Monthly income contributions from clients have increased by up to 30% of their disposable income.
- Introduce a residency test so that only those with a strong connection to the UK are able to receive civil legal aid.
- Make it more difficult for claimants to use civil legal aid to bring speculative cases by ensuring all cases must have at least a 50% chance of success to be funded.

Legal aid and criminal cases

Following LASPO, overseen by the **Legal Aid Agency** and now referred to as **criminal legal aid**. Criminal defence accounts for more than half of legal aid expenditure.

In September 2013 the Law Society and the Ministry of Justice agreed new proposals for criminal legal aid. These will ensure that all those solicitors who currently provide criminal legal aid work to their clients will continue to be able to do so, as long as they meet quality requirements. The proposals are also considering an updated tendering model for duty work, such as in police stations.

The main reforms include:

- Stop criminal legal aid being given to prisoners where their disputes can be solved through the prisoner complaints system and do not require a lawyer. This will prevent around 11,000 cases each year being funded unnecessarily by criminal legal aid.
- Introduce a threshold on Crown Court legal aid to stop the wealthiest defendants with an annual household disposable income of £37,500 or more being automatically granted legal aid.
- Reduce the cost of the long-running criminal cases, which place too much of a burden on taxpayers, by 30%.
- Cap on contracts for duty solicitor work at police stations.
- Funding is still demand led, no set budget. Funding for criminal matters is divided into three types of service. **Advice and Assistance**, this provides for general advice, e.g. getting a barrister's opinion, it does not cover representation in court, a means test is applied. **Advocacy Assistance**, this covers a solicitor preparing the case and initial court proceedings, there is a merits test. **Representation**, this covers the cost of a solicitor preparing the defence and representation in court.
- **Public defenders** – set up in 2001. The Legal Aid Agency employs criminal defence solicitors, known as public defenders. There has been opposition to public defenders, with some questioning whether a conflict of interest lies in the fact that the government employs both prosecution and defence lawyers.
- **Duty solicitors** – free of charge, available at police stations and Magistrates' Courts
- **Contract** required from Legal Aid Agency. Only those firms with a contract can offer state-funded criminal defence work. Solicitors who have a contract can provide the range of services from arrest to the end of the case. In certain cases defendants are not free to choose their own solicitor/barrister, e.g. serious fraud cases; here there is a panel of experts from whom the suspect will have to choose.
- Means test was abolished by AJA 1999, instead for those cases in the Crown Court an order was given at the end of the trial for those who had been convicted and had the necessary income, to pay back the defence costs.
- ***Criminal Defence Service Act 2006*** – reintroduced means test for cases in the Magistrates' Courts. In 2010 the means test was reintroduced for cases in the Crown Court, now if a defendant is found not guilty then any contributions they have made towards their case will be refunded to them with interest.
- Criminal Defence Service Direct (now Criminal Defence Direct) – set up in 2005. A free telephone advice service particularly for those in police detention for non-imprisonable offences.

Two tests must be passed to get criminal legal aid:

- **Interests of Justice test** considers the 'merits' of the case, e.g. a person's previous convictions, the nature of the offence and the risk of custody.
- **Means test** considers the person's financial position, e.g. household income, capital, and outgoings. This test determines whether a client will be liable for any of their defence costs.

- If a person fails the means test and their case is being heard in the Magistrates' Court, they will not be given legal aid and will be expected to pay privately.
- If a person's case is being heard in the Crown Court, the means test will determine how much they need to contribute towards their defence costs; this could be from their income, their capital or a combination of both.

Passported applications

Who is passported?

Some applications for legal aid are 'passported' through the means test. In other words, the application passes the means test automatically.

This will apply to a client if they are under 18, or in receipt of any of the following benefits:

- Income support
- Income-based job seeker's allowance
- Universal credit
- Guaranteed state pension credit
- Income-related employment and support allowance.

Conditional fee agreements

Introduced by the ***Courts and Legal Services Act 1990*** and ***Access to Justice Act 1999***.

How do they work?

- Solicitors can agree to take no fee, or a reduced fee if they lose, and raise their fee by a agreed percentage if they win (maximum of double usual fee).
- Extra fee is called the **'uplift' or 'success fee'**.
- Loser pays winner's costs and the uplift and if the court orders the insurance premium also, if insurance has been taken out.
- ***Access to Justice Act 1999*** – conditional fee available for all cases except medical negligence.

From 1 April 2013 new rules on conditional fee agreements (CFAs) came into force. These changes have been brought about by sections 44 and 46 of the ***Legal Aid, Sentencing and Punishment of Offenders Act 2012*** and the ***Conditional Fee Agreements Order 2013***.

Summary of the key changes to CFAs following LASPO

- No win no fee conditional fee agreements remain available in civil cases, but the additional costs involved (success fee and insurance premiums) are no longer payable by the losing side.
- Referral fees are banned in personal injury cases.
- Claimants' damages are protected: the fee that a successful claimant has to pay the lawyer – the lawyer's 'success fee' is capped at 25% of the damages recovered.
- Claimants who lose, but whose claims are conducted in accordance with the rules, are protected from having to pay the defendant's costs.

Key terminology

Conditional fee agreements = also known as 'no win, no fee' agreements. They provide for litigation and advocacy. A solicitor shares the risk in that if a case is lost the solicitor will not be paid, but if the case is won the solicitor will charge a success fee

Advantages and disadvantages of conditional fee agreements

Advantages	Disadvantages
Widens access to justice – allows those who are ineligible for state help to bring a case.	High risk: uncertain cases may not be taken on because of the fear of losing.
Cost the state nothing.	Claimants misled – many believe that they will pay no costs but in practice this is not always true.
Financial incentive to win – could encourage better performance by solicitors.	Insurance can be costly.
Widens coverage – e.g. defamation and tribunal cases.	Pressure from insurance companies to settle early.
Insurance requirement – mitigate against losing.	Should lawyers be so heavily involved in the financial outcome of a case?
Very popular with the public.	

stretch&challenge

Lord Jackson's Report 2010 – Review of Civil Litigation – this review was carried out because of concerns over the huge rise in civil litigation costs, and disputes over the cost-shifting rule, where the loser pays the winner's costs. Research the proposals of Lord's Jackson's report. What impact do you think they will have, if implemented, on conditional fee agreements?

The future of legal funding

Lord Carter's review

- Lord Carter's review, **Legal aid: a market-based approach to reform (2006)**
- Government paper, **Legal Aid: a sustainable future (2006)**
- Government paper, **Best Value Tendering for Criminal Defence Services (2007)**

The aim of the reforms to control costs and quality.

Carter's recommendations include:

Recommendation	Reforms
Procurement contracts and Competitive tendering – here providers will have to bid to deliver certain legal services within a geographical area	This reform is due to come into force in 2013 for criminal work and 2015 for civil work.
Introduction of fixed fees for cases. Lawyers should not be paid by the hour but by the case	Fixed fees are due to be introduced for all criminal cases.
Granting fewer and larger contracts.	Lord Carter's review stated that larger firms are more efficient than small firms and therefore the Legal Services Commission is planning to grant larger legal aid contracts to either an individual firm or a number of firms who will work together. This will have an effect in Wales where the number of sole practitioners is high, and may see many go out of business as they fail to compete with the larger firms for the contracts

The European Convention on Human Rights and the Human Rights Act 1998

Background to the European Convention on Human Rights

The Council of Europe drew up the European Convention on Human Rights; the Council of Europe was set up after World War 2 to achieve unity among countries in matters such as protection of fundamental human rights. The Council now has 45 members.

The European Convention on Human Rights and Fundamental Freedoms was drafted and signed in 1950 and ratified by UK in 1951 and became binding in 1953.

The Convention contains rights known as Articles.

Articles	Rights
Article 1	Imposes obligation on state to secure the rights within their own country
Article 2	Right to life
Article 3	Right not to be subjected to torture or inhumane or degrading treatment
Article 4	Freedom from slavery and forced labour
Article 5	Right to liberty and security of the person, e.g. to question validity of detention
Article 6	Right to a fair trial (includes right to a solicitor and the trial itself)
Article 7	Laws should not act retrospectively (i.e. laws when passed come in on that day or a day in the future, they do not work back in time)
Article 8	Right to privacy
Article 9	Freedom of thought, conscience and religion
Article 10	Right to freedom of expression
Article 11	Right to peaceful protest and assembly (including right to join a trade union)
Article 12	Right to marry and have a family
Article 13	The country (in our case the UK) must have a court system where the person complaining about a breach of rights can have their case heard
Article 14	The rights in the Convention are enjoyed free from discrimination

New rights were added in 1952 in Protocol 1, these include:
- Article 1 – Right to peaceful enjoyment of your possessions
- Article 2 – Right to education
- Article 3 – Right to free elections by secret ballot.

The rights in the Convention are not absolute rights; the Articles contain exceptions as to when the rights can be withheld from us. Only one right in the Convention is an absolute right, this is Article 3.

You can enforce the rights in the Convention ONLY AGAINST PUBLIC BODIES.

It is very important to note that you SUE (Civil law) for a breach of human rights.

Grade boost

You must discuss, with cases, the meaning of 'public authority' for section 6 of the Human Rights Act 1998. The definition was considered in ***Donoghue v Poplar Housing and Regeneration Community Association Ltd (2001)*** – public authority could include a housing association as by providing accommodation it was fulfilling the Local Authority's statutory obligation. Further a private body can be included within section 6 if it is performing functions that are of a public nature; however, this will be decided on a case-by-case basis – ***YL v Birmingham City Council (2007)***.

Machinery for the enforcement of human rights

The European Commission of Human Rights used to consider the admissibility of any application. The **Committee of Ministers**, consisting of politicians, supervises the execution of the Court judgments. **The European Court of Human Rights and Grand Chamber, set up in 1951,** handles claims made by one state against another and by individuals against a state. The Court is in Strasbourg and is not to be confused with the Court of Justice of the European Union, which is a separate court.

The European Court of Human Rights can only hear individual claims where the state has recognised the right of individuals to bring a case to it – the **right of individual petition**, the UK agreed to this right in 1966.

Taking a case to Europe was often very slow and expensive, remedies were often inadequate. To take a case you must:

- have exhausted all domestic remedies first; and
- file the case within six months of final domestic decision.

Note: after the passing of the **Human Rights Act 1998** you can still take a case to the European Court as the final appeal court.

Grade boost

Further ***Andrews v Reading BC (2005)*** shows the duty on public bodies to act in a way which is compatible with human rights – Reading Borough Council had to pay compensation for failing to consider Andrews' Convention right to peaceful enjoyment of his possessions when implementing transport policy in Reading which resulted in more traffic passing his home.

Key sections of the Human Rights Act 1998

How has the ***Human Rights Act 1998*** affected how our rights are protected?

HRA 1998 incorporated the European Convention (and 1st protocol) into domestic law; the Act came into force in October 2000.

Section 7 HRA – Convention now directly applicable in UK courts, no need to go to the European Court of Human Rights (but possible as a last resort).

Before the *Human Rights Act* taking a case to Strasbourg could take up to 6 years.

Section 2 – *domestic judiciary 'must take into account'* any relevant jurisprudence – this requires the courts to take into account any relevant judgments from the European Court of Human Rights, but they are not bound by them. Section 2 creates a weak obligation on judges.

Section 3 – requires that: 'So far as it is possible to do so legislation must be read and given effect in a way which is compatible with the Convention rights'.

Section 6 – unlawful for public authorities to act in a way which is incompatible with Convention rights. Meaning of 'public authority' considered in ***Donoghue v Poplar Housing and Regeneration Community Association Ltd (2001)*** – public authority could include a housing association as by providing accommodation it was fulfilling the Local Authority's statutory obligation. Further a private body can be included within section 6 if it is performing functions that are of a public nature; however, this will be decided on a case-by-case basis – ***YL v Birmingham City Council (2007).***

Andrews v Reading BC (2005) – Reading Borough Council had to pay compensation for failing to consider Andrews' Convention right to peaceful enjoyment of his possessions when implementing transport policy in Reading which resulted in more traffic passing his home.

Section 19 – All Bills must contain a written statement as to whether the Bill is compatible with the Convention.

Section 4 – The HRA 1998 has limitations – laws which are incompatible with Convention rights are still valid – judges CANNOT strike them out (upholds principle of parliamentary sovereignty). However, if Courts find legislation to be incompatible, they can issue a

declaration of incompatibility under section 4, where a Minister can then amend the law by a fast track process.

*Section 4 – declarations of incompatibility – **Wilson v First County Trust (2003)*** – House of Lords issued a declaration that a provision of the Consumer Credit Act 1974 was incompatible with the Convention. *Other important cases to note on* **section 4:**

- *Procurator Fiscal v Brown (2000)*
- *Bellenger v Bellenger (2003)*
- *A and Z and others v Secretary of State for the Home Department (2004)*

Current issues and debates see:

- *Re JJ (control orders)(2006)*
- *Re MB (2006)*
- *R (on the application of Shabina Begum) v Head Teacher and Governors of Denbigh School (2006)*
- *Ali v Head Teacher and Governors of Lord Grey School (2006)*

Advantages and disadvantages of the Human Rights Act 1998

Advantages	Disadvantages
- Improved access - Encourages conformity with domestic law and the European Convention - Avoids conflict between UK domestic law and international law - Better awareness of rights by citizens - ECHR has been tried and tested over 30 years.	- HRA NOT entrenched. The main problem with the Human Rights Act is that it is not ENTRENCHED – this means it is not permanent, any new government could scrap it. There is only one entrenched law in the UK constitution, that the monarch may not be a catholic, there are no other laws that are entrenched, unlike America that has a Bill of Rights. - Too much judicial power? - Too little judicial power? – judges cannot strike out laws. - Rights in the Convention only enforceable against the state and not private individuals. - ECHR is old, out-dated, does not include social or economic rights.

Grade boost

You must be aware of current debates surrounding the Human Rights Act. The Prime Minister, David Cameron, says he intends to replace the UK's Human Rights Act with a 'British Bill of Rights'. Do you think the Human Rights Act should be scrapped? Research the debates surrounding this issue, look at the UK Bill of Rights Commission that was established in March 2012. Some suggest the reforms would lead to the Supreme Court's powers to hold the executive to account being weakened further. Do you agree? Do you think the reforms will go ahead?

stretch&challenge

Should the UK resist giving prisoners the right to vote despite the ruling of the European Court of Human Rights? Do you think prisoners should have the right to vote?

stretch&challenge

Research the cases of Abu Hamza and Abu Qatada. Do you think they should be deported? What are the human rights arguments against deportation in these cases?

Grade boost

Very important to be able to discuss, with relevant authority, sections 2, 3, 4 and 6 of the HRA in detail. When you are discussing section 4 declarations of incompatibility you must include cases where they have been issued or considered.

Grade boost

Human rights also links to statutory interpretation, particularly sections 3 and 4 of the Human Rights Act and the implications for statutory interpretation. Ensure that you know all of these topics thoroughly for the examination

Grade boost

Also important to be able to include examples of the rights in the European Convention.

It is a common examination error for students to mix up the Court of Justice of the European Union with the European Convention of Human Rights, they are separate institutions.

stretch&challenge

Article 6, of the Lisbon Treaty, which came into force in 2009, brings the European Union a step closer to protecting human rights, in that Article 6 recognises the rights contained in the European Charter of Fundamental Rights. This contains more extensive rights than the European Convention, including social and economic rights. However, the Charter will not create new rights in the UK. Why is this? Do you think we should have social and economic rights also?

Summary of protection of Human Rights pre- and post-HRA

	Pre-Act	Post-Act
Applicability of the ECHR	No direct effect – Convention had persuasive influence	Convention rights now directly applicable
Case law of ECtHR	Courts reluctant to apply case law of the Convention	Under s.2 duty to take into account case law of the ECtHR
Interpretation of statutes	Presumption against interference with fundamental rights	Must interpret laws in light of Convention rights wherever possible – S.3
Validity of primary legislation	No power to question or strike out an Act of Parliament	Power of higher courts to issue declarations of incompatibility – S.4

Future of human rights

Commission for Equality and Human Rights was set up in 2007, became fully operational in 2009. Functions include:

- Providing advice and guidance
- Conducting inquiries
- Bringing cases
- Monitoring the ECHR in domestic law
- Scrutinising new laws
- Publishing reports.

Bill of Rights

- Among Western democracies only the UK and Israel do not have a Bill of Rights, does that matter?
- America, China, Iraq, South Africa, most of Europe does. A Bill of Rights is only as effective as the state that enforces it.
- Do you think that the Human Rights Act has given greater protection to people against breaches of Human Rights, or do we need a Bill of Rights?

Advantages and disadvantages of a Bill of Rights

Advantages	Disadvantages
- Control on the executive – Bill of Rights offers a check on the huge powers of the executive (the government and its agencies, e.g. police, etc.). Courts could refuse to apply legislation that was incompatible with the Bill of Rights. - The judiciary – under the HRA section 3 – judges must interpret all laws to be compatible with human rights BUT only so far as it is possible to do so. This means that an Act that breaches rights in the Convention still prevails. This would not be the case with a Bill of Rights. - The HRA is not entrenched, therefore it can be repealed. A Bill of Rights would be entrenched. - The HRA did not bring in any new rights; a Bill of Rights would introduce new rights.	- Not needed – our rights are adequately protected. - Inflexible – hard to change. - Difficult to draft – what would you include? - Could lead to uncertainty – loose drafting style of a Bill of Rights. - A Bill of Rights is only as effective as the government that underpins it. - Increased power to the judiciary – judges not elected and power would be removed from Parliament.

European Union: Institutions

The UK joined the European Union on 1 January 1973 by passing the *European Communities Act 1972*. Each of the current 28 **Member States** remain independent sovereign states but have agreed to recognise the **supremacy** of the EU law created by the **institutions** of the EU. They have also delegated some of their decision-making powers to the EU Institutions. The latest addition, and the 28th Member State of the EU, was Croatia, who joined in July 2013.

There are five Key Institutions (though seven in total).

European Parliament

The Parliament currently has 766 *MEPs* from all 28 countries. They are elected every five years by the citizens of the Member States. MEPs do not sit with others from their country, but in seven Europe-wide political blocks representing broad political parties. The number of MEPs depends on the population of the Member State, with smaller States being over represented. For examples, the UK has 73, Germany has 99 and Malta has 6 MEPs. Seats are distributed among countries according to '*degressive proportionality*', i.e. MEPs from more populous countries will each represent more people than those from smaller countries. The Parliament's main function is to discuss proposals put forward by the Commission, and to act in conjunction with the Council to pass EU law via the **ordinary legislative procedure** (ex co-decision). The Parliament also exercises democratic supervision over the other EU Institutions, particularly the Commission, and shares control over the EU budget.

European Commission

The **executive** arm of the EU, it manages the day-to-day running of the EU, implementing EU policies and the budget. The Commission is a political body whose role is to propose ideas for legislation to the Parliament and Council. It acts as 'Guardian of the Treaties' and ensures Member States comply with their EU obligations. If they do not, the Commission can take action against them in the CJEU. The 28 Commissioners are independent of their national governments and they represent and uphold the interests of the EU as a whole. They also represent the EU internationally, negotiating agreements between the EU and other countries.

The Council of the European Union

The Council of the European Union is the main decision-making body of the EU. It is the **legislative** arm of the EU. Its membership varies according to the topic under discussion. For example, if the topic is environmental issues, the Environmental Minister from each Member State will attend on that occasion. The Council Ministers represent national interests thereby balancing the role of the Commission. They approve the budget jointly with the European Parliament.

The European Council

The European Council became an official institution after the *Treaty of Lisbon* in 2009. It consists of the Heads of State or Government of the Member States, together with its President. The European Council meets every six months or more often if the President requires. The meetings are known as **summits** and are used to set overall EU policy.

Key terminology

Executive = government.

Legislative = Parliament.

Judicial = judges.

Sovereignty (parliamentary sovereignty) = Parliament is the supreme legal authority. It has the power to make or repeal any law it wants. The courts cannot overrule its legislation and no Parliament can pass laws that future Parliaments cannot change. Parliament has lost some of its sovereignty since joining the EU.

stretch & challenge

To find out more about the EU, visit the official website of the European Union: www.europa.eu

The Council continues to play an important role in the passing of EU legislation. There are three systems of voting in the Council:

- **Unanimity**: in sensitive areas such as security and external affairs and taxation, decisions by the Council have to be unanimous, meaning all Members must vote for them. Effectively, one single country can therefore veto a decision.

- **Double majority**: this is a new system from 2014, where a majority of countries will be needed **and** a majority of the **total population** of the EU, for a proposal to go through.

- **Qualified majority**, which allows each state a specified number of votes (the larger the state, the more votes it has), and provides that a proposal can only be agreed if there are a specified number of votes in its favour.

Grade boost

The case of **Marshall v Southampton Area Health Authority (1986)** demonstrates how UK courts have used the preliminary ruling procedure. Find out about this case and why the UK courts needed to ask for guidance from the CJEU.

Use this unit and the unit on European Union Sources of Law to examine how Parliament has lost some of its sovereignty since joining the EU.

The Court of Justice of the European Union

Based in Luxembourg, the court of the European Union known as the CJEU, ensures that EU legislation is applied and interpreted consistently throughout the Member States and that they uphold their EU obligations. There is one judge from each Member State assisted by eight **Advocates General**. Cases can be brought to the CJEU by businesses, individuals and EU Institutions. It has the power to issue sanctions and settle disputes but does not follow a system of precedent, instead deciding cases by a majority. For the sake of efficiency the Court rarely sits as a full court with all 28 judges present. It generally sits as a 'Grand Chamber' of just 13 judges or in chambers of five or three judges. Since 1988, the CJEU has been assisted by a **Court of First Instance** to help it cope with the large number of cases brought before it.

It has two main functions – **Judicial** and **Supervisory**.

Judicial function

It hears cases to decide whether Member States have failed to fulfil their Treaty obligations. These actions are usually started by the European Commission, although they can also be started by another Member State. If found to be at fault, the accused Member State must change their practice at once. If they don't comply, the court may impose a fine on the Member State.

CASE – *Re Tachographs: The Commission v United Kingdom (1979)*

The UK was not enforcing the EU Regulation for road vehicles used in the carriage of goods to have tachographs fitted. **Held**: The United Kingdom had to fulfil its EU obligation and make it compulsory for these road users to fit tachographs.

Supervisory function

Known as the **preliminary ruling procedure.** It helps to ensure that EU law is consistently applied in all Member States. The power is given in **art.267 Treaty on the Functioning of the European Union.** If a national court is in any doubt about the interpretation or validity of an EU law, it may ask the CJEU for advice. This advice is given in the form of a 'preliminary ruling' and they use this ruling to help them come to a decision in the national case. This should only be done if the ruling is necessary to allow the court to give a ruling. Due to the potential volume of referrals, the case of **Bulmer v Bollinger (1974)** laid down guidelines as to when national Courts should refer a question to the CJEU. Generally only the highest court in a State should refer questions to the CJEU under the principle that Member States should first exhaust their own national appeal process to see if they can reach a conclusion in the case.

The guidelines state that a referral should only be made where **a ruling by the CJEU is necessary to enable the English court to give judgement in the case, i.e. where the ruling would be conclusive**. The courts should also take into account:

- Whether the CJEU has already made a judgement on the meaning.
- Whether the point is clear.
- The circumstances of the case, e.g. the length of time that may elapse before a ruling is given, possible overloading of the CJEU, the expense, the wishes of the parties.

LA2: Understanding Legal Reasoning, Personnel and Methods

LA2 focuses on developing students' understanding of Legal Reasoning, Personnel and Methods. LA2 looks to develop additional skills of applying the law to the facts and dealing with stimulus response questions. Students look at the passage of an Act of Parliament and the importance of delegated legislation along with considering the importance of keeping the law up to date with law reform. Two important legal doctrines are explored in this unit: statutory interpretation and judicial precedent. Students look at the different rules of interpretation that judges use when dealing with Acts of Parliament along with examining the operation of a consistent body of case law within a court hierarchy. Students will further their knowledge of the EU by looking at the different sources of EU law along with evaluating the effects of EU law on domestic legislation. Finally, students will also look at key legal personnel, their work, training and possible reforms. As with LA1, human rights remains a key topic that is pervasive throughout AS level.

Revision checklist

Tick column 1 when you have completed brief revision notes.
Tick column 2 when you think you have a good grasp of the topic.
Tick column 3 during final revision when you feel you have mastery of the topic.

			1	2	3
Magistrates	p59	Appointment of Magistrates			
	p60	Role of Magistrates			
	p61	Background of Magistrates			
	p61	Advantages and disadvantages of Magistrates			
The Judiciary	p62	Role of Judges			
	p62	The Lord Chancellor			
	p63	Judicial appointments process			
	p64	Training, dismissal, promotion and termination			
	p64	Judicial independence			
	p65	Criticisms of the judiciary/Reforms of the judiciary			
	p65	Role of the Supreme Court and reasons for establishment			
The Legal Profession	p66	Role of solicitors			
	p67	Complaints against solicitors			
	p67	Role of barristers			
	p68	Complaints against barristers			
	p68	Representation issues surrounding barristers and solicitors			
	p69	Reforms and the future of the legal profession			
Law Reform	p70	Advisory committees			
	p71	Law Commission			
	p72	Pressure groups			

				1	2	3
Judicial Precedent	p73	Elements of precedent				
	p75	House of Lords Practice Statement 1966				
	p75	Court of Appeal				
	p75	The Privy Council				
	p76	Judges as law makers?				
	p77	Advantages and disadvantages of judicial precedent				
	p77	The Supreme Court and precedent				
Statutory Interpretation	p78	How are statutes formed?				
	p78	Approaches to statutory interpretation				
	p80	Aids to interpretation – internal (intrinsic)				
	p81	Aids to interpretation – external (extrinsic)				
Delegated Legislation	p82	What is delegated legislation?				
	p82	Forms of delegated legislation				
	p83	Control of delegated legislation				
	p84	Advantages and disadvantages of delegated legislation				
European Union: Sources of Law	p85	Sources of EU law				
	p86	Direct and indirect effect				
	p88	The supervisory role of the CJEU				
	p89	The impact of EU law on parliamentary sovereignty				

Magistrates

The role of a Magistrate or **Justice of the Peace** was established with the **Justices of the Peace Act 1361**. They are **lay** people and volunteer to hear cases in the Magistrates' Court. There are also professional judges known as **District Judges** who sit alone in Magistrates' Courts who are considered in the unit on the judiciary. Volunteering as a Magistrate is seen as a way of giving something back to the community and gaining valuable skills. Today, Magistrates' powers and functions are governed by the ***Justices of the Peace Act 1997*** and ***Courts Act 2003.***

Magistrates must be able to commit at least 26 half-days per year to sit in court. An employer is required by law to allow reasonable time off work for an employee's service as a Magistrate. Though this time off does not have to be paid, many employers will allow paid time off. If a Magistrate suffers loss of earnings, they can claim a set rate for this loss. Expenses are also paid for travel and subsistence. There are approximately 30,000 lay Magistrates.

Cases in the Magistrates' Courts are usually heard by a panel of three Magistrates called a **Bench** supported by a legally qualified **Justices' Clerk** and **legal advisor**.

Appointment of Magistrates

- Appointed from the age of 18.
- Must retire at 70, though generally won't be appointed if over 65.
- Appointed by the Lord Chancellor on behalf of the Crown assisted by local advisory committees who vet and recommend suitable candidates.
- Individuals can now apply to become a Magistrate as well as being approached by the local advisory committee. Advertisements are published inviting applications.
- Potential magistrates complete an application form.
- For those shortlisted, there is usually a two-stage interview.
- They may also be required to participate in judicial aptitude tests and case studies.
- Selection is based on merit.
- The local advisory committee will ensure that the magistrate can demonstrate six key qualities: good character, understanding and communication, social awareness, maturity and sound temperament, sound judgement, commitment and reliability.
- Local advisory committees try to meet the needs of local benches in terms of the numbers required, with the aim of maintaining a balance of gender, ethnic origin, geographical spread, occupation, age and social background.
- Magistrates must be able to commit to 26 half-day sittings per year.
- Magistrates are unpaid but may claim expenses and an allowance for loss of earnings.
- Applications welcome from all sections of the community regardless of gender, ethnicity, religion or sexual orientation.
- No legal or academic qualifications required to be a Magistrate and full training is provided.
- Certain individuals are excluded from appointment such as police officers and traffic wardens.

Role of Magistrates

Grade boost

The **Justices Clerk** assists the Magistrates with the law. They are qualified lawyers with a Magistrates' Court qualification. They have to give their advice in open court and cannot influence the Magistrates' decision. This is an important role and some have recommended increasing the role of the Clerk to aid the efficiency of Magistrates.

stretch&challenge

Consider how the magistracy may be reformed particularly in light of reports calling for the lay element to be abolished.

Criminal jurisdiction

Magistrates play an important role in the criminal justice system, dealing with approximately 95% of cases. They hear **summary** and some **triable either way** offences. Their role is to decide the guilt or innocence of the defendant and to sentence. They also issue warrants for arrest and decide on bail applications. They have a limited sentencing jurisdiction. They cannot order sentences of imprisonment that exceed 6 months (or 12 months for consecutive sentences), or fines exceeding £5000. In triable either way cases, the offender may be committed by the Magistrates to the Crown Court for sentencing if a more severe sentence is thought necessary. They also try cases in the **Youth Court** where the defendants are aged 10 to 17.

Civil jurisdiction

They have a limited role in civil cases. They used to deal with the issuing of alcohol, betting and gaming licences but these are now dealt with by local authorities. They can issue some debt actions, e.g. enforcing Council Tax demands and issuing rights of entry warrants for gas and electricity authorities.

The Family Proceedings Court has jurisdiction over various family law matters such as orders for protection against violence, maintenance orders and proceedings concerning the welfare of children.

Training

As lay Magistrates are rarely from a legal background, they receive mandatory training. They will also be assisted by a **Justices' Clerk** and **legal advisor**. Magistrates' training is based on **competences** or what a Magistrate needs to know and be able to do so that they can carry out the role. The **Judicial Studies Board** is responsible nationally for training and at a local level this responsibility lies with the Magistrates' Association and the Justices' Clerks' Society.

Training in the first year

- Initial training – basics of the role. Then, will sit in court with two other experienced magistrates.
- Mentoring – a specially trained magistrate mentor to guide them through first months. Six formal mentored sittings in the first 12–18 months. New magistrate will review learning progress and talk over any training needs. A personal development log will be kept.
- Core training – over first year, further training, visits to penal institutions and/or observations take place to equip magistrates with the key knowledge they need. Every magistrate is given a core workbook for further optional self-study.
- Consolidation training – at the end of the first year, this builds on the learning from sittings and core training. Designed to help magistrates plan for ongoing development and prepare for first appraisal.
- First appraisal – about 12–18 months after appointment, when both mentor and magistrate agree he/she is ready, the new justice is appraised. Another specially trained magistrate appraiser will sit as part of the bench, observing whether the new magistrate is demonstrating he/she is competent in the role, against the competences. When successful, the magistrate is deemed fully competent.

Ongoing training and development

- Magistrates continue training throughout their magisterial career
- Appraisals
- Continuation training every three years before having an appraisal.
- Threshold training
- They receive additional training for Youth Court work.

Background of Magistrates

There is an argument that Magistrates do not represent the people whom they serve. They face similar criticisms to the judiciary in that they are 'middle class, middle aged and middle minded'. There are reasons why they tend to come from professional or middle-class backgrounds such as availability to sit as a Magistrate. Similarly, they tend to be middle aged or older as a result of the impact on career prospects by taking time to sit as a Magistrate. However, magistrates are generally evenly balanced in terms of gender with around 50.6% women and 49.4% men and they also well represent the proportion of ethnic minorities in the population with around 8% of Magistrates from an ethnic minority – almost exactly the proportion found in the population as a whole.

Advantages and disadvantages of Magistrates

Advantages	Disadvantages
Lay involvement – public participation in the justice system	**Not representative** – similar criticisms to judiciary being from middle-class and professional backgrounds
Local knowledge – community concerns and interests represented	**Inconsistent** – Magistrates' Courts have a tendency to come to different decisions and sentences for the same crime
Balanced view – a bench of three Magistrates provides a balanced view	**Inefficient** – Magistrates can be slow to reach a decision often retiring to consider their verdict where a professional district judge would come to a decision straight away
Cost – they are volunteers and therefore relatively cheap, though do take longer to make decisions than professional judges.	**Bias towards the police** – sitting in local areas, Magistrates get to know the police officers that come to give evidence and tend to be more sympathetic to this.

Justices of the Peace Appointed by Gender 2006/7 – 2010/11

Year	Men	Women	Total
2006/7	1,225	1,875	2,412
2007/8	927	972	1,189
2008/9	814	959	1,773
2009/10	759	873	1,632
2010/11	464	548	1,012

[Source: Ministry of Justice - Magistrates Recruitment and Appointments Bench]

The Judiciary

Role of Judges

The independence of the judiciary is a fundamental principle of the **Rule of Law**.

Judges have a key role in controlling the exercise of power by the state through **judicial review** and through the ***Human Rights Act 1998***, with the power to issue section 4 **declarations of incompatibility** – ***A and X and others v Secretary of State for the Home Department (2004)***.

Key terminology

Rule of Law = this simply means that the state should govern its citizens in accordance with rules that have been agreed upon.

Judicial review = a system whereby the High Court oversees decisions of public bodies, officials, local authorities, and members of the Executive to ascertain whether the body had the power to make the decision.

Declarations of incompatibility = issued under Section 4 of the ***Human Rights Act 1998***, this gives senior judges the power to question the compatibility of legislation with human rights. The declaration is sent to Parliament. It does not allow judges to strike out laws.

Separation of powers = state power is divided into three types: the executive, judicial and the legislative, and that each type of power should be exercised by a different body/people.

Executive = the government.

Hierarchy

Head of the Judiciary – President of the Courts of England and Wales
(in practice the Lord Chief Justice)
(***Constitutional Reform Act 2005***)

Most senior judges – Justice of the Supreme Court – 12 judges; President and Deputy President and 10 puisne Justices of the Supreme Court – Supreme Court and **Privy Council** (***Constitutional Reform Act 2005*** replaced the House of Lords with the Supreme Court in 2009)

Court of Appeal – 38 judges known as Lord and Lady Justices of Appeal
Head of Criminal Division – Lord Chief Justice; Head of Civil Division – Master of the Rolls

High Court – 110 full-time judges

Circuit Judges – Crown Court and County Court

District Judges – Crown Court

District Judge (Magistrates' Court) – Magistrates' Court

Recorder – (part-time) County Court and Crown Court

The Lord Chancellor

The role of the Lord Chancellor has existed for over 1,400 years; recently the role of the Lord Chancellor has been seen to be in conflict with the doctrine of **separation of powers**. In 2003 the government announced the intention to abolish the role; however, this has not happened. The ***Constitutional Reform Act 2005*** has maintained the role but the powers of the Lord Chancellor have been severely curtailed as a result of the Act.

Changes to the role of the Lord Chancellor by the Constitutional Reform Act 2005

Lord Chancellor no longer	The Lord Chancellor now
Sits as a judge (the Lord Chancellor used to be able to sit as a Judge in the House of Lords)	Head of the newly created Ministry for Justice
Heads the judiciary	Responsible for legal aid, the Law Commission and the court system
Takes a role in judicial appointments process	No longer required to be a member of the **House of Lords**
Automatically becomes Speaker of the **House of Lords** (the law-making chamber in Parliament)	No longer a requirement that the Lord Chancellor be a lawyer – section 2 *Constitutional Reform Act 2005*

Judicial Appointments process

Old procedure	New procedure
Lord Chancellor central role in appointments	*Constitutional Reform Act 2005* – Establishment of *Judicial Appointments Commission*
Secret soundings	Judicial Appointments Commission – 14 members (5 **lay**, 5 judges, 2 legal professionals, a **lay** Magistrate and a tribunal member) appointed by the Queen on the recommendation of the Lord Chancellor
Until recently no advertisements for judicial appointments	The procedure for the selection of judges to the Supreme Court is set out in sections 23–31 of the *Constitutional Reform Act 2005*. The Judicial Appointments Commission does have a role in appointing judges to the Supreme Court.
Secretive	*Tribunals, Courts and Enforcement Act 2007* – eligibility to become a judge no longer based on numbers of years of rights of audience, but now on number of years post-qualification experience

Other countries have different systems for appointing judges. In France, judges choose at the beginning of their career to be a judge, rather than being a lawyer first, and follow a career judiciary path. In the United States judges are appointed by two methods, appointment and election.

Key terminology

Lay = a non-legally qualified person.

Oxbridge = Oxford and Cambridge University.

Secret soundings = the old appointments process whereby information on a potential judge would be gathered informally over time from leading barristers and judges.

Privy Council = the final appeal court for Commonwealth countries.

House of Lords = the name of the Upper House in Parliament = the legislative chamber. Confusion arose before the establishment of the Supreme Court, as the highest appeal court was also called the House of Lords.

Grade boost

It is important that you are aware of how judges are appointed to the Supreme Court. When a vacancy arises, the Lord Chancellor calls a selection commission, he usually does this by way of a letter; members of the Commission include a member of each of the Judicial Appointments Commission for England and Wales, the Judicial Appointments Board in Scotland, and the Judicial Appointments Commission in Northern Ireland. At least one of those representatives has to be a lay person. The Commission reports its selection to the Lord Chancellor. The Lord Chancellor then undertakes further consultation and can either notify the selection to the Prime Minister, reject it, or ask the commission to reconsider.

Grade boost

High Court judges and above can only be removed from office by the Queen after successful petition of both the House of Commons and the House of Lords. There has only been one such dismissal since the Act of Settlement. In 1830 Sir Jonah Barrington was dismissed from the High Court for taking £922 for his own personal use.

Grade boost

When discussing judicial appointments it is important to remember that since the Courts & Legal Services Act 1990 solicitors are now eligible to join the judiciary.

stretch&challenge

The position of the Lord Chancellor, prior to 2005, appeared to be in breach of the doctrine of separation of powers. Do you think that the reforms to the role of the Lord Chancellor, in the Constitutional Reform Act 2005 have been successful in addressing this breach of a fundamental doctrine?

Training, dismissal, promotion and termination

Training

Judges receive little formal training, the training they do receive is organised by the Judicial Studies Board. Training includes:

- one-week residential course
- one-week sitting alongside an experienced judge
- refresher courses and seminars; and specialised training when needed, e.g. passing of the **Human Rights Act 1998.**

Dismissal

Five ways a judge may leave office:

1. Dismissal – High Court judges and above – **Act of Settlement 1701; Courts Act 1971 and Constitutional Reform Act 2005**
2. Suspension from office (**Constitutional Reform Act 2005** – set up disciplinary procedures)
3. Resignation
4. Retirement – usually retire at 70
5. Removal due to infirmity.

Promotion

There is no formal system of promotion of judges, as it is believed that the desire to be promoted may affect their decision making. Any promotion is dealt with in the same way as the initial appointment process through the Judicial Appointments Commission.

Judicial independence

Judicial independence is of paramount importance, it is a necessary condition of impartiality and, therefore, of a fair trial. Judges should:

- be independent from: **Executive**, interest groups and litigants
- have an independent pay review
- have no other paid appointment or profession or business
- not sit on a case where has or appears to have personal interest/bias, e.g. Lord Hoffmann in **Re Pinochet Urgarte (1999)**.

Threats to judicial independence from:

- Supremacy of Parliament – judges subordinate to the will of Parliament.
- Judges have been seen to show political bias, see **McIlkenny v Chief Constable of the West Midlands(1980); R v Ponting (1985)**.
- As well as political bias these cases tend to show a bias towards the right wing of the political spectrum, see – **Bromley London Borough Council v Greater London Council (1982); Council of Civil Service Union v Minister for the Civil Service (1984); Thomas v NUM (1985)**.

- Bias against women – attitudes towards women by some judges are out of date and stereotypical. This is of particular concern in cases involving sexual offences such as rape.

Criticisms of the judiciary

- Mostly white, male, attended public school / **Oxbridge**
- Limited training
- Lack of specialisation.

Reforms of the judiciary

- Further reform of the appointment process – remove the government from the appointment process
- Increase training
- Improve organisation of court hours.

Role of the Supreme Court and reasons for establishment

The Constitutional Reform Act 2005 established the Supreme Court, it has replaced the House of Lords to achieve a complete separation between the United Kingdom's senior Judges, and the Upper House of Parliament, which is also called the House of Lords, thereby emphasising the independence of the Law Lords and removing them from the legislature.

In August 2009 the Justices moved out of the House of Lords (where they sat as the Appellate Committee of the House of Lords) into their own building. They sat for the first time as the Supreme Court in October 2009. The Supreme Court is the highest appeal court in the land.

The impact of Supreme Court decisions will extend far beyond the parties involved in any given case, shaping society, and affecting our everyday lives.

S.23 Constitutional Reform Act 2005 – 12 judges appointed by the Queen on recommendation of the Prime Minister – notified to Prime Minister by the Lord Chancellor following selection by a selection commission set up by the Lord Chancellor, the number of judges can be increased. The senior Lord of Appeal is President of the Court. To qualify for appointment to the Supreme Court a judge must have held high judicial office for at least two years *Section.25 Constitutional Reform Act 2005* or been a qualifying practitioner for at least 15 years, e.g. in the Court of Appeal or House of Lords.

Grade boost

It is a common examination error when discussing the appointment process to only discuss the old procedure, it is vital that you can fully discuss both the old and new procedures and that you can evaluate the new procedure. You must also be able to discuss whether judges are representative of society; this is affected by factors such as their class, background and ethnicity.

A judiciary question could also ask you to discuss the role of the Supreme Court and the reasons for the establishment of the Supreme Court.

stretch&challenge

Research ways in which judges can be more representative of society, research the Lord Chancellor's Diversity Strategy of 2006.

Consider more reforms to the appointment process, research the findings of the Government's Consultation Paper in 2007 – 'Constitutional reform: a new way of appointing judges'.

Grade boost

It is important that you are aware of the connection between the Rule of Law and the Supreme Court. The *Constitutional Reform Act 2005* recognises the Rule of Law and the importance of the independence of the judiciary. Judges hold a position of central importance in relation to the Rule of Law. Research current decisions of the Supreme Court and see how they impact upon the Rule of Law.

The Legal Profession

The legal profession in England and Wales is divided into two separate branches, barristers and solicitors; each branch does similar work, both do advocacy and legal paperwork, but they differ in the amount of time dedicated to this work, with barristers spending more of their time in court. A simple analogy can be made with the medical profession with the barrister being the consultant (the specialist) and the solicitor being the general practitioner. The legal profession also includes paralegals, e.g. legal executives.

Role of solicitors

There are approximately 100,000 solicitors, with 80% being in private practice. The solicitors' governing body is called The Law Society; in 2005 membership of the Law Society became voluntary. The Solicitors Regulation Authority regulates solicitors.

What types of work do solicitors do?

Most solicitors' work and income comes from commercial, conveyancing, family/matrimonial and probate work. In 1985 solicitors lost their monopoly on conveyancing work.

Solicitors do almost all of their advocacy work in the Magistrates' Court. Until recently solicitors did not have full rights of audience upon qualification, a right barristers have always had; having full **rights of audience** means that you can appear in any court. However, the ***Courts and Legal Services Act 1990 and Access to Justice Act 1999*** changed this, solicitors now acquire full rights of audience when admitted to the roll, and solicitors can exercise this right upon completion of extra training.

Solicitors can form partnerships, and since 2001 they can form Limited Liability Partnerships. Solicitor's offices range from large firms to sole practitioners. However, most law firms are small, 85% having four or fewer partners, 50% having only one partner. The average annual salary is £51,000.

Qualifications

After qualification: Continuous professional development

⬆

Solicitor

⬆

2-year training contract

⬆

Legal practice course (1 year)

⬆

Law degree or for non-law graduates the Common Professional Exam

⬆

Legal executives can progress to become solicitors though it is a long process.

Promotion to the judiciary

Before 1990 solicitors were only eligible to apply for junior judicial appointments, e.g. circuit judges. Since the *Courts and Legal Services Act 1990* they are eligible for appointment to the higher courts.

Complaints against solicitors

Complaints can be made in the following ways:

- Legal Complaints Service – set up in 2007 (replaced Consumer Complaints Service) an independent complaints service.
- The **Legal Ombudsman and Office for Legal Complaints** was set up following the *Legal Services Act 2007* and is the final appeal regarding complaints against legal professionals in England and Wales. This body replaced the Legal Services Ombudsman and started taking complaints on 6 October 2010.
- Action for negligence through the courts – *Arthur JS Hall and Co v Simons (2000).*

Role of barristers

- There are approximately 14,000 barristers, known collectively as the Bar.
- The governing body of barristers is the Bar Council.
- The Bar Standards Board is responsible for regulating the Bar.

What types of work do barristers do?

Their main role is advocacy (presenting cases in court). A great deal of their work is pre-trial work, 'opinions' (considered assessment of case), and conferences with solicitors and clients.

A key difference with solicitors, barristers must be self-employed, they cannot form partnerships; they share offices called Chambers with other barristers, and the sets of Chambers are managed by the clerk who arranges meetings with solicitors, and negotiates barristers' fees. Not all barristers work as advocates, some barristers work for law centres, government and private industry.

Before 2004, members of the public were not allowed to directly contact a barrister; a barrister had to be appointed through a solicitor. In 2004 direct access was introduced, members of the public can now contact a barrister without going through a solicitor.

Barristers work according to the **'cab rank' rule**. This means that a barrister is obliged to accept any work in a field in which they profess themselves competent to practise, at a court at which they normally appear and at their usual rates.

Key terminology

Cab rank rule = a barrister is obliged to accept any work in a field in which they themselves are competent to practise, at a court at which they normally appear and at their usual rates.

Chambers = office space where barristers group together to share clerks (administrators) and operating expenses.

Inns of Court = the four Inns of Court are Inner Temple, Middle Temple, Gray's Inn and Lincoln's Inn. The Inns originated in the 13th century, barristers must join one of the Inns of Court, the Inns provide accommodation, education and they promote activities.

Pupillage = a one year apprenticeship in which a pupil works alongside a qualified barrister, who is known as the pupil master.

Tenancy = a permanent place in chambers.

Queen's Counsel (to take silk) = a senior barrister who has practised for at least 10 years and is then appointed QC, they can then wear silk gowns, hence 'to take silk'.

Qualifications

Continuous professional development

⬆

Tenancy in chambers

⬆

Pupillage (1 year)

⬆

Called to the Bar

⬆

Bar Vocational Course (1 year) renamed the Bar Professional Training Course in 2010

⬆

Join one of the four **Inns of Court** (dine at their Inn 12 times)

⬆

Law degree or for non-law graduates the Common Professional Exam

Barristers remain 'junior' unless made '**QC**' (Queen's Counsel). Barristers are eligible to become a QC after 10 years in practice, the Bar Council and Law Society appoints QCs, on appointment they '**take silk**'. Average annual earnings of a QC are in the region of £300,000.

Promotion to the judiciary

Barristers are eligible for appointment to all judicial posts, provided they have the necessary experience.

Complaints against barristers

Complaints can be made in the following ways:
- Barristers are no longer immune from liability for negligent work in court, – *Rondel v Worsley (1969)* overruled by *Arthur JS Hall v Simons (2000)*. However, see – *Moy v Pettman Smith (2005)* lenient treatment of a barrister by the House of Lords compared to other professionals.
- Bar Standards Board and Independent Complaints Commissioner, responsible for complaints against barristers.
- Professional Conduct and Complaints Committee.
- Legal Ombudsman and Office for Legal Complaints

Representation issues surrounding barristers and solicitors

Solicitors

The Solicitors Regulation Authority, since 2012, has required firms to collect and publish data to gain a view of the diversity profile of the legal profession.

In 2012, the Diversity and Inclusion Charter Annual Report showed that:
- 59.6% of solicitors are female
- 70% of partners are male
- 10% of solicitors are from BAME backgrounds, which is proportionate to the national percentage.

The full report can be viewed at www.lawsociety.org.uk

Barristers

In 2010, the Bar Council reported:

- 35% of practising barristers are female
- 10% of barristers are from BME backgrounds
- 12% of QCs are female.

Reforms and the future of the legal profession

Should the two professions merge and become one? This is a question that has dominated for many years.

Recent moves towards fusion

1990	***Courts and Legal Services Act***
1992	Solicitor-advocates introduced
1999	***Access to Justice Act*** – all barristers and solicitors acquire full rights of audience
2004	Clementi Report – regulation of the profession
2007	***Legal Services Act*** – allows for alternative business structures

Clementi Report

Sir David Clementi's report (2004) *Review of the Regulatory Framework for Legal Services in England and Wales* was followed by a White paper – The Future of Legal Services – Putting Consumers First.

Key reforms in the Legal Services Act 2007

- Legal Services Board set up in 2009 responsible for maintaining standards in regulation, training and education.
- **Legal disciplinary practices** (LDPs) maximum of 25% of partners can be non-lawyers.
- **Multi-disciplinary partnerships** (MDPs) – this structure would allow for other professionals, e.g. surveyors, estate agents, to work in partnerships with lawyers.
- Other alternative business structures – allowed for in the ***Legal Services Act 2007***, e.g. **Tesco law** – big companies will be able to buy legal firms.
- Office for Legal Complaints – to hear complaints against all legal professions.

Other legal personnel

Legal executives

- Perform professional work under solicitors – tend to specialise, e.g. conveyancing.
- Can go on to qualify as a solicitor.
- Governing body – Institute of Legal Executives.
- ***Tribunals, Courts and Enforcement Act 2007*** – legal executives to be given right to apply for junior judicial appointments.

Licensed conveyancers

- ***Courts and Legal Services Act 1990*** – abolished solicitors' monopoly on conveyancing.

stretch & challenge

- Research whether QC status is a reliable indicator of excellence and expertise.
- The Solicitors Regulation Authority wishes to broaden access to the profession. In 2005, they issued a paper, '*Qualifying as a solicitor – a framework for the future*' and a 2006 paper, '*A new framework for work-based learning*'. Research their proposals for increasing access to the profession, including changing qualification rules.
- Andy Howells, tutor2u website article on: Inequality in the Profession – 'more needs to be done' March 2011 – research his findings on increasing access to the legal profession.

Grade boost

For the examination it is important that you can show the examiner that you are fully aware of all current proposals/reforms to the legal profession,, e.g. Clementi, **Legal Services Act 2007**, Legal Disciplinary Practices, and Multi-Disciplinary Practices.

Examination questions sometimes focus on the unmet need for legal services, so ensure that you are able to discuss this fully.

Law Reform

Codification = the process of gathering together all Acts and case law in a particular area and making them into one Act.

Repeal = the process of modernising statutes, and making obsolete those statutes that are no longer of any use or needed in modern society.

Consolidation = a similar process to codification, only instead of taking all the Acts and the case law, this process merely brings together all the Acts into one place, with no new provisions.

Consultation = a part of the process whereby the Law Commission's proposals are circulated to the legal professionals, academics, the media, the public and interest groups in order that the Commission can glean their comments and opinions to provide the best solution possible.

Law is predominantly made and reformed by Parliament through the usual legislative process, but there are occasions when other reform bodies play a part in reforming the law. This has many advantages, including saving parliamentary time, and allowing specialist bodies to suggest recommendations in their area of expertise. Sometimes, the law is reformed in response to a major incident, or sometimes the government will commission a body to investigate a certain area, or the Law Commission, a permanent body of law reform, takes charge of changing the law. Alternatively, the public can cause a change in the law by joining a pressure group or lobbying their MPs.

There are many reasons why the law needs to be reformed:

- There is no **codified** law in the United Kingdom; that is to say, the law is not written down all in one place.
- Parliament 's role is much bigger than just law making; reforming the law will not always get them votes, so it is not always the top priority.
- Changes in society and technology means laws can become outdated, and therefore need to be **repealed**.

Advisory committees

There are three main types of committe or enquiry which you will need to know about: committes, public inquiries and Royal Commissions. These are 'ad-hoc' bodies that are set up to investigate a particular area of the law in need of reform. Once their report has been published, they cease to exist. The average duration of a Commission is two to four years. Fewer ad-hoc agencies have been established over the last 50 years, but they have led to significant changes in the law:

Type of advisory committee	Name of committee	Result
Royal Commissions	Phillips Commission	*Police and Criminal Evidence Act 1984*
	Runciman Commission	Established **Criminal Cases Review Commission**
Ad-hoc committees	Auld Report	*Criminal Justice Act 2003*
	Woolf Report	*Access to Justice Act 1999*
Public inquiries (as a response to a major incident)	Stephen Lawrence Inquiry (Macpherson Report)	Some recommendations enacted by the *Race Relations (Amendment) Act 2000*
	Bloody Sunday Inquiry	British soldiers were found to have shot dead unarmed civilians in Ireland

These ad-hoc agencies are often criticised for being very expensive and taking a long time, often resulting in only minor changes to the law.

Law Commission

The **Law Commission** is an independent law reform body, that was set up by Parliament in the ***Law Commission Act 1965***,— where ***s3(1)*** stipulated its role to '...*take and keep under review all the law...*'. At any one time, the Commission is dealing with many consultations passed by the government. The Law Commission's work is essentially split into four roles.

Reform

Although Parliament is often reluctant to dedicate the time to consider the Law Commission's proposals, it has been successful in bringing about the reform of some key pieces of legislation, including ***Unfair Contract Terms Act 1977, Children Act 1989***, ***Computer Misuse Act 1990***.

Repeal

This is where the Law Commission concedes that the law in a particular area is outdated or no longer needed and therefore decides to abolish it. A ***Statute Law (Repeals) Act*** acts as the 'dustbin' enabling the obsolete Acts to be put in one place.

Codify

This is where all statutes and cases relating to one area are brought together in one Act, and the Law Commission was responsible for this in the ***Sale of Goods Act 1994***.

Consolidate

This is where just the statutes relating to one area are brought together under one Act. The Law Commission has been working tirelessly to produce a Single Criminal Code, as exists in almost every country in the world, whereby all the criminal law will be in one place and easily understandable to everyone who uses it. It is still a project that is ongoing, and to date, Parliament has not implemented any of the recommendations.

The Law Commission recommend changes by researching, consulting and reporting and finding ways in which the law can be modernised, improved and simplified. These reports will then be considered by the Lord Chancellor and the Secretary of State for Justice, who will then introduce the proposals to Parliament with a draft Bill, who will then decide whether they should be enacted through the usual legislative process.

There are five full-time Commissioners who work at the Law Commission and all of these are experienced legal professionals. The chairman of the Commission is a High Court Judge and all the Commission is appointed by the Lord Chancellor for five years at a time.

Grade boost

When talking about Law Reform, be sure to read the question because often it will be asking you to specifically look at one area of Law Reform, such as the Law Commission or Pressure Groups.

stretch&challenge

Visit the Law Commission's website at www.lawcom.gov.uk and research current issues that are being investigated by the Commission.

Grade boost

Very often, an examination question will ask solely about the Law Commission, so it is very important to have a good understanding, not only of its role, but recent consultations and advantages and disadvantages of having the Law Commission.

It is always good practice to outline the process the Law Commission uses in outlining its recommendations for reform:

Research
⬇
Consultation
⬇
Report of Recommendations
⬇
Draft Bill
⬇
Parliament

Pressure groups

Pressure groups represent the views and opinions of their members and spend their time campaigning for a change in the law and making people aware of their causes. Here are some examples:

- **Fathers 4 Justice** – this is a pressure group which campaigns for equality in the law for fathers to have access to their children when a relationship breaks down. They feel that fathers are not treated with the same equality as mothers, and wish for the law to be reformed. Although they have not been successful yet in bringing about any change in the law, they have had a huge impact in terms of the awareness that has been generated by some rather outrageous publicity stunts. These have included one of their members climbing onto Buckingham Palace dressed as Batman.

- **Friends of the Earth** – this is an environmental pressure group, whose main aims are to encourage people to be more 'green', and improving the environment. They have been very successful in their campaigns; most notably being responsible for the ***Household Waste Recycling Act 2003*** which made doorstep recycling a reality. They have also recently forced the government to consider their ***Climate Change Bill*** in 2008, which later became law and committed the government to implementing measures to reduce carbon emissions and cut greenhouse gases by 80%.

- **Liberty** – this is a Human Rights pressure group which promotes people's liberties and helps those whose Human Rights have been breached. Liberty have campaigned in high profile miscarriages of justice such as the ***Birmingham Six***, where they persistently recommended changes to the criminal justice system and also intervened in the case of ***A and others v Secretary of State for the Home Department (2004)***, where it was held to be a breach of human rights for prisoners to be detained without charge indefinitely. Indeed, they were significant campaigners to get the ***Human Rights Act 1998*** passed in the first place and have been heavily involved with many high profile cases, particularly that of ***Diane Pretty***, campaigning for a change in the law for assisted suicide.

- **Welsh Language Society** – this is a campaign group whose most significant campaign has been the introduction of the ***Welsh Language Act 1993***, which encourages bilingualism in all sectors throughout Wales, and more recently the campaign to get both English and Welsh spoken throughout the National Assembly for Wales, following the ***Welsh Language (Wales) Measure 2011***.

Judicial Precedent

The Anglo-Welsh Legal System is a common law system; this means that much of the law has been developed over time by the courts, through cases. The basis of this system of precedent is the principle of *stare decisis*, this requires a later court to use the same reasoning as an earlier court where the two cases raise the same legal issues, this in turn ensures a just process.

Elements of precedent

The Court hierarchy

This establishes which decisions are binding on which courts. Decisions of higher courts are binding on lower courts.

Court of Justice of the European Union (CJEU)

Decisions from this court on European matters bind all Anglo-Welsh Courts. The CJEU is not bound by its own decisions

---

Supreme Court

(previously called the House of Lords)

Highest appeal court on civil and criminal matters, the Supreme Court binds all other Anglo-Welsh Courts. Bound by its own decisions until 1966 – see 1966 Practice Statement below

---

Court of Appeal

Criminal and Civil divisions, they do not bind each other. The Supreme Court and the old House of Lords bind both divisions. The criminal division is not usually bound by its previous decisions

---

High Court

The High Court consists of the Divisional Courts (**Queen's Bench Division** – criminal appeals and **judicial review**; the Chancery division and Family division) and the ordinary High Court. The Court of Appeal, the Supreme Court and the old House of Lords bind the High Court

---

Crown Court

All the courts above bind this court. Decisions from the Crown Court do not form binding precedent but can form **persuasive precedent**; they are not bound by their previous decisions

---

Magistrates' and County Courts

Bound by the High Court, Court of Appeal, old House of Lords and Supreme Court. They do not produce precedents; are not bound by their previous decisions

---

European Court of Human Rights

Under section 2 of the **_Human Rights Act 1998_** Anglo-Welsh courts must take account of decisions from the European Court of Human Rights but are not bound by them.

Grade boost

Though a general awareness of the operation of precedent is important, you will need to apply the rules of precedent in LA2. For example, LA2 May 2009:

b) Read the following cases and consider whether and, if so, on what grounds the House of Lords could depart from precedent.

In 1884 it was held that there was no defence of killing by necessity when members of a crew on a sunken vessel off the Cape of Good Hope put to sea on a small boat and, left with nothing to eat, decided to kill the cabin boy and fed on his body. It was accepted that they would not have survived without doing this.

In 2007, Lucy gave birth to twins. Both babies were joined at the head and it was impossible to separate them without it becoming inevitable that one of the twins would die. The hospital is now seeking a declaration from the House of Lords whether such action is lawful.   *[11 marks]*

Grade boost

Remember when you are answering a precedent question that is always good practice to make the link with human rights. Under section 2 of the HRA judges must take into account cases from the European Court of Human Rights but they do not have to follow them. This creates a weak obligation on judges. Do you think that judges should be bound by decisions from the European Court?

stretch&challenge

Research the case of
SW v United Kingdom (1995)
involving the issue of rape within
marriage and breach of Article 7
of the European Convention,
which provides that criminal laws
should not act retrospectively.
Why do you think the European
Court gave the decision that it did?

stretch&challenge

Emergency Applications

In some cases the judge needs to
make a ruling very quickly. There
is no time to wait for a court date,
prepare a case file or even give
notice to both parties involved.
The parties are often seeking an
injunction to make someone do
something (mandatory) or prevent
someone from doing something
(prohibitory). In order to help
make a speedy judgement, the
judge may use *reasoning by
analogy*.

Examples can include:

- Injunctions to make an
  emergency caesarean go
  ahead despite the mother's
  refusal to give consent even
  though the foetus is at risk.
- Injunctions to prevent a child
  from being removed from the
  country after they have been
  snatched by an estranged
  parent.
- Injunctions to make sure that
  an individual is not made
  homeless, e.g. because of the
  actions of Local Authorities or
  Housing Associations.

Accurate law reporting

This allows legal principles to be collated; identified and accessed; the earliest
form of law reporting was in the Year Books from around 1272. Modern reporting
dates from the Council on Law Reporting established in 1865; also private series of
reports, examples of this are the All England Law Reports (ALL ER); journals (e.g.
New Law Journal) and newspapers (e.g. *The Times*). More recent innovations include
on-line systems (e.g. LEXIS), and the Internet.

The binding element

The judgment contains four elements:

- statement of material (relevant) facts
- statement of legal principle(s) relevant to the decision – **the *ratio decidendi*
  (the reason for the decision)**
- discussion of legal principles raised in argument but not relevant to the decision –
  ***obiter dicta* (things said by the way)**; and
- the decision or verdict.

The binding element in future cases is the ***ratio decidendi***; this is the part of the
judgment that future judges, depending on their position in the court hierarchy,
have to follow. The ***obiter dicta***, while never binding, may have strong persuasive
force, this is known as persuasive precedent, and the strength of this depends on
which court it comes from. It will have strong persuasive force if coming from the
higher courts like the Court of Appeal, the Supreme Court and the old House of
Lords.

Other forms of persuasive authority include:

- decisions of other common law jurisdictions (esp. Australia, Canada and New
  Zealand)
- decisions of the Privy Council – *see **Attorney General for Jersey v Holley
  (2005)***
- writing of legal academics.

Flexibility and certainty

The system of binding precedent, sometimes referred to as the doctrine of judicial
precedent, does create certainty, this is needed to allow people to plan, and lawyers
to advise. It also creates flexibility, as precedent enables the common law to develop.

How judicial precedent works

- Overruling – higher courts can overrule lower courts.
- Following – with similar facts the precedent set by the earlier court is followed.
- Distinguishing – where a lower court points to material differences that justify the
  application of different principles.
- Departing – in certain circumstances a court can depart from its own previous
  decision.
- Reverse – on appeal a higher court may change the decision of a lower court.

House of Lords Practice Statement 1966

Until 1966, the House of Lords was bound by its own previous decisions *(London Tramways v LCC (1898))* unless the decision had been made *per incuriam* – by mistake. In 1966 the House of Lords issued the *Practice Statement*. This stated that the House of Lords will normally be bound by their previous decisions, but may depart, as well as on the grounds of *per incuriam*, when it is right to do so.

The following cases show where the House of Lords have departed from previous decisions:

- *Anderton v Ryan (1985)* precedent overruled in *R v Shivpuri (1987)*
- *Rondel v Worsley (1969)* precedent overruled in *Hall v Simons (2000)*
- *R v Caldwell (1981)* precedent overruled in *R v G and another (2003)*
- *R v R (1991)* set new precedent for the law on rape within marriage overruling a precedent set hundreds of years before.

stretch & challenge

Research the cases of *R v Smith (Morgan) (2001)*, *Attorney General for Jersey v Holley (2005)* and *R v James and Karimi (2006)*. Discuss what were the justifications for the Court of Appeal in departing from the traditional rules of precedent in applying the Privy Council's decision in *Holley* rather than the House of Lords decision in *Smith (Morgan)*.

Court of Appeal

Court of Appeal (Civil Division). Normally bound by their own previous decisions; however, they can depart from their previous decisions if any of the exceptions established in *Young v Bristol Aeroplane Co (1944)* and *R (on the application of Kadhim) v Brent London Borough Housing Benefit Review Board (2001)* apply. They can depart when:

- the previous decision was made *per incuriam*
- there are two previous conflicting decisions
- there is a later, conflicting, House of Lords' decision
- a proposition of law was assumed to exist by an earlier court and was not subject to argument or consideration by that court.

The Court of Appeal is also not bound to follow its previous decisions where, in the previous case, the law was misapplied or misunderstood, resulting in a conviction *(R v Taylor (1950))*; extra flexibility is given to the Criminal division due to dealing with the liberty of the citizen.

Grade boost

There are many common examination errors seen in precedent question answers: they include lack of understanding and application of precedent, and the court hierarchy, and lack of case law. Ensure that you know all the elements of the doctrine of precedent and you support your answer with relevant case law.

The Privy Council

The Privy Council is the final appeal court for Commonwealth countries. The general rule is that decisions of the Privy Council do not bind English Courts; however, their decisions have strong persuasive authority, see: *R v James and Karimi (2006)* – Court of Appeal applied the Privy Council's judgment in *Attorney General for Jersey v Holley (2005)* rather than the House of Lords' judgment in *R v Smith (Morgan) (2001)*.

Judges as law makers?

Are judges making law, or are they simply interpreting existing law? Should judges make law or should this be left to Parliament? The following cases clearly support the view that judges do make law:

- **_Airedale NHS Trust v Bland (1993)_** – the House of Lords stated that this case raised wholly moral and social issues which should be left to Parliament to legislate for, nevertheless they had no option but to give a decision.

- **_R v Dica (2004)_** – the Court of Appeal overruled a previous decision, and held that a defendant could be criminally liable for recklessly infecting another with HIV; the Court gave this decision despite Parliament refusing to introduce legislation to impose such liability.

- **_Kleinwort Benson Ltd v Lincoln City Council (1998)_** – in this case the House of Lords changed a longstanding rule regarding contract law, despite the Law Commission's recommendations that this rule be changed by Parliament.

- **_DPP v Jones (1999)_** – the House of Lords concluded that statutory highway laws placed unrealistic restrictions on the public.

- **_Fitzpatrick v Sterling Housing Association Ltd (2000)_** House of Lords established that same sex partners could establish a familial link for the purposes of the **_Rent Act 1977_**, overruling the Court of Appeal's decision that this should be left to Parliament to determine.

- **_Gillick v West Norfolk and Wisbech Area Health Authority (1985)_** the House of Lords, faced with no lead from Parliament on the issue in this case, held that a girl under 16 could be given contraceptive services without her parents' consent, if she was mature enough to make up her own mind.

- **_Donoghue v Stevenson (1932)_** In this famous case Lord Aitken developed the law of negligence, the principle that those who harm others should compensate for damage _done_.

- **_R v R (1991)_** House of Lords established that rape within marriage was a crime, overruling a precedent set hundreds of years before, and after pleas from the House of Lords for several years to Parliament to change the law in this area.

Advantages and disadvantages of judicial precedent

Advantages	Disadvantages
A just system – like cases will be treated the same	Developments contingent on accidents of litigation – case law only changes if someone is determined enough to pursue a case through the courts
Impartial system – again like cases are treated in a similar way, this promoted impartiality	**Retrospective effect** – unlike legislation, case law applies to events which took place before the case came to court, see *SW v UK (1996); R v C (2004)*
Practical rules – case law is always responding to real-life situations, as a result there is a large body of detailed rules which give more information than statutes	Complex – whilst case law gives us detailed practical rules, it also means that there are thousands of cases and identifying relevant principles and the *ratio decidendi* can be difficult and time consuming
Certainty – claimants can be advised that like cases will be treated in a similar way and not by random decisions of judges	Rigid – depending on the place of the court in the hierarchy, precedent can be very rigid, as lower courts are bound to follow decisions of higher courts even where they think the decision is bad or wrong
Flexibility – case law can change quickly to meet changes in society	Undemocratic – judges are not elected and should therefore not be changing or creating laws, unlike Parliament that has been elected to do so

The Supreme Court and precedent

The Constitutional Reform Act 2005 established the Supreme Court, it has replaced the House of Lords to achieve a complete separation between the United Kingdom's senior judges, and the Upper House of Parliament, which is also called the House of Lords, thereby emphasising the independence of the Law Lords and removing them from the legislature.

In August 2009 the Justices moved out of the House of Lords (where they sat as the Appellate Committee of the House of Lords) into their own building. The court sat for the first time as the Supreme Court in October 2009. The Supreme Court is the highest appeal court in the land, and hears appeals from the whole of the United Kingdom; it has also taken over the role from the Privy Council of hearing cases concerned with the devolution of Wales, Scotland and Northern Ireland. However, the Supreme Court does not have the power to strike out legislation. The Supreme Court has 12 full-time judges though normally five sit together to hear a case; in exceptional cases all 12 can sit.

The impact of Supreme Court decisions will not just affect the parties involved in a case, the decisions will extend far beyond that, shaping society, and affecting our everyday lives.

Grade boost

It is a common exam question to be asked to apply the principles of precedent to a scenario type question, so you must fully understand how it works and be able to apply the principles with supporting legal authority.

It is also important that you are up to date with the new Supreme Court and recent cases decided there.

When applying each avoidance technique, include a case as authority for each option:

- Follow
  – *Re Pinochet (1999)*
- Distinguish
  – *Merritt v Merritt (1971)* distinguished from *Balfour v Balfour (1919)*
- Reverse
- Overrule
  – *R v R (1991)* (marital rape case); *R v Shivpuri (1986)* overruled *Anderton v Ryan (1985)*.

stretch & challenge

Research recent cases from the Supreme Court www.supremecourt.gov.uk, try and distinguish between the *ratio decidendi* and the *obiter dicta* in the judgements.

Grade boost

Think of some reasons why the wording of an Act can be unclear for judges and therefore require interpretation: e.g. words left out, words change meaning over time, error, events not foreseen or in existence when the Act was made. Be able to explain these in the exam and give an example if needed.

Statutory Interpretation

How are statutes formed?

All statutes start as **Bills**. Bills propose the idea for the legislation and need to pass through various stages in the **House of Commons** and **House of Lords** before receiving the **Royal Assent** and becoming an **Act of Parliament**. The three types of Bill are: **Public Bills**, **Private Members' Bills** and **Private Bills**. Bills are usually preceded by a **Green Paper,** which is a consultation document outlining the idea for the new law, followed by a **White Paper**, which gives more detail on the outcome of the consultation and details the specific reform proposal. The stages a Bill goes through to become an Act are:

First Reading

Title of Bill read to House of Commons

Second Reading

Proposals debated, amendments made, members vote

Committee Stage

Committee of House of Commons examines the Bill and may amend

Report Stage

Committee reports back, debates and any amendments made are voted upon

Third Reading

Amended Bill re-presented to Commons who vote on whether to accept/reject

House of Lords

Three Readings. If any changes made, Bill returns to Commons who agree, disagree or propose an alternative

Royal Assent

Queen gives her consent to the legislation which then becomes law

---

Approaches to statutory interpretation

Judges use four different rules or 'approaches' when dealing with a statute that requires interpretation. They are free to use any of the four approaches in combination with the other aids to interpretation discussed in this section.

Literal rule

The judge will give the words contained in the statute their ordinary and plain meaning even if this causes an absurd result. Many feel this should be the first rule applied by judges in the interpretation of an unclear statute.

Case – **Whiteley v Chappel (1968):** in this case, it was an offence to 'impersonate anyone entitled to vote' at an election. The defendant in question had pretended to be a dead person and taken their vote. He was found not guilty of the offence as the judge interpreted the word 'entitled' literally. As a dead person is no longer 'entitled' to vote, the defendant had done nothing wrong.

Golden rule

If the literal rule causes an absurd result, the judge can take a more flexible approach to rectify the absurdity. Courts can take either a narrow or a wide interpretation considering the statute as a whole. With both the golden and literal rules, judges *use internal (intrinsic) aids*.

Case – **Adler v George (1964):** S.3 of the Official Secrets Act 1920 states that it is an offence to obstruct a member of the armed forces 'in the vicinity of' a 'prohibited place'. The defendant in the case had obstructed an officer *in* an army base (a 'prohibited place') and argued that the natural meaning of 'in the vicinity of' means in the surrounding area or 'near to' and not directly within. Had the judge applied the literal rule, he could have escaped prosecution but the judge used the golden rule to reasonably assume the statute to include both within and around the prohibited place.

Mischief rule

Laid down in **Haydon's** case and allows the judge to look for the 'mischief' or problem the statute in question was passed to remedy. It directs the judge to use *external (extrinsic) aids* and look for Parliament's intention in passing the Act.

Case – **Elliot v Grey (1960):** it is an offence under the Road Traffic Act 1930 to 'use' an uninsured car on the road. In this case, a broken down car was parked on the road but was not able to be 'used' as a result of its wheels being off the ground and its battery removed. The judge decided that the Road Traffic Act 1930 was passed to remedy this type of hazard and even though the car could not be 'used' on the road, it was indeed a hazard to other road users.

Purposive approach

Similar to the mischief rule in that it looks for the intention or aim of the Act. This approach has increased in popularity since joining the European Union, due in part to the different way that European laws are drafted. Whilst our laws are more verbose and suit a literal interpretation, European laws are more vaguely written, requiring the judge to construct a meaning. Lord Denning was a supporter of the use of the purposive approach and giving judges more discretion when interpreting Acts. As the title of the approach suggests, with this rule, judges are looking for the 'purpose' of the Act or, as Lord Denning said, the 'spirit of the legislation'.

Case – **Magor and St. Mellons Rural District Council v Newport Corporation (1950):** Lord Denning sitting in the Court of Appeal stated *'we sit here to find out the intention of Parliament and of ministers and carry it out, and we do this better by filling in the gaps and making sense of the enactment by opening it up to destructive analysis'.*

Lord Simmons criticised this approach when the case was appealed to the House of Lords, calling this approach *'a naked usurpation of the legislative function under the thin disguise of interpretation'.* He suggested that *'if a gap is disclosed, the remedy lies in an amending Act'.*

stretch&challenge

Try to think of an advantage and disadvantage for each of the four rules to provide some evaluation.

Literal rule:

Advantage – respects parliamentary sovereignty.

Disadvantage – can cause absurd results.

Golden rule:

Advantage – gives judges discretion and puts right absurdities caused by literal rule.

Disadvantage – judges given power to interpret what is constitutionally the role of the legislator.

Mischief rule:

Advantage – the most flexible of the rules and allows judges flexibility when dealing with statutes.

Disadvantage – this approach was developed when parliamentary supremacy was not fully established and common law was the primary source of law. It is felt that the mischief rule gives too much power to the unelected judiciary to interpret the 'will of Parliament'.

Purposive approach:

Advantage – flexible and seeks the purpose or reason why the Act was passed.

Disadvantage – described by Lord Simonds as 'a naked usurpation of the judicial function, under the thin disguise of interpretation'.

Aids to interpretation – internal (intrinsic)

Grade boost

Look carefully for what the question is asking. Some exam questions ask for *all* of the aids available to judges, whereas others focus on just one or two of the other types of aid such as Hansard. Remember to include as many case examples as you can, not just for the rules of interpretation but the other aids, too.

Be prepared to discuss sections 3 and 4 of the Human Rights Act 1998 in a statutory interpretation question and the implications for statutory interpretation of these sections.

Grade boost

When answering a question on statutory interpretation, it is important to apply all four rules and give a case example for each. Other aids to interpretation may also be needed to give a complete answer to a problem scenario style question.

stretch&challenge

Try to think of your own hypothetical example for each of the rules of language.

Presumptions

The court will start with the **presumption** that certain points are applicable in all statutes, unless explicitly stated otherwise. Some of the main presumptions are:

- Statutes do not change the common law.
- **Mens rea** ('guilty mind') is required in criminal cases.
- The Crown is not bound by any statute.
- Statutes do not apply **retrospectively**.

Internal aids

Internal aids are found within the Act itself. Examples are:
- **The Long Title to the Act**
- **Preamble** – normally states the aim of the Act and intended scope
- **Headings**
- **Schedules**
- **Interpretation sections.**

Rules of language

Judges can use other words in the statute to help them give meaning to specific words that require interpretation:

Ejusdem generis ('of the same kind')

Where there are general words which follow a list of specific ones, the general words are limited to the same kind/class/nature as the specific words.

Case – *Powell v Kempton (1899)*: a statute stated that it was an offence to use a 'house, office, room or other place for betting'. The defendant was using a ring at a racecourse. The court held that the general term 'other place' had to include other indoor places because the specific words in the list were indoor places and so he was found not guilty.

Expressio unius est exclusio alterius ('express mention of one thing is the exclusion of all others')

Case – *R v Inhabitants of Sedgley (1831)*: in this case, it was held that that due to the fact the statute stated 'lands, houses and coalmines' specifically in the Act, this excluded application to other types of mine.

Noscitur a sociis ('a word is known by the company it keeps')

Words in a statute must be read in context of the other words around them.

Case – *Muir v Keay (1875)*: a statute required the licensing of all venues that provided 'public refreshment, resort and entertainment'. Defendant argued his café did not fall within the Act because he did not provide entertainment. Court held the word 'entertainment' in the Act referred to refreshment houses, receptions and accommodation of the public, not musical entertainment and therefore did include the defendant's café.

Aids to interpretation – external (extrinsic)

With both the mischief and purposive approach, the judge is directed to use **external** or **extrinsic aids**. These are found outside of the Act and include:

- Dictionaries and textbooks
- Reports, e.g. Law Commission
- Historical setting
- Treaties
- Previous case law.

Hansard

Perhaps the external aid that has caused the most problems is **Hansard**. Hansard is the daily record of parliamentary debate during the passage of legislation. Some argue that it acts as a good indicator of Parliament's intention; however, over the years its use has been subject to limitations. Traditionally, judges were not allowed to consult Hansard to assist them in the interpretation of statutes. Lord Denning disagreed with this approach and said in the case of ***Davis v Johnson (1979)*** that: '*Some may say, and indeed have said, that judges should not pay any attention to what is said in Parliament. They should grope about in the dark for the meaning of an Act without switching on the light. I do not accede to this view....*' The House of Lords disagreed with him and held that the prohibition on using Hansard should stand. However, the key case of ***Pepper v Hart (1993)*** finally permitted the use of Handard, albeit in limited circumstances. This was confirmed in the case of ***Three Rivers District Council v Bank of England (No. 2) (1996)***.

The recent case of ***Wilson v Secretary of State for Trade and Industry (2003)*** has once again restricted the use of Hansard. Currently, only statements made by a Minister or other promoter of legislation can be looked at by the court, other statements recorded in *Hansard* must be ignored.

Human Rights Act 1998

The Human Rights Act incorporates into UK law the European Convention on Human Rights. Under **s.3** of the HRA courts are required: 'So far as it is possible to do so, primary and subordinate legislation must be read and given effect in a way which is compatible with convention rights.' If the statute cannot be interpreted to be compatible, then the court can issue a **declaration of incompatibility** under **s.4**. This asks the government to change the law to bring it in line with the convention. **S.2** also requires judges to take into account any previous decision of the ECHR, though they are not bound by it.

Grade boost

Remember the link with Human Rights for this topic. Make sure you cite sections 3 and 4 and understand how they apply to this topic. Often, the exams mix and match topics and human rights and statutory interpretation are a popular mix.

In addition, be sure to know some cases on the use of Hansard, as discussed above. Examiners are looking for a range of case law and an understanding of how the law has evolved.

stretch&challenge

Research and find the case of ***Ghaidan v Godin-Mendoza (2004)*** regarding the issue of human rights when interpreting statutes. What happened in the case and how did human rights apply to this case?

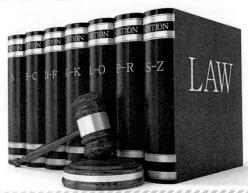

Delegated Legislation

stretch&challenge

When answering a question on delegated legislation it is important to be aware of the role of devolution. The changing arrangements, for example, in Wales, following the implementation of Part 4 of the *Government of Wales Act 2006*. Research some Bills put forward by the Welsh Government, for example the controversial Bill relating to a change in organ donation, and the Local Government (Byelaws) (Wales) Bill which was challenged by the UK Government.

What is delegated legislation?

Delegated (sometimes called secondary or subordinate) legislation is law made by a body other than Parliament but with authority given to it by Parliament. Parliament normally passes an **enabling (or parent) Act** to delegate the authority to make law to the other body and they have to stay within the terms and conditions set out in the enabling Act. If they do not, any law made may be declared as *ultra vires.* Delegated legislation is often used to 'flesh out' a piece of legislation or make changes to an Act where it is not practical to pass a new Act. It can also be used for technical reasons such as changing the amount of a fine.

Forms of delegated legislation

There are four main forms of delegated legislation.

Statutory Instruments

These are made by government departments and make up the majority of delegated legislation passed each year (approximately 3000). They are normally drafted by the legal office of the relevant government department who will consult with interested bodies and parties. They are made via either **affirmative resolution** or **negative resolution,** which are part of the parliamentary controls on delegated legislation.

Byelaws

Byelaws are made by local authorities, public corporations and companies and usually concern local issues or matters relating to their area of responsibility. For example, County Councils make byelaws that affect the whole county, whilst district or town councils only make byelaws solely for the particular district or town. The laws are made with awareness of the needs of the locality.

The proposed law must be advertised to allow local people to view and comment. The law then has to be approved by central government before becoming law. They normally concern matters such as parking and traffic management in an area or library provision.

Orders in Council

These are generally made in times of emergency and have to be approved by the Privy Council and signed by the Queen. They can also be used to amend law and to give effect to EU law, e.g. *The Misuse of Drugs Act 1971 (Modification) (No. 2) Order 2003* downgraded cannabis from a Class B to a Class C drug.

The Welsh government

Following devolution and the referendum in Wales in 2011, the Welsh government has now been granted full lawmaking powers under Part 4 of the *Government of Wales Act 2006*. Under the system of devolution before May 2011, the UK government had to approve all bids for powers to legislation from the Welsh

Assembly. Under the new system, the Welsh government can legislate right across the devolved fields without reference to the UK government. However, the **Government of Wales Act 2006** gives the Attorney General four weeks from the date of the Welsh government passing a Bill to raise an objection and refer it to the Supreme Court.

Control of delegated legislation

A huge amount of delegated legislation is passed each year by non-elected individuals and bodies. For that reason, it is important that control is exercised over the passing of this legislation. There are two types of control – **Parliamentary** and **Judicial**.

Parliamentary controls

- **Affirmative resolution** – this is where the statutory instrument has to be laid before both Houses of Parliament and they have to expressly approve the measure. Where used, this is an effective control.
- **Negative resolution** – this is where the statutory instrument is published but no debate or vote takes place. It may be annulled by a resolution of either House of Parliament.
- About two-thirds of Statutory Instruments are passed via negative resolution and therefore are not actually considered before Parliament. They merely become law on a future specified date and for that reason have limited control over the delegated authority.
- **Consultation** – many enabling Acts require the undertaking of consultation with interested parties or those who will be affected by the delegated legislation. Where consultation is required, it is an effective control, but not all enabling Acts require consultation, thereby limiting its usefulness.
- **Joint Committee on Statutory Instruments** – all Statutory Instruments are subject to review by the JCSI. The report to the House of Commons or House of Lords on any statutory instrument which they think requires special consideration and could cause problems. Their control is limited by the fact that they can only make recommendations to the Houses.

Judicial controls

- A statutory instrument can be challenged by someone who has been directly affected by the law. The process for challenge is called a **Judicial Review** and takes place in the **Queen's Bench Division of the High Court**. The person making the challenge will be asking the judge to review the legislation and decide whether it is **ultra vires** ('beyond powers'). If it is declared to be *ultra vires*, the delegated legislation will be declared **void**.
- **Procedural *ultra vires*** – this is where the procedures laid down in the enabling Act for making the Statutory Instrument have not been followed (e.g. consultation was required but not carried out).
- **Substantive *ultra vires*** – this is where the delegated legislation goes beyond what Parliament intended.
- **Unreasonableness** – the delegated legislation is challenged as being unreasonable. To be unreasonable, the person making it must have taken into account matters which they ought not to, or not taken into account matters which they ought to. Even if that test is passed, then it needs to be proved to be a decision that no reasonable body could have come to.

Advantages and disadvantages of delegated legislation

Flexibility

Delegated legislation is often used to amend existing legislation. It is easier to use delegated legislation than pass a completely new Act of Parliament.

Speed

It is far quicker to introduce a piece of delegated legislation than a full Act of Parliament. Orders in Council can be used in times of emergency when a law is needed very quickly.

Advantages

Time

Parliament does not have time to debate and pass all of the laws needed to run the country effectively. It barely has time to pass around 70 Acts of Parliament per year, let alone the 3000 Statutory Instruments that are needed.

Expertise

Delegated legislation is made by specialised government departments who have experts in the relevant field of the legislation. Ordinary MPs would not have the same level of technical expertise.

Local knowledge

Byelaws are made by local authorities who have knowledge of the needs of their local area and people. Parliament would not have the same local awareness.

Lack of control

As highlighted above, most Statutory Instruments are passed using the negative resolution procedure. This is a loose control of delegated legislation. In addition, if consultation is not required, it is not carried out and is also a limited control.

Disadvantages

Undemocratic

Law should be made by those elected to do so. Delegated legislation is made by unelected individuals/bodies.

Sub-delegation

The power to make the delegated legislation is often sub-delegated to those not given the original authority to pass law. For example, from a Government Minister to a department and then to a group of experts. The democratic process is even further removed.

stretch&challenge

Take a look around your local area and see if you can spot any byelaws. For example: no ball games in the park. Make a list. Why are these made at a local level?

Volume

There is a vast amount of delegated legislation made each year (approx. 3000 Statutory Instruments). As a result, the correct law can be difficult to find and keep up to date with.

European Union: Sources of Law

The UK joined the European Community (now known as the European Union) on 1 January 1973. The European Community had been in existence since 1957, when six Member States (France, Germany, Italy, Belgium, Netherlands and Luxembourg) signed the Treaty of Rome. There are currently 28 Member States. European law was incorporated into UK law by the ***European Communities Act 1972***.

Sources of EU law

The main sources of EU law are:

- EU **primary legislation** – the Treaties
- EU **secondary legislation** – Regulations, Directives, Decisions, Recommendations and Opinions
- **Rulings** on cases brought before the Court of Justice of the European Union.

EU law is created by the EU institutions. This law is binding on all EU Member States who must: *'take all appropriate measures, whether general or particular, to ensure fulfilment of the obligations arising out of this Treaty ...'*

Treaties

Treaties are agreements between all 28 Member States and are the highest source of EU law. The Treaties form the basis of the law that is passed by the institutions and set out the aims of the EU overall. Treaties include: Treaty of Rome, Maastricht Treaty, Treaty of Amsterdam, Lisbon Treaty and Treaty on the Functioning of the European Union. Treaties have both **vertical** and **horizontal direct effect** (see later in this section).

Regulations

Regulations are **directly applicable**. This means that they become part of domestic law as soon as they are passed and take effect. No intervention is needed from Parliament to give the law effect. They are similar to an Act of Parliament and are binding in their entirety on each Member State. If there is a conflict between a Regulation and an existing national law, the Regulation prevails, thereby limiting the sovereignty of the Member State in areas of EU law and creating legislative uniformity in the EU. Regulations have both **vertical** and **horizontal direct effect**.

Directives

Directives are formal instructions that require Member States to change their national laws within a stated period of time in order to give effect to the Directive and achieve a particular result. In the UK, Directives can be implemented either by statute or by delegated legislation under the ***European Communities Act 1972***. Directives may concern one or more Member States, or all of them and create legislative harmony in the EU. Directives only have **vertical direct effect.**

Decisions

A decision is an individual act addressed to a specified person or persons, firm or Member State. Decisions are binding only on those to whom they are addressed without any need for implementation into national law (directly applicable).

Recommendations and Opinions

Non-binding and of persuasive value only. Aimed at promoting the implementation of common practices throughout the EU.

Key terminology

Vertical direct effect = allows individuals to rely upon a European provision against the State.

Horizontal direct effect = allows individuals to rely upon a European provision against another individual or private company.

Indirect effect = compels national courts to interpret 'so far as possible' national legislation in accordance with the aims of a Directive.

Direct and indirect effect

The principle of direct effect allows individuals to rely upon European laws before a national or European court even if their Member State has not implemented the legislation. There are two types of direct effect: **vertical direct effect** and **horizontal direct effect**:

- **Vertical direct effect** allows individuals to invoke a European provision against the State.
- **Horizontal direct effect** allows individuals to invoke a European provision against another individual or private company.

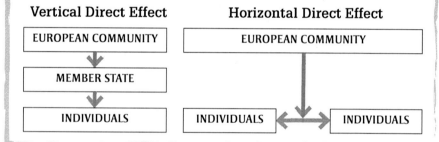

Treaties and direct effect

The direct effect of Treaty articles was established by the case of **Van Gend en Loos**. For a Treaty provision to have direct effect, it must be *unconditional, clear and precise as to the rights or obligations it creates, and leave Member States no discretion on implementing it.* Treaties have both vertical and horizontal direct effect.

This can be illustrated in the case of **Macarthy's Ltd v Smith (1979)**. Article 157 Treaty on the Functioning of the EU provides that men and women should be treated equally and receive the same pay for work of equal value and status. Ms Smith had taken over from a male predecessor and was doing the same job but being paid around 20% less. The UK Equal Pay Act 1970 said that men and women employed at the same time should receive equal pay, but provided no protection for those having taken over a job from a person of the opposite sex. The CJEU held that the Treaty provision was directly effective (horizontally against her employer) and Ms Smith could rely upon the rights contained within, even though there was no such law protecting her in the UK.

Regulations and direct effect

If there is a conflict between an EU Regulation and a domestic law, the EU Regulation takes precedence. Courts must apply the EU Regulation even if there is a directly conflicting domestic law, confirming the supremacy of EU law over domestic law and the dilution of the sovereignty of Member States. In **Leonesio v Italian Ministry of Agriculture (1973)**, an EU regulation aimed at reducing dairy production provided that a cash premium would be payable to farmers who slaughtered cows and agreed not to produce milk for five years. Leonesio, a farmer, had satisfied all the necessary pre-conditions but the Italian constitution conflictingly required domestic legislation to authorise government expenditure. The CJEU held that Leonesio was entitled to the payment as the EU Regulation was directly applicable in Italian law. The Italian government could not use their own laws to block payment. Leonesio could rely upon the directly effective right given in the regulation.

Directives and direct effect

Directives are not directly applicable as they require further enactment by a Member State before they can take effect within its domestic law. Member States have no discretion as to what is to be achieved by the implementation of the Directive, but do have discretion as to how it is achieved. In the UK the implementation of a Directive may take the form of primary or secondary legislation. Directives have only vertical direct effect, as it is only the government that has control over their implementation. The principle that Directives have direct effect is important in compelling Member States to enact Directives as required by their EU obligations.

The case that ruled Directives can have direct effect is **Van Duyn v Home Office (1974)**. In this case, Miss Van Duyn was prohibited from entering the UK as she was a member of the Church of Scientologists. At the time, the UK wanted to exclude members of this religious group. Miss Van Duyn attempted to rely on article 48 of the Treaty of Rome which allowed free movement of workers in the EU and Art 3 of Directive 64/221, which held that exceptions to freedom of movement must be based exclusively on conduct. The CJEU had to decide whether the Directive in question had direct effect, i.e. was it capable of being relied upon by a private individual before national courts. The CJEU held that the Directive was not directly applicable as it relied on further legislation to enact it by the Member States, but as the Directive imposed a clear obligation then the exceptions could be based solely on conduct. This would be directly effective as long as three conditions were filled: the Directive must be (i) clear, precise and unconditional, (ii) not dependent on further legislation/action by the Member State or the Community, and (iii) the date of implementation must have passed.

The case of **Marshall v Southampton Area Health Authority (1986)** confirmed that Directives can only have vertical direct effect and are not effective against individuals. Ms Marshall could invoke the rights given by the Directive (for equal treatment of men and women) even though she was not suing the government. She was claiming against a health authority which was held to be a public body and therefore an 'emanation' of the State.

Grade boost

Remember to use case law to support your point. On LA2, a popular question is: 'consider the impact of EU law'. For this question you would demonstrate the impact through explaining key principles such as direct effect and direct applicability but also through decided case law and the impact of the **European Communities Act 1972**. It is also important to consider the different effect of different sources of EU law.

Grade boost

Include a range of case law to illustrate how the position of EU laws has been decided by the courts.

In **Defrenne v Sabeena (1976)**, Ms Defrenne, an airline stewardess employed by the Belgian airline Sabeena, was paid less and had to retire earlier than male stewards. She claimed that this was in breach of the equal treatment of men and women. The CJEU held that Treaty provisions are capable of creating direct effects both vertically between an individual and the State, and also horizontally between individuals. It was held by the CJEU, via an Article 234 reference, that Treaty provisions created direct effects both vertically and horizontally. Again it had to be clear, unconditional and not requiring further action by the Member State.

In **Pubblico Ministerio v Ratti (1979)** it was held that after the implementation date, the Directive will have vertical direct effect so that it is enforceable against the State (or 'emanations' of the State).

Indirect effect

The principle of indirect effect was established in the case of **Von Colson v Land Nordrhein-Westfahlen**. It compels national courts to interpret 'so far as possible' national legislation in accordance with the aims of a Directive. Directives require implementation by the Member State government and while the Member State has the freedom to decide on the form of implementing law, the law must comply with the aim of the original Directive.

The case of **Francovich v Italy (1991)** raises the possibility that, should a Member State fail to implement a Directive, individuals can sue the government for any losses as a result of this failure.

The supervisory role of the CJEU

As seen in the earlier section on EU Institutions, the CJEU has a dual role – judicial and supervisory. Here, the supervisory function will be explored.

The supervisory function

Known as the **preliminary ruling procedure**, it helps to ensure that EU law is consistently applied in all Member States. The power is given in **art.267 Treaty on the Functioning of the European Union**. If a national court is in any doubt about the interpretation or validity of an EU law it may ask the CJEU for advice. This advice is given in the form of a 'preliminary ruling' and they use this ruling to help them come to a decision in the national case.

Due to the potential volume of referrals, the case of **Bulmer v Bollinger (1974)** laid down guidelines as to when national courts should refer a question to the CJEU. Generally only the highest court in a State should refer questions to the CJEU under the principle that Member States should first exhaust their own national appeal process to see if they can reach a conclusion in the case. A reference should only be made if a ruling by the European Court is 'necessary' (meaning conclusive to the case) to enable the national court to give judgment in the case. If other matters remain to be decided then the ruling would not be considered necessary. All courts have a power to refer, whereas the final appeal court in any Member State has a duty to refer.

The other guidelines are:

1. There is no need to refer a question that has already been decided by the CJEU in a previous case.
2. No need to refer a point which is reasonably clear and free from doubt – *acte clair* doctrine.
3. Courts must refer if the case is in a court from which there is no further appeal (e.g. Supreme Court in the UK).

A case that demonstrates the use of art. 267 preliminary ruling procedure is: **Marshall v Southampton Area Health Authority (1986)** At the time of this case, the retirement age for men and women the UK was different – men could retire at 65 but women at 60. Ms Marshall was 62 and was compulsorily retired by the Local Authority. She argued that the UK law contravened EU law on the equal treatment of men and women. The UK tribunal referred this question to the CJEU under art. 267 who responded by stating that there was a conflict between EU and UK law and that EU law should take precedence. As a result of this case the UK changed the State pension age to 65 for both men and women.

The impact of EU law on parliamentary sovereignty

Parliamentary sovereignty is a principle of the UK constitution. It makes Parliament the supreme legal authority in the UK, which can create or end any law. Generally, the courts cannot overrule its legislation and no Parliament can pass laws that future Parliaments cannot change.

As seen above, direct effect and the direct applicability of EU laws in domestic law has eroded the sovereignty of Member States. In the UK, membership of the EU came via the **European Communities Act 1972** which set out the position of UK law in relation to the UK's new EU obligations. It is important to remember that the UK chose to become a Member of the EU and did do with the passing of this Act. As per the doctrine of parliamentary sovereignty, in theory, if the Act were repealed, the UK Parliament would regain its full sovereignty once again.

The case of **Costa v ENEL (1964)** was a landmark ruling that confirmed the supremacy of EU law over the domestic laws of the Member States.

Section 2(1) of the **European Communities Act 1972** cements the **supremacy** of EU law over domestic legislation, providing that:

'All such rights, powers, liabilities, obligations and restrictions from time to time created or arising under the Treaties, and all such remedies and procedures from time to time provided for by or under the Treaties, as in accordance with the Treaties are without further enactment to be given legal effect or used in the United Kingdom shall be recognised and available in law, and be enforced, allowed and followed accordingly; and the expression "enforceable Community right" and similar expressions shall be read as referring to one to which this subsection applies.'

Section 2(4) is an important section that provides that UK law should be interpreted in accordance with EU law and that EU law takes precedence over all domestic sources of law where there is a conflict. It also requires judges to construe all domestic laws, so far as possible, to conform with EU law. This is evident in the key case of **R v. Secretary of State for Transport, ex parte Factortame (No.2) (1990)** regarding the application of provisions of the **Merchant Shipping Act 1988.** In the House of Lords, Lord Bridge conceded that:

'Under the 1972 Act it has always been the duty of a United Kingdom court, when delivering final judgement, to override any rules of national law found to be in conflict with any directly enforceable Community law. ...Thus ...to insist that, in the protection of rights under Community law, national courts must not be inhibited by rules of national law from granting interim relief in appropriate cases is no more than a logical recognition of that supremacy.'

It can be clearly seen that membership of the EU has diluted parliamentary sovereignty. As Lord Denning said in **Bulmer v Bollinge (1974)**:

'Our sovereignty has been taken away by the European Court of Justice ... Our courts must no longer enforce our national laws.

They must enforce Community law ... No longer is European law an incoming tide flowing up the estuaries of England. It is now like a tidal wave bringing down our sea walls and flowing inland over our fields and houses — to the dismay of all.'

Grade boost

Think about what s.2(1) means.

This section provides for the direct application of EC law in the UK and the recognition that where there is a conflict, EU law is supreme. Make a list of cases mentioned earlier in this unit that confirm the supremacy of EU law over domestic law.

Section 2(2) provides a general power for further implementation of Community obligations by means of **secondary legislation**.

stretch&challenge

It is important to understand the facts of the Factortame case. This was the first time the House of Lords had refused to apply a UK Act of Parliament in favour of EU law. There are several further cases that confirm this approach such as:

- **Pickstone v Freemans PLC (1988)** – UK law should be interpreted in accordance with EU law.

- The case of **Marleasing (1990)** which provides that judges have a new external aid to statutory interpretation and emphasises the duty of a Member State to achieve the objects of a directive.

Exam Practice and Technique

Exam Advice and Guidance

How exam questions are set

WJEC AS Law aims to encourage students to:

- develop and sustain their enjoyment of, and interest in, law;
- develop knowledge and understanding of selected areas of law and the legal system in England and Wales;
- develop an understanding of legal method and reasoning;
- develop the techniques of logical thinking, and the skills necessary to analyse and solve problems by applying legal rules;
- develop the ability to communicate legal arguments and conclusions with reference to appropriate legal authority;
- develop a critical awareness of the changing nature of law in society;
- gain a sound basis for further study;
- develop knowledge of the rights and responsibilities of individuals as citizens including, where appropriate, an understanding of moral, spiritual and cultural issues;
- develop, where appropriate, skills in communication, application of number and information technology;
- improve, where appropriate, their own learning and performance, to facilitate work with others and solve problems in the context of their study of law.

Examination questions are written well in advance of the examination. They are written by the Principal examiner responsible for the unit. A committee of experienced examiners discuss the quality of every question and changes are made to the questions until the committee agree that they are appropriate. The questions are written to reflect the substantive content and the success criteria outlined in the specification.

Each of the papers LA1 and LA2 are worth 50% of the overall AS mark and 25% of the overall A Level grade.

Exam answers are marked in relation to three assessment objectives:

- **Assessment Objective 1 (AO1) – Knowledge and Understanding**
  This is knowledge and understanding and it accounts for 52% of the marks at AS.

  This assessment objective (AO) is assessing candidates' underlying knowledge and understanding of the workings of the law as described in the subject content. It is also assessing candidates' ability to describe how the law operates and applies in practice. To achieve the higher mark boundaries, candidates would be expected to bring in current debates, criticism and major proposals for the law if applicable. Candidates are expected to bring in legal authority to support their answers as appropriate and required by the specification.

- **Assessment Objective 2 (AO2) – Skills**
  This is analysis and evaluation and accounts for 36% of the marks at AS.

  This assessment objective (AO) is assessing candidates' ability to evaluate how the law operates and is implemented, and the extent to which it protects rights and imposes duties. It looks at how well candidates can categorise factual problems in order to apply relevant legal principles and conduct legal argument, applying law to facts and supporting conclusions by the citation of authority and by analysis and analogy. In this AO, candidates are expected to analyse and evaluate, interpret and use legal material including statutes and other sources of law

- **Assessment Objective 3 (AO3) – Language and Argument**
  This accounts for 12% of marks at AS.

  Use of key terminology and development of an argument is important in law. This assessment objective is looking at candidates' ability to present a logical and coherent argument and communicate relevant material in a clear and effective manner using appropriate legal terminology. It considers the extent to which candidates refer to specialist terms and conventions appropriate to the question and how they organise and present information, ideas, descriptions and arguments. It is also assessing candidates' ability to clearly express ideas and present their answers with accuracy in spelling, punctuation and grammar.

The AS Law exam comprises two papers sat on separate days:

LA1

This paper is 1½ hours long and consists of six essay questions. Each question is broken down into parts a and b totalling 25 marks. Part a will assess knowledge and understanding and be worth a maximum of 14 marks and part b will assess skills of analysis and evaluation and will be worth a maximum of 11 marks. Students have to answer two full questions from a choice of six (parts a and b of two questions). The paper is out of 50 marks in total.

LA2

This paper is 1½ hours long and consists of four 'stimulus response' questions. These questions test knowledge and understanding but also the ability to extract the relevant information from the source or apply the law to the source. Each question is broken down into parts a and b totalling 25 marks. Part a will assess knowledge and understanding and be worth a maximum of 14 marks and part b will assess skills of analysis and evaluation and will be worth a maximum of 11 marks. Students have to answer two full questions from a choice of four (part a and b of two questions). The paper is out of 50 marks in total.

How Exam questions are marked

Questions are split into parts a and b. Students are assessed on three 'assessment objectives' as summarised above and below.

Part a

For part a questions, which are worth 14 marks, candidates can achieve a maximum of 13 marks for AO1 for a 'sound' answer. WJEC marking guidelines for law dictate that examiners can award either the top or bottom of a mark boundary (for example, if an answer

is 'adequate', it can achieve either 7 marks or 10). This can seem strange but it allows for a good spread of marks and if a candidate's answer is 'safely' within a mark boundary, it generally achieves the top of the boundary and if an answer is 'just' within a boundary, it achieves the bottom of the mark boundary. One of the three marks available for AO3 is awarded for part a. This is generally always awarded unless a candidate has not answered the question or spelling and punctuation are exceptionally poor.

Marks are allocated as below:

MARKS	AO3
1	Presents effective communication using appropriate legal terminology. Nonetheless, there may be several errors in grammar, punctuation and spelling, although not enough to detract from communication of meaning.
0	Fails to communicate and present logical argument, including inadequate use of legal terminology. There are significant errors of grammar, punctuation and spelling which detract from communication of meaning.

MARKS	AO1 Knowledge and Understanding
11–13	Candidates display a sound knowledge and understanding of the subject content relevant to the question and a good perception of the concepts and principles underlying that subject content. They display a sound understanding of the practical application of the law and are aware of current debate and criticism including the major proposals for reform.
7–10	Candidates display an adequate knowledge and understanding of the subject content relevant to the question and have a perception of some of the concepts and principles underlying that subject content. They display a general understanding of the practical application of the law and are aware of aspects of current debate and criticism.
3–6	Candidates display a limited knowledge and understanding of the subject content relevant to the question with limited insight into some of the concepts and principles underlying that subject content. They display a limited understanding of the practical application of the law and are aware in general terms of some of the current criticisms.
0–2	Candidates display a basic knowledge and understanding of the subject content relevant to the question and/or identify some of the relevant principles. They demonstrate occasional basic insights into some of the concepts and principles underlying the subject content. They display a basic understanding of the practical application of the law.

Part b

For part b questions which are worth 11 marks, candidates can achieve a maximum of nine marks for AO2 for a 'sound' answer. Two of the three marks available for AO3 are awarded for part b. Here the two marks are awarded based on the general overall quality of a candidate's answer and assessed according to the definition of AO3 below.

Marks are allocated as below:

MARKS	AO3
2	Presents a wholly logical and coherent argument and provides clear application using appropriate legal terminology. This does not mean that there are no errors in grammar, punctuation and spelling but these will only be occasional.
1	Presents a mostly logical and coherent argument and provides a reasonably adequate application using appropriate legal terminology. Whilst there may be errors in grammar, punctuation and spelling, these are not enough to detract from a mostly effective communication of meaning.

MARKS	AO2 Skills
8–9	Candidates demonstrate a sound evaluation of how the law operates, or an accurate and well-substantiated application of the law to a given fact situation. This is achieved through their selection of legal authorities, by appropriate methodologies and by their ability to apply the law to a given question. They support their conclusions by citation, analysis and analogy.
6–7	Candidates demonstrate an adequate evaluation of how the law operates, or a generally accurate and substantiated application of the law to a given factual situation. This is achieved through their selection of legal authorities, by appropriate methodologies and by their ability to apply the law to a given question and support their conclusions by citation.
4–5	Candidates demonstrate a limited evaluation of some of the points of how the law operates, or apply the law to a given fact situation in a partly accurate and occasionally unsubstantiated way. This is achieved through a limited selection of legal authorities and limited ability to apply the law to a given question.
0–3	Candidates demonstrate a basic evaluation of one of the simpler points of how the law operates or apply the law to a given factual situation in a generally inaccurate and unsubstantiated way. There will be little or no reference to legal authorities and points will not be developed. There will be very limited evidence of structure in the candidate's response.

Improving your exam performance

There are a few important things to remember and common errors that occur year on year:

- Both examinations require you to answer TWO questions; BOTH these questions have a part a) and a part b). You MUST answer part a) and b) from the SAME question. Many candidates year after year pick and choose, but these rubric errors will get you no marks.
- It is good practice to write a good introduction to your answer because it shows the examiner that you understand the topic from the start. Do not fall into the trap of writing a 'waffly' introduction; spend a couple of minutes thinking and planning before you begin to write.

In your introduction, you should begin with a definition of key terms contained in the question. Some examples are highlighted below:

'Outline the role of the Crown Prosecution Service'.

'Discuss the extent to which the law promotes morality'.

'Evaluate the reliability of jury trial'

'Discuss the approaches used by judges in statutory interpretation'

- Use as much **legal authority** as you can remember – this is especially important in part b) where you are being tested on your skills of application. You also need to make sure you explain the relevance of the case.

Example: R v Young (1995)

Answer A: *Another disadvantage of juries is that you do not know how the jury arrived at their verdict; this was seen in the case of R v Young (1995).*

Answer B: *Another disadvantage of juries is that you do not know how the jury arrived at their verdict; this was seen in the case of R v Young (1995), where the jury used a Ouija board to contact the dead victim.*

The highlighted section of Answer B shows that the candidate knows and understands the relevance of the case, whereas the candidate in Answer A has just used the case to support her point and not actually made the progression in showing HOW.

- Part a questions are generally testing your knowledge and understanding of a topic, and command words such as **Explain, Describe, Outline** are all indicative of this.
- Part b requires you to provide a **balanced** argument; there will always be an opportunity to look at two sides of an argument, and you should make sure that

you explore both sides thoroughly. The command words are indicative of this requirement to analyse and evaluate. Common questions have included:

'Consider the effectiveness of…'
'To what extent…'
'Consider the advantages and disadvantages of…'
'Discuss the impact of…'
'Evaluate the importance of…'

The wording of all these questions opens the opportunity for you to look at both sides of the argument and the examiner is looking for a reasoned, balanced argument, supported with relevant legal authority and a rounded conclusion.

- Where possible, try to cite the legal authority in full. An attempt at citation will be credited, but obviously it is more appropriate to learn the cases and relevant legal authority.

    Answer A: *Another disadvantage of the jury system is that you do not know how the jury reached their verdict as was seen in the case where the jury used a Ouija Board.*

    Answer B: *Another disadvantage of juries is that you do not know how the jury arrived at their verdict; this was seen in the case of **R v Young (1995)**, where the jury used a Ouija board to contact the dead victim.*

    It is quite clear that Answer A knows the case, but obviously the fact that the candidate in Answer B has actually cited it in full makes it more clear to the examiner that there is a **sound** knowledge, rather than just an **adequate** knowledge.

- Make sure you answer the question; many candidates will have learned essays off by heart, and then merely repeat this in the examination, only to find that it does not actually answer the question at all. Read and re-read the question to ensure that your planned answer actually answers the question.

- Be aware of recent reforms, criticisms and current affairs in the area. Your lecturer may have made you aware of some such reports and news, but it is always good practice to keep abreast of recent developments. Bookmark these websites:

- When you are revising, be careful if you are taking the decision to omit certain topics. It is very likely that a question may be asked which 'mixes' up topics, and you may find that you can answer part a but have not done enough revision to answer part b as competently. Look back over past papers and see what combination of topics have been asked.

- The LA2 paper is NOT a comprehension exercise. You are required to use the stimulus as a source to support what you are saying, but ultimately, you are being examined on YOUR knowledge. Re-writing a table in your own words, or quoting copious amounts from the source is not going to get you any marks.

- You are marked on your use of appropriate legal terminology and your understanding of core legal principles; yet candidates often make very simple errors.

    Do you know the difference between:

    - *CJEU and ECHR?*
    - *CPS and CPR?*
    - *Guilty and Liable?*
    - *Magistrates and Juries?*
    - *'Should of' and 'Should have'?*

    As obvious as these errors may seem, they are very common, so make sure you have a good grasp and watch your spelling:

    - *Defendant*
    - *Sentence*
    - *Precedent*
    - *Trial*

- Human Rights are an underpinning principle of most of the legal system now, and as such it is expected to be present across the examination in every topic. Therefore, it is important that you have a good grasp of the **Human Rights Act 1998**, as well as the key Articles of the **European Convention on Human Rights** – see p.49 for a detailed breakdown of the key elements.

General websites – these are good for news articles and provide examples of recent developments that are of general public importance.

BBC – www.bbc.co.uk
The Guardian – www.guardian.co.uk
The Times – www.thetimes.co.uk
The Independent – www.independent.co.uk
The Daily Telegraph – www.telegraph.co.uk

Subject-specific websites – these are websites that will give you access to specific information on certain topics.

ACAS – www.acas.org.uk
Crown Prosecution Service – www.cps.gov.uk
Home Office – www.homeoffice.gov.uk
Parliament – www.parliament.uk
Ministry of Justice – www.justice.gov.uk
Directgov – www.direct.gov.uk
National Assembly of Wales – www.assemblywales.org
Welsh Government – wales.gov.uk

Questions and Answers

1. The Rule of Law; Law and Morality	p95	a) Explain the role of judges in promoting the Rule of Law.	(14 marks)
	p96	b) Discuss the extent to which morality should be enforced by the law.	(11 marks)
2. Juries	p98	a) Explain the different types of jury trial available in England and Wales.	(14 marks)
	p99	b) To what extent is trial by jury reliable?	(11 marks)
3. Common Law and Equity	p101	a) Outline the development of common law and equity.	(14 marks)
	p102	b) Discuss the impact of equity upon the development of the common law.	(11 marks)
4. Criminal Procedure: Bail/CPS	p104	a) Explain the powers available to grant bail.	(14 marks)
	p105	b) Discuss the role of the CPS within the English and Welsh legal system.	(11 marks)
5. Criminal Procedure: CCRC	p107	a) Outline the role of the Crown Court in hearing criminal cases.	(14 marks)
	p109	b) Discuss the impact of the Criminal Cases Review Commission.	(11 marks)
6. Civil Procedure	p110	a) Outline the major reforms introduced to the Civil Justice System in 1999.	(14 marks)
	p111	b) Discuss the impact on the Civil Justice System of these reforms.	(11 marks)
7. ADR; Tribunals	p113	a) Outline the different forms of ADR.	(14 marks)
	p114	b) Evaluate the role of tribunals in England and Wales.	(11 marks)
8. European Union: Institutions	p115	a) What is the role of the Court of Justice of the European Union?	(14 marks)
	p117	b) Discuss the powers and decision-making procedures of the Council, Commission and European Parliament.	(11 marks)
9. The Supreme Court; Judicial Precedent	p118	a) Explain the role of the Supreme Court.	(14 marks)
	p120	b) Consider the application of the doctrine of precedent.	(11 marks)
10. Human Rights Act 1998	p121	a) Explain the effect of the Human Rights Act 1998 on English and Welsh law.	(14 marks)
	p123	b) Evaluate the role of the European Court of Human Rights in English and Welsh law.	(11 marks)
11. Judiciary	p124	a) Explain the way in which judges are appointed.	(14 marks)
	p126	b) To what extent are judges representative of society?	(11 marks)
12. Law Reform	p128	a) Explain, with examples, the role of pressure groups in promoting law reform.	(14 marks)
	p130	b) Evaluate the role of the Law Commission in the law reform process in England and Wales.	(11 marks)
13. Statutory Interpretation	p132	a) Explain the role of Hansard in the interpretation of statutes.	(14 marks)
	p133	b) Using your knowledge of statutory interpretation, consider whether an offence has been committed in the situation set out.	(11 marks)
14. Statutory Interpretation	p135	a) Outline the ways in which the Courts have interpreted statutes.	(14 marks)
	p137	b) Using your knowledge of statutory interpretation, consider whether an offence has been committed in the situation set out.	(11 marks)
15. European Union: Sources of Law	p139	a) Explain the role of European Directives in English and Welsh law.	(14 marks)
	p140	b) Evaluate the primary and secondary sources of EU law.	(11 marks)

1. The Rule of Law; Law and Morality

a) Explain the role of judges in promoting the Rule of Law.

(14 marks)

Tom's answer

① The Rule of Law is based on the principle that no one is above the law – even the Queen. The principle came about in the 19th century. Many consider parliamentary sovereignty and the Rule of Law to be the most important principles of the constitution.

② The Rule of Law has three elements: No sanction without Breach meaning that nobody should be punished by the state unless they have broken a law, one law should govern everyone, the law should be given equally and Rights of individual are not secured by a written constitution, but by judges. Judges should be free to decide cases with no influence from outside.

③ Right to a fair trial supports no sanction without breach, but bail and remand do not support it. In today's society everyone is equally treated with the laws which follow the principle that one law should govern everyone. The first element talks about how no one should be punished when they haven't broken a law. This element is included for an obvious reason, that it isn't right for anyone to be punished if they have don't nothing wrong. Unfortunately this cannot always be applied. This is because people can be wrongly convicted, such as murder, for example– which if found guilty, can end with a harsh punishment. This happens less and less now due to forensics giving better results. But if this were to happen, people who may have never committed a crime in their life may be punished for a crime. Also, if a person is held in remand for any reason, and then released with no charge, the remand can be seen as a punishment to the individual as they were held against their will. Looking at these two examples, I can see that even though the law can go against this element, it is not on purpose; as they assume that the individual has either broken the law, or suspected to have done, so they are carrying out their duties.

④ The third element is that the rights of the individual were not secured by a written constitution, but by the decisions of judges. This means that the final decision should be based on what the judge of the case thinks, and shouldn't be influenced by a constitution, or any other outside influences. This is a good idea because it means that the decision will be based on the facts of the case and not and rules that are laid down by a document.

Examiner commentary

① A very brief introduction, Tom has identified what the rule of law is but has failed to mention Dicey's name. Tom has introduced here, though, the concept of parliamentary sovereignty. This is good as this affects judges' ability to promote the rule of law.

② Tom has highlighted the three parts to the rule of law well; however, no mention of the doctrine of separation of powers or Montesquieu.

③ Some good points have been made in this paragraph but it is far too long, and should have been broken down into separate paragraphs, where the points made would have had more of an impact. The discussion of fair trial, remand and bail is good, but appears a little confused as Tom is attempting to discuss the right that everyone is innocent until proven guilty.

④ No real conclusion offered by Tom.

Mark awarded:
AO1 – 6
AO3 – 1
Total = 7 out of 14 (50%)

Whilst Tom has shown some knowledge of the principles of the rule of law, no case to support or statutes, no current examples of breaches of the rule of law and a very limited attempt to answer the question.

Seren's answer

① The Rule of Law is a fundamental principle which underpins our legal system by ensuring that all individuals are protected from abuses of power by the State. The Rule of Law is based on the principle that no one is above the law – even the Monarchy. It is in place to protect all citizens from any breach of human rights and secures the supremacy of the law.

② The Rule of Law was developed by the great British philosopher Dicey in the 19th century. He believed that for the Rule of Law to operate in UK law, it was necessary to establish three important principles: no one should be punished unless they have broken the law, all rights of individuals derive from the law and that all individuals are equal before the law and must obey it. The third element that the rights of the individual were not secured by a written constitution, but by the decisions of judges in ordinary law, this is really important in ensuring that judges promote the rule of law.

③ The principle of the separation of powers, developed by French philosopher Montesquieu, states that full power of our constitution cannot be given to one party, therefore was split into three arms: the legislature who make the law, and the judiciary who interpret the law, and the executive who enforce the law. This has helped uphold the Rule of Law through Judicial Independence.

④ Judicial Independence is one of the most important principles in helping judges to promote the rule of law. It states that the judiciary should not be influenced by the legislature or the executive. This is now the case in the UK under the Constitutional Reform Act 2005. This Act reformed many parts of the law enshrining that judges should promote the rule of law and deal with any breaches of the Rule of Law.

⑤ The Constitutional Reform Act 2005 created the Supreme Court which was established and opened in 2009 and is now the highest court in England and Wales. It also created the Judicial Appointments Commission which plays the role of appointing judges, removing the responsibility from the government. It also reformed the role of the Lord Chancellor, who was considered the most unconstitutional role because he was a Member of Parliament, part of the government and was also head of, and a member of, the judiciary. This also is not a pure separation of powers, and so was removed as head of and member of the judiciary which ensured the independence of the judiciary.

⑥ Another important aspect which helps judges promote law is judicial review, which basically ensures that all actions of the government are legal. This demonstrates that all men and women and government officials are equal before the law and they must obey it. It was confirmed in R v Horseferry (1994) that an important role of the judiciary is to uphold the rule of law in the UK and to protect all citizens from any breach of human rights.

⑦ The UK has an unwritten constitution and can be altered easily, unlike some modern Western democracies that have written constitutions that require a special procedure to be acted upon to change the constitution. With our unwritten constitution it can be seen as a danger for the Rule of Law and could prevent judges from performing their role fully.

⑧ Another principle that could prevent judges from promoting the rule of law is Parliamentary Sovereignty. The Magna Carta 1215 secures Dicey's theory that 'all rights of individuals should derive from the law', because it created the Habeas Corpus, which said that the King could not imprison a baron without taking him to court to determine his guilt. This could be argued to be a clear breach under the Terrorism Act 2001 which gave the police the power to detain any suspect without trial; this is a clear breach of the rule of law and an example of how Parliament is sovereign to judges.

⑨ In conclusion, the role of promoting the rule of law is protected by our constitution, but threatened by Parliamentary Sovereignty. It treats all citizens equally and the judicial role is extremely important in our constitution.

Examiner commentary

① Good opening paragraph defining the rule of law. It is good as Seren has done well here to define any key terms, though this could have been in a little more in depth saying that the rule of law simply means that the state should govern its citizens in accordance with rules that have been agreed upon.

② Seren has done well to mention Dicey as he is a key person within the rule of law debate.

③ Seren's answer has a good logical structure to it, she moves from Dicey to Montesquieu, two key people that must be discussed in a rule of law answer.

④ In this paragraph Seren addresses the question of how judges promote the rule of law, very good to include key statutes.

⑤ Seren does well to include how judges are appointed and the removal of powers from the Lord Chancellor, as both are key to ensuring the independence of the judiciary and in turn promoting the rule of law.

⑥ Excellent to support your arguments with key cases, Seren has done very well here linking this case to the question.

⑦ This paragraph could have been developed more, Seren has not really explained why our unwritten constitution is a danger for the rule of law and how it prevents judges from performing their role fully.

⑧ However, Seren should have gone on here to consider the impact of the Human Rights Act 1998, particularly sections 3 and 4 on the role of judges in enforcing human rights and promoting the rule of law, a good case to illustrate this is A & others v Home Office (2004) where House of Lords judges declared that the Terrorism Act 2001 was incompatible with human rights, which in turn forced a change in the law by Parliament.

⑨ A conclusion is a very important feature of an essay, in Seren's answer the conclusion is a little brief, and the conclusion should tie the main strands of the essay together. Seren could have also included some more current examples of breaches of the rule of law, e.g. extraordinary rendition.

Mark awarded:
AO1 – 11
AO3 – 1
Total = 12 out of 14 (86%)

This is a good sound answer that demonstrates a sound knowledge of the rule of law. Most importantly Seren has really tried to answer the question throughout the whole of the essay, rather than writing everything she knows about the rule of law, she has linked it to how judges promote the rule of law. Seren has used correct terminology and citation throughout. Seren would have gained top marks if she had also discussed the impact of the Human Rights Act 1998 on judges promoting the rule of law.

b) Discuss the extent to which morality should be enforced by the law.

(11 marks)

Tom's answer

① Some parts of our law are obviously influenced by morality, for example abortion law. Many laws that we have come about because of things in the bible, and religious groups today, for example in this country we do not have a law which allows you to kill someone if they are dying, but in some other countries this is allowed.

② Also in our country we do not have the death penalty this is a very moral issue, where our government has decided that morally this is wrong, but if they had asked the people I believe a majority would be in favour of it, so our law does not really take into account the morals of everyone.

③ There have been some people who believe that the law should enforce morality and others who believe that the law should not enforce morality and that people should be free to do whatever they want as long as they don't harm others.

④ There are many moral issues in today's society. Should people be able to choose the sex of their baby, if they have boys and want a girl, or choose their eye colour? The law does have to get involved in cases like these and say it is wrong as this could lead to people abusing the law.

Examiner commentary

① Tom has identified where moral influences possibly come from and given one example, but overall this is a fairly weak opening paragraph.

② Again Tom has identified another moral issue, and this is a good one to discuss, but this could have been developed further, and Tom could have talked about free votes in Parliament where MPs are able to vote on moral issues within the law according to their conscience.

③ Tom is attempting here to discuss the Hart Devlin debate, but he has failed to name them and develop the debate any more than in a very limited way.

④ Once again the final paragraph does touch upon current moral issues, but there is no supporting legal authority. The answer is very chatty, dealing with general moral issues that most people would be aware of regardless of whether they were studying law.

Mark awarded:
AO2 – 5
AO3 – 1
Total = 6 out of 11 (55%)

This is a limited answer which touches upon some of the main areas but the lack of explanation or legal authority to support points meant that he could not achieve more than 5 marks. No discussion of the Hart Devlin debate.

Seren's answer

① Morals are normative; they vary between different people and different religious groups. Many principles of the English legal system are derived from religious concepts and therefore maintain a degree of morality in the system.

② In the case of Pretty v UK a woman suffering from motor neurone disease wished to take her own life but she was unable to. She exhausted the UK court system in search of the reassurance that if her husband assisted her in dying that he would be immune from prosecution. On appeal to the European Court of Human Rights it was ruled that article 2 – a right to life – should not be distorted in any way to allow right to death. Some would argue that this ruling was morally right because they believe in the religious principle that life is sacred. On the other hand, some would argue that pain and suffering is immoral and providing that the person is of sound mind they should increase the enforcement of morality to enable people to take their own lives with help if that is their wish.

③ In the case of R v Cox a doctor injected a terminally ill patient causing almost instant death. He claimed falsely in his defence that the drug was being trialled as a pain killer. Some people would argue that unlawfully taking someone's life is immoral and that they should be punished. Although others might disagree and think that it is moral to end a person's pain and suffering, they might also think that this view of morality should not be properly enforced by the law because it could lead to potential unnecessary 'murders' which would be deemed immoral.

④ In the case of R v Brown six adult consenting males who were homosexual took part in the acts of sadomasochistic violence and were charged with assault. The House of Lords refused their arguments that they were all consenting and said that pleasure from pain was an awful thing and the men were convicted. This would support some people's view of morality, for example religious people and they would agree with the House of Lords' statement.

⑤ The Wolfenden report was commissioned after a succession of well-known men were charged with homosexual actions. This led to legalisation of homosexual actions between consenting adults in private and also the Hart Devlin debate.

⑥ Devlin believed that it was society's role to protect people on the basis of what was viewed as good and evil and Hart believed that morality should be left to the individual and that acts in private were not a threat to society. The six men in the Brown case were convicted despite the legalisation of homosexual acts in private, upholding Devlin's view of morality.

⑦ In conclusion, morality to a certain extent is enforced in the law, although it is not always recognised. Morality in the law is an equal compromise of the diverse views of what the concept of morality really is.

Examiner commentary

① Good opening paragraph, clearly setting the scene for the rest of the answer.

② Almost straightaway Seren has used case law to back up her points on morality; this is very good and directly links to the question of should morality be enforced by the law.

③ Again use of case law to illustrate how the law enforces morality, the points made in this paragraph are slightly repetitive as to the previous paragraph, perhaps Seren could have used a more recent case as well, e.g. Re A (Children) (Conjoined Twins: Surgical Separation) (2001).

④ This is an excellent case to use to illustrate how the law has enforced morality even for acts done in private.

⑤ Seren has done well to mention the Wolfenden report and the Hart Devlin debate, this must be included in any essay on morality; however, more recent debates and legislation could also be mentioned, e.g. embryo testing, Human Fertilisation and Embryology Act 2008.

⑥ Good application of the Brown case to the Hart Devlin debate.

⑦ Conclusion a little brief, perhaps Seren could have extended this further to include more recent and topical morality issues, e.g. cloning, IVF, designer babies.

Mark awarded:
AO2 – 8
AO3 – 2
Total = 10 out of 11 (91%)

Overall this is a good answer; there is a real danger with morality questions that the answers become very general, vague and chatty with very little back up of any legal authority. Seren has avoided doing this and has really attempted to answer the question. Remember to always include current cases and debates within morality and current legislation, e.g. HFEA 2008.

2. Juries

a) Explain the different types of jury trial available in England and Wales.

(14 marks)

Tom's answer

① The jury is an ancient and democratic institution that has been used since the 12th century. Lord Devlin described the jury as 'the lamp which shows freedom lives'.

② Originally the jury wasn't independent and its decisions weren't respected. But Edward Bushell appealed and took the issue to the Court of Common Pleas where Sir James Vaughn announced that any verdict made by the jury must be final.

③ Today juries are used in the Crown Court and also sometimes in the civil courts. In the Crown Court the judge will decide questions of law and the jury will decide questions of

fact. Their role is to evaluate the cases presented by the prosecution and defence and retire to discuss their views. Whilst doing this they will reach a verdict and decide if the defendant is guilty or not guilty. In the civil courts, the jury is rarely used.

④ The verdict of a jury is really important, before 1976 the verdict had to be unanimous. But today the verdict can be majority of either 10-2 or 11-1 if allowed following the judge asking for a unanimous one but it not being possible.

⑤ Juries are selected from the electoral register and have to be between 18 and 70.

Examiner commentary

① Tom has done well to include an introduction here to put his answer in context. He has used a key quotation from Lord Devlin.

② Again some good history provided but will Tom focus enough on the question below?

③ Tom has done well to identify the jury's role in both criminal and civil cases here. He has identified the jury as trier of fact but could also comment on the judge as trier of law as a comparison. He could also have explained the proportion of cases tried by a jury in comparison to those in the Magistrates' Court. He has used some good key terminology but needed some further depth on the standard of proof (beyond reasonable doubt) and he could also mention the secrecy of the jury room.
Tom has only introduced the jury in civil trials but not expanded at all. He

should have explained the civil cases in which a jury can be used such as fraud and slander. He could also have brought in the limits on the role of the jury in complex fraud cases and dangerous cases following the Criminal Justice Act 2003.

④ The end of this sentence is a little unclear but Tom has still done well to include the unanimous verdict and majority verdict. To provide some extra depth of explanation he could have linked the requirement of a 10-2 or 11-1 majority to the standard of proof – beyond reasonable doubt.

⑤ Tom perhaps ran out of ideas here as this part is not strictly relevant to the question of the role of the jury. Tom should also have included a brief conclusion to sum up the main strands of his answer and 'focus' on the question posed.

Mark awarded:
AO1 – 7
AO3 – 1
Total = 8 out of 14 (57%)

Overall this is a limited/adequate answer which, though touching upon two key roles of the jury in criminal and civil cases, has failed to identify the role in the Coroner's Court. His explanation of the role in criminal cases was good but he didn't expand on their role in civil cases. He also needed some broader evidence of knowledge and understanding by considering wider issues such as the standard of proof, the new limits on the role of the jury and the courts in which they are present. Tom has used some key terminology accurately and gave an introduction. He needed to sum up his answer with a brief conclusion.

Seren's answer

① Juries have been used to try people ever since the introduction of the Magna Carta, which stated that individuals had a right to be tried by their peers. Lord Devlin described the jury as 'the lamp that shows that freedom lives'.

② In criminal cases, the role of a jury is to be deciders of the facts and to determine a verdict based on these facts, guilty or not guilty beyond reasonable doubt. The judge's role is to decide on matters of law.

③ The most common types of cases that juries are used to try are indictable offences in the Crown Court such as murder or rape. A total of 12 jurors will serve throughout the duration of the trial and the reasoning for this is believed to have come from the religious principle that there were 12 disciples.

④ The jury has two hours to deliberate the arguments presented by the prosecution and defence in the secrecy of the jury room and if they cannot

reach a unanimous verdict, s.17 of the Juries Act 1974 allows a majority verdict to be given of either 11-1 or 10-2.

⑤ Trial by jury is also used in the County Court to listen to cases regarding malicious prosecution, false imprisonment, defamation and fraud (Supreme Court Act 1981). Usually eight jurors serve on such cases and their role is to determine liability and if appropriate, to decide the amount that should be awarded to the claimant in damages. Here the standard of proof is on the balance of probabilities.

⑥ Juries listen to cases in the High Court regarding the same matter as in the County Court but of a much higher monetary value. Similarly to the Crown Court, a total of twelve jurors usually serve. The role of a jury in complex and dangerous cases has been limited by the Criminal Justice Act 2003.

⑦ As well as being used in civil and criminal cases, juries are sometimes used in the Coroner's Court. In this case, the role of the jury is to hold inquests on deaths in police custody, in prison, or deaths as a result of breach of health and safety. They have to decide on the cause of death. Usually between seven and eleven jurors serve in this type of case.

⑧ In conclusion, the role of the jury varies in different courts but in their most common role in the Crown Court they are used to be the deciders of the facts and to evaluate from this any responsibility.

Examiner commentary

① Good to see an introduction here to put the answer in context. This is a good place to start for any essay style question.

② Seren has also done well to mention the role of the jury as trier of fact and the verdict and to bring in judge as trier of law as a comparison. Good mention of the standard of proof.

③ Seren has done well to recognise the role of the jury in the Crown Court. She could also have commented on the proportion of cases in the Magistrates'(95%) and Crown Courts and why a jury is only present in around 2% of criminal cases (e.g. no need for jury where defendant pleads guilty).

She has done well to include some examples of indictable offences such as murder, rape, etc.

④ Seren has demonstrated sound knowledge and understanding here to bring in the majority and unanimous verdicts. She could also provide some evaluation by linking to the standard of proof. E.g. by requiring either 10-2 or 11-1 jurors to be in agreement on the verdict, it ensures that guilt is proved 'beyond reasonable doubt'.

⑤ Seren has provided a balanced answer here by bringing in the role of the jury in a civil case and drawing some comparisons to its role in a criminal case. Good examples of civil cases where jurors serve. Good reference to legal authority.

Good mention of the standard of proof as a comparison with the criminal standard of proof mentioned earlier. Seren is working logically through the issues.

⑥ Very good mention of the change to the limits on jury trial and legal authority to substantiate.

⑦ Seren has done very well here to also comment on the role of the jury in the Coroner's Court. This is the area most students omit.

⑧ A conclusion is an important feature of an essay style question. It should draw together the main strands from the main body of the work but not bring in any new information. Seren has done well to comment on the varied role of the jury with its most common role in the Crown Court. If she had more time, she could round up this essay in a bit more depth perhaps drawing on 'lay participation' and 'trial by one's peers', but overall, good to see a conclusion which many students omit under exam conditions.

Mark awarded:
AO1 – 11
AO3 – 1
Total = 12 out of 14 (86%)

Overall this is a very good answer which demonstrates a sound knowledge and understanding of the role of the jury in the three key areas of criminal, civil and Coroner's Court cases. Seren has used key terminology accurately and logically progressed through the issues presented. She has focused on the question posed and provided a comprehensive answer.

b) To what extent is trial by jury reliable? *(11 marks)*

Tom's answer: Grade C

① Trial by jury was perceived to be the new more open and fairer way in which to try a case. However, there have been some criticisms of juries in the past.

② Firstly the selection process for juries does not obtain a fair representative selection of the public. Whilst this has improved recently, with the previous selection process being anyone who owned property would be eligible to sit on a jury, it is still ripe for criticism. The current selection process is still based on citizenship, so anybody who is registered to vote is eligible to be selected to sit on a jury. This immediately excludes anyone who is homeless, anyone who is young and anyone who has lived in this country less than five years. It also excludes anyone who chooses not to vote.

③ In addition to this there are excusals whereby anyone within set criteria may be excused from jury service. Such people can be members of the armed forces, medical staff or anyone with illness (severe). Again narrowing down our selection and making the jury less reliable. Although these people may simply be deferred as opposed to excused.

④ Whilst the jury has been decided there are still potential risks such as jury nobbling. This was a major issue when juries were required to obtain a unanimous vote; therefore the majority vote has been put in place to prevent this.

⑤ In previous cases such as Fraser 1988 where the defendant was black and the jurors were all white, there is a concern that the lack of representation may create a bias result.

⑥ There is also the possibility of a perverse verdict if there is an inadmissible piece of evidence submitted.

⑦ In summary, trial by jury is not always reliable. Our alternatives would be to allow single judge trials, much like the civil courts, have a panel of judges or have a judge and lay magistrates to sit as a 'mini' jury. Ultimately, if we lose juries, we risk case hardened judges deciding on these cases.

Examiner commentary

① A limited introduction given.

② Tom has done well here to mention the selection of juries and how representative they are. This is one of the reasons why they are (not) reliable. However, his answer is quite general in terms of evaluating how the changes made with the Criminal Justice Act 2003 have improved selection. This would certainly have enhanced his answer. He would also have benefited from citing this legal authority.

③ He touches upon selection criteria here but needs to expand more specifically on who is eligible to sit on a jury as per the Juries Act 1974 as amended by the Criminal Justice Act 2003. In addition, he needs to be careful with his use of key terms 'excusal' and 'deferral' and to explain these more clearly.

④ A good mention here of the risk of jury nobbling and link to the verdict. He could also bring in the standards of proof to evaluate how reliable a jury verdict is based on how convinced they need to be of guilt (in a criminal trial) before delivering a guilty verdict.

⑤ Good mention of relevant case law here. This adds legal weight to the answer. Tom has also done well to focus this example on the issue of reliability and representation.

⑥ Good mention of perverse verdicts here but the end of the sentence is unclear. In addition, he should have given a case example to illustrate the problem of perverse verdicts. Ones he could have cited are: Young, R v Owen, Kronlid.

⑦ Good to see a focused conclusion here where Tom brings in some alternatives to the current system to evaluate. A good final sentence.

Mark awarded:
AO2 – 6
AO3 – 1
Total = 7 out of 11 (64%) Grade C

This is an 'adequate' answer which touches upon some of the main areas but the lack of explanation or legal authority to support earlier points meant that he could not achieve more than 6 marks. He did well later on to mention a key case but other areas also demanded some authority. However, he did well to use a logical structure and to give an introduction, albeit brief, and conclusion.

Seren's answer

① Juries play an important part in the legal system and therefore their decisions should be reliable.

② Firstly, those eligible to serve as a juror has changed throughout time. Prior to the Juries Act 1974, it was only property owners that were allowed to serve as a juror and this was mainly middle aged, white males. A report by the Morris Committee showed that 95% of women were ineligible.

③ The Juries Act 1974 widened the range of people eligible to serve in an attempt to make them more representative of society. It stated that those aged 18-70, those that were registered on the electoral role and those that had been a UK resident for 5 years since 13 were eligible providing that they do not count as disqualified, mentally disordered or lacking in capacity. This increased the reliability of the jury because prior to the Act, wealthy property owners would possibly be more inclined in favour of defendants of their social class, thus making them unreliable.

④ The Criminal Justice Act 2003 allowed even more people to be eligible to serve as a juror. It removed the categories of ineligibility which meant judges, magistrates, prison officers and police could now serve as jurors. This, it can be argued, increased the reliability of the jury because they would make decisions that incorporated their view and the law and some might argue that professional people make more calculated judgements.

⑤ On the other hand, jurors are supposed to be representative of society and the general presumption is that they are 'lay' otherwise a judge could determine a verdict. Some might argue that a jury consisting of legal personnel is not reliable because they might be more likely to convict in accordance with the law and be biased against defendants.

⑥ The deliberations in the jury room are secret and so it could be argued that a jury trial is not reliable because they could decide a verdict by any means. For example, they could methodically consider the evidence or guess whether or not the defendant is guilty or they could use an unconventional and unreliable method to determine guilt or innocence. In the case of Young, the jury were found to have used a Ouija board to contact the deceased victim and ask him who had killed him. Clearly this is unreliable and a risk of the deliberations remaining secret.

⑦ In addition, the jury are 'free' to make any decision they like, even if directed otherwise by the judge. As Lord Devlin said, they are 'the lamp that shows that freedom lives'. This can sometimes lead to a 'perverse verdict' which is a decision that goes against the evidence presented. A case to show this is R v Owen where a lorry driver killed a man's son. The man shot the lorry driver but didn't kill him. The jury refused to find the man guilty despite him having shot the lorry driver. This was known as a perverse verdict as they should have found the man guilty but went against the evidence.

⑧ Jury trials have recently been limited by the Criminal Justice Act 2003 where there is a risk of jury tampering or where they would not understand the evidence in a complex fraud case. This should increase the reliability of the jury.

⑨ To conclude, juries are used in thousands of cases per year and play an important role but their decisions are not always reliable. There are suggestions of allowing a judge to try cases alone or to have lay members sit with judges to improve reliability but for the time being, juries remain.

Examiner commentary

① Introduction present, albeit brief.

② A logical place to start considering representation of the jury. Good discussion of this important report.

③ Seren has focused on the question posed here. She has linked in her example on eligibility to the reliability of juries. Good understanding of the previous selection criteria.

④ Seren has done well here to progress to the important changes made as a result of the CJA 2003. She has also linked this in to the main issue of the question – the reliability of the jury – and evaluated well.

⑤ Good balanced argument here. It is important to consider both sides.

⑥ Seren is discussing a wide range of relevant issues and she has done well here to back up her answer with reference to an appropriate case.

⑦ A good paragraph where she has initially put it in context with reference to Lord Devlin's quote. She has then done well to draw in perverse verdicts and cite a relevant case to substantiate.

⑧ Good discussion of a recent reform and again linked in to the question posed.

⑨ Seren has included a focused conclusion here that incorporates the suggestion about judges sitting alone to try cases or with lay members. Good range and understanding demonstrated.

Mark awarded
AO2 – 9
AO3 – 2
Total = 11 out of 11 (100%)

This is a very good answer. Seren has provided a well-structured and detailed answer supported by a good range of correct and appropriate legal authority. She continuously linked her evaluation back to the question posed and discussed a good range of relevant issues including proposals for reform. Though not a 'perfect' answer, she has done enough to gain full marks for this question.

3. Common Law and Equity

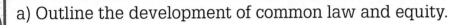

a) Outline the development of common law and equity.

(14 marks)

Tom's answer

① When William I came upon the throne in 1066, there was not a system which was common, i.e. the same throughout the country. Therefore there were different rules and regulations throughout the country, so in one place, for example, where theft may have been considered a crime, another area it may not have. William laid the basis for the development of the common law from customs.

② The judges who solved disputes throughout the country used the system of local courts; rules were also applied that were used on the previous cases. However the Normans were adamant to create a unified government and legal system, this slowly incorporated the best local systems and it created common law. The most senior official, the Chancellor would deal with cases where common law was unable to offer a remedy. When the cases were dealt by the Chancellor, he would do what he thought was acceptable and fair, he was criticised by saying the system was too flexible and that the decision depended too much on the personal opinion of the Chancellor. Gradually many principles and ideologies were built up to create 'Equity'. Equity was rather different from Common law because it was not as rigid and did not have to follow a specific set of rules like common law.

③ One of the problems with common law was that it simply offered one remedy, which was monetary compensation; therefore this was not adequate to every dilemma. The second main problem was that the case had to fit with an existing 'writ'. So new cases that were not dealt with before by other judges were not taken into consideration, they were rejected. Equity helped to counter these two main problems because it was fair and provided additional remedies besides compensation, individuals could take their cases to court, even if they were previously denied remedy in common law.

④ The Earl of Oxford's case was extremely important in the history of equity because it determined the status of equity and whether or not it should prevail when in conflict with common law, which it did succeed. Without this decision, equity would have been worthless, so it had to be more dominant if it was to succeed. Equity was created to rectify the problems in common law and to provide adequate remedies that common law was not capable of providing.

Examiner commentary

① There is no mention of the Curia Regis here or the importance of the judges travelling the country to find the best laws.

② This is a good paragraph, but there is no mention of some of the problems with equity – a common citation is that equity 'varied with the length of the Chancellor's foot'. More detail needs to be given about the administration of the two systems.

③ The Provisions of Oxford Case is another significant piece of legal authority that needs to be mentioned. Although Tom has mentioned the problems with the common law, this is not done in a great amount of detail, and remains 'adequate' in terms of evaluation and analysis.

④ This answer comes to a rather abrupt ending, and Tom has not mentioned the significance of the Judicature Acts and why there was a need for equity to develop.

Mark awarded:
AO1 – 7
AO3 – 1
Total = 8 out of 14 (57%)

This is an 'adequate' answer, but is lacking detail in places – there is a lack of substance and depth to convince that it is well into the level. Increased use of legal authority and greater utilisation of detail would have increased Tom's marks. He also needs to take care to provide a rounded conclusion to his answers.

Seren's answer

① Common law began to develop during the reign of William I in 1066. When he conquered England, he found it had no single system of law common to the whole country, only sets of rules that differed from area to area. He wanted to develop an 'English law' that would be common to the whole country. To do this, he would have to be in control of the whole country.

② He began to take control of the country by introducing the feudal system. This meant that all the land in the country belonged to him, and the people who helped and supported him would be rewarded with land and a job. William made himself or one of his advisers available to any landholder who had a dispute or a problem, and could not seek redress from their lord. This was known as the Curia Regis, which would administer a set of rules which applied to the whole country, in order to solve the problem. This practice eventually developed into common law.

③ However this new development of common law still had flaws. It had two main problems – the only remedy that could be granted was damages, and that after the 13th century, a case could only be started with an existing writ. Although in many cases damages is a sufficient remedy, in some it is not. An example of this is if the claimant has been denied the opportunity to buy a piece of land they were promised. If they have already made arrangement based on the knowledge that they would own said piece of land, money may not be an adequate remedy for the problems this may incur.

④ After the 13th century, new cases could only be started by way of an existing writ. This caused problems because if there was not an existing writ to the claimant's case, they would not be able to take it to court. People were dissatisfied with this, and began to petition to the King for a remedy.

⑤ The King and his court dealt with these petitions until they became too numerous, he began to delegate responsibility to his chancellor. Cases would be settled on what the chancellor thought was fair, or 'equitable'. Over the years, the chancellor developed a large body of principles, which eventually developed into what we now call 'Equity'. Equity is very important historically, as it overcame the problems associated with common law. However, it took a while before equity was accepted. People said that it was too flexible and lacked certainty.

⑥ An important case in the acceptance of equity was the Earl of Oxford's case in 1615, where it was held that whenever common law and equity are in conflict, equity will always prevail.

⑦ After the realisation that a case could require both common law and equity, the idea came about that the two courts should not be completely separate. Despite this, it was not until the Judicature Acts in 1873–1875 that the two courts became officially combined. This had a positive effect on people's cases because they could have their case heard in one court, and seek both common law and equitable remedies. Although the two courts were combined, they still are entirely different systems with different outcomes. When they are in conflict, equity will always prevail.

⑧ Overall equity seems to have filled in the gaps in common law, and made the entire system fairer.

Examiner commentary

① An immediately sound opening paragraph with an outline of where common law came from; which is precisely what the question is asking.

④ Good use of examples here showing that Seren is able to develop the topic and accurately trace the history of the common law. Good mention of the flaws in the common law and thus why equity needed to develop. At all times, Seren is sticking to what the question is asking and providing sufficient detail.

⑥ This is a key case in the development of equity, and is a vital point to make when talking about the history of equity.

Mark awarded:
AO1 – 13
AO3 – 1
Total = 14 out of 14 (100%)

Common Law and Equity is an extremely popular question, answered by many candidates. However, in order to get the higher range of marks, you need to provide the level of detail that demonstrates a 'sound' knowledge. Just like Seren has done above, make sure that you illustrate with examples where necessary and use the relevant terminology and legal authority throughout. Further, it is a common error for students to repeat themselves in part b) where both parts ask about equity. You will only be credited once for the knowledge so try not to do this.

b) Discuss the impact of equity upon the development of the common law.
(11 marks)

Tom's answer

① Common law offered one remedy which was damages, this is monetary compensation but as said before this did not qualify to satisfy every problem because it would be inappropriate. For instance if an individual wanted to purchase a car that was extremely special to them and after entering an agreement to purchase, the owner changes their decision to sell, monetary compensation would not satisfy this problem, so common law would not provide justice for the claimant.

② The four most important equitable remedies are:

Injunction – this orders defendant to do or not do something.

Specific performance – forces a party to comply with a previous decision.

Rectification – this is an order which alters the words in a document, which does not express the correct intentions of the parties.

Rescission – this is a remedy that reinstates the parties involved to the position they were in before signing the contract.

③ These equitable remedies are discretionary; therefore it is not compulsory for the court to award claimants with an equitable remedy.

④ Maxims of equity were created from equity's previous decisions. The belief behind the maxims is to ensure moral fairness and it assumed that the use of maxims has restrained the application of equity by restricting the times it can be used. One maxim of equity is 'He who comes to equity must come with clean hands'. This simply means that the claimants who have been in some type of wrong regardless of how minor this is won't be granted an equitable remedy. Other common maxims are 'Delay defeats equity' and 'He who seeks equity must do equity'.

⑤ Equity has proved itself capable of adapting to a changing society, therefore changing to meet new needs of society. Equity gives a decision that is generally fair and new remedies can be created if new cases emerge. However, only six decades ago, in 1948 the Court of Appeal said any claim in equity must show ancestry founded in history, simply saying that the judgements must follow precedents and the decision made by predecessors. He also said that because even if it is thought by judges that the case requires different jurisdiction from precedents, this is not sufficient to invent a new jurisdiction.

Examiner commentary

② Tom outlines all the main equitable remedies, but does not refer back to the question and more importantly has not used legal authority to illustrate the use of these remedies. His descriptions are quite simplistic.

③ This is an important point to have made and is crucial.

④ Again, there is an awareness shown, but it is lacking in legal authority, and although maxims are mentioned, there is limited description and no supporting authority.

⑤ Tom has not made any reference to the importance of equity today in helping to develop the common law; meaning that he has not actually answered the question posed. Tom needs to have mentioned the Mareva Injunction and the Anton Piller Order, and thought about how equity may be relevant today in terms of technological advances, with a rounded conclusion.

Mark awarded:
AO2 – 5
AO3 – 1
Total = 6 out of 11 (55%)

A limited answer showing little reference to legal authority and the importance of understanding the need to answer the question and make specific reference to what the question is asking. Although there is a broad understanding of the relevant concepts, there is a lack of substance and coherence.

Seren's answer

① After the development of common law, problems started to emerge. Common law could only provide damages as a remedy, which sometimes wasn't adequate. Equity developed, along with new remedies for the problems it is faced with. Equity has been described as 'the gloss on common law' and 'common law's safety valve'. This is because people feel the system is more just, and can provide them with the outcome they need, not just monetary compensation. Maxims mean that when a claimant's case is based on a rule of equity, the rule can only be applied if the maxims are satisfied.

② Equity has four main remedies: injunction, specific performance, rectification and rescission. Injunction means that the court can order the defendant to do or not to do something. For example, the defendant could be ordered not to play loud music after a certain hour if this has upset or disturbed the claimant.

③ Specific performance means that a party has to fulfil a previous agreement. For example, if the sale of a house has been agreed, but one party wants to back out, the sale still has to take place if one of the parties wants it to. It can also be awarded in cases where a contract for a unique item has been made; as in the case of Sky Petroleum v VIP Petroleum where petrol was regarded as a unique item.

④ Rectification can alter the words of a document or contract which does not express the true intentions of the parties to it. This makes the document reflect what the parties actually agreed, not what the contract may state, despite the fact that it may have been signed. This was seen in the case of Craddock v Hunt.

⑤ Rescission restores parties to the position they were in before the contract was signed. For example, if you were to buy a car, only to find out it didn't work. If the seller did not specify that it did work, you could not necessarily get them to give you the money back. However, via rescission, the car can be returned to the seller, and the money returned to the buyer, as in the case of Grist v Bailey where a mistake was made in the contract.

⑥ To make sure administering these remedies was morally fair, maxims were developed. They are basic principles aiming to protect both the claimant and defendant from unfairness. An example of a maxim is: 'He who comes to equity must come with clean hands'. This basically means that if the claimant themselves is in the wrong somehow, they will not be granted an equitable remedy. This is shown in the D&C Builders v Rees case, in which some builders did some work which was supposedly not up to standard and they accepted a drop in agreed payment from their employer as they were in financial difficulty. The builder later sued the Rees for the outstanding amount. The Rees asked for the doctrine of equitable estoppel to be applied to make the acceptance of the lower payment binding. This was refused as the Rees had taken unfair advantage of the builder's financial situation and therefore had not 'come with clean hands'.

⑦ Another maxim of equity is 'Delay defeats equities'. This means that if a claimant takes an unreasonable amount of time to bring an action, the remedies will not be available to them. The amount of time that is classed as unreasonable will be assessed in each case. An example of this is the Leaf v International Galleries case. The claimant bought a painting described as genuine; only to find five years later that it was not genuine. He tried to claim the equitable remedy of rescission, but the delay had been too long.

⑧ Equity has shown that it can develop along with current times, by making new rules and principles such as promissory estoppel. Promissory estoppel is an act that can stop a party to a contract enforcing his legal rights when he has given his word he will not. This was useful in the High Trees case. (Central London Property Trust v High Trees House Ltd). The defendants were leased a block of flats at a set rent, which was then agreed to be reduced by 50% because of the economic climate during the war. No time limit was set on this reduction of rent. Five years later the flats were full, and the claimants company wrote to the defendants asking for the full amount of rent for the last two quarters of the year (when the flats became full). In defence, the defendants claimed that the agreement of half rent related to the whole term of the lease. The claimants claim was successful and they put the rent back up. However, on the basis of promissory estoppel, if the claimant had tried to claim back the rent for the previous 5 years, he would have been stopped as the promise was intended to be binding until the flats were full.

⑨ Overall equity can provide alternative remedies to common law, which are required in many cases. It developed and changes along with times and new situations it is presented with.

Examiner commentary

① A good introduction which summarises the problems with common law, and thus why equity needed to develop. This illustrates the impact that equity has in resolving problems in the common law.

②–⑤ Very pleasing to see a description of all four remedies and relevant supporting cases This shows a 'sound knowledge' of the relevance of equity and how these remedies are more preferable to the common law remedy of damages.

⑧ Again, this shows a good knowledge of equity developing with the times, alongside common law to provide a claimant with an adequate remedy. Seren has missed some of the more obvious modern methods of equitable remedies – such as the Mareva Injunction and the Anton Piller Order. These are key to the modern use of equity and should be included.

Mark awarded:
AO2 – 8
AO3 – 2
Total = 10 out of 11 (91%)

A 'sound' evaluation of the development of equity with a good overall understanding of all the key features demonstrated. Care needs to be taken to answer the question set and not to produce a well-rehearsed answer that does not acknowledge the question.

4. Criminal Procedure: Bail/CPS

a) Explain the powers available to grant bail. *(14 marks)*

Tom's answer

① After a person has been arrested, sometimes questioned and had all their details taken, they can be granted bail. This means they are free to leave and return to their lives pending trials/ further investigation.

② The powers available to grant bail can come from the police themselves on most occasions or if the police refuse to grant bail, which is in their power, the defendant can appeal to the courts who also have the power to grant bail.

③ Police may refuse bail if the crime is more serious, for example drug dealing or rape. They may also refuse bail if they fear the person may skip bail or break the conditions of bail. Also, if the person is seen to be any threat to themselves or others.

④ It is likely for a person to appeal to the court for bail and win.

⑤ Bail can hold different terms and conditions, you may be forbidden from contacting certain people or may be given a curfew. If these are broken, your bail can be revoked or you may have the time lengthened.

⑥ For example, the case of Hagans who had 28 previous convictions was granted bail but raped and killed a woman despite the conditions.

⑦ As long as a person is not seen as a threat and has a clean or good record of sticking to their bail, they are likely to be granted it.

Examiner commentary

① Tom has done well here to provide a definition of bail as a brief introduction. He should have substantiated his answer with reference to Acts. This is a weak opening paragraph.

② Tom has identified the two types of bail but does this superficially. He needs to reference s.38 PACE 1984 for police bail and s.4 Bail Act 1976 for court bail and make the point that the courts start with the presumption that everyone is entitled to bail. He also mentions the appeal to the courts, which is a separate issue and needs to be considered on its own. Again, he could reference a case to back up his point. Here the case of Nottingham Justices is relevant regarding the appeal.

③ Tom has done well to mention some of the reasons why bail can be denied. Again this is done without depth or development. He could have brought in the Criminal Justice Act 2003 and the effect of drug use on the bail application.

④ This is a strange sentence as it is on its own and not expanded at all. This point could have been made in the paragraph above, in terms of structure, and as with the points above, he needed further depth on the appeal and a case as legal authority.

⑤ Tom has briefly mentioned some conditions though the final sentence is unclear. It is not clear what he means by the 'time lengthened'. There are several other conditions he could have discussed such as: surrender passport, live in a bail hostel, obtain legal advice, etc.

⑥ It is good to see Tom bring in a case for authority here. This provides some development on the above paragraph on conditions.

⑦ A weak conclusion here. A conclusion should summarise the main strands of the main body of the essay. Tom could have commented on the balancing act between bail and remand and referred to a case such as Hagans to illustrate the problems with bail.

Mark awarded:
AO1 – 7
AO3 – 1
Total = 8 out of 14 (57%)

This is a 'just' adequate answer at the lower end of the band. There are some errors of expression and Tom doesn't always convey his points clearly or sophisticatedly. There is a general lack of legal authority with only one case mentioned. He does highlight that there are two types of bail – police and court but does not expand on this.

Seren's answer

① The majority of bail is covered in the Bail Act 1976. It is stated in section 4 that there should be a presumption that everyone is entitled to bail, except in specific circumstances. This supports the principle that everyone is innocent until proven guilty.

② Both the police and courts have the power to grant bail. Police bail comes under s.38 PACE 1984 and court bail comes under s.4 Bail Act 1976. The presumption of the right to bail can be overturned if a person is charged with an indictable offence, if they have lots of previous conditions, if they may interfere with witnesses or obstruct the course of justice or if they are a danger to themselves or others.

③ Under the Criminal Justice Act 2003, a defendant is refused bail if he tests positive for a class A drug and refuses treatment. This is because he may be committing crime to fund his drug addiction therefore the cause of his criminal activity needs to be taken into account.

④ If a person is charged with murder, rape or manslaughter and has a previous conviction for such an offence, the Criminal Justice and Public Order Act 1994 said that he would be automatically denied bail.

However, the case of Caballero challenged this automatic denial of bail in the European Court of Human Rights saying that this breached his right to liberty (article 5) and his right to a fair trial (article 6). He won his case and the UK changed the law with the Crime and Disorder Act 1998. Now a person charged with a serious offence who has previous convictions for such offences can get bail in 'exceptional circumstances'.

⑤ Bail is either conditional or unconditional. Conditions that can be imposed are: surety, which is where a person other than the defendant promises to pay a sum of money if the defendant skips bail or a security where the money is paid upfront and the defendant gets it back if he returns on the day of his trial. Other conditions may be surrendering passport, reporting to police station, staying away from a person or place, staying in a bail hostel or wearing an electronic tag.

⑥ However, sometimes bail is granted to people who shouldn't get bail with dire consequences. An example of this is the Gary Newlove case where he was killed by youths on bail or Hagans who was given bail despite previous convictions and raped and killed a woman.

Examiner commentary

① A good opening paragraph including the presumption of innocent until proven guilty. Good mention of the Bail Act 1976 and the important presumption under s.4.

② Seren has done well here to comment on both police bail and court bail as both are needed for the question. Students should check the wording of the question as it may ask about either court bail or police bail or, more commonly, require both to be discussed.
Seren has again done well to back up with reference to the relevant and correct law.

③ Good discussion of this important development in the granting of bail with explanation to show understanding.

④ This is a good paragraph with a lot of detail and discussion of wider elements.

Seren has done very well to quote Acts and articles from the ECHR along with the case of Caballero. She needed the specific section numbers of the CJPOA and CDA as a small criticism.

⑤ Good progression onto conditional/unconditional bail with a range of conditions mentioned.

⑥ A brief final paragraph which isn't really a conclusion. Seren also needed to evaluate the impact of bail upon the defendant balanced with how it protects the public. This could have formed the basis of a conclusion to round off the answer. In addition, Seren could have discussed potential appeals against the decision to refuse bail and the case of Nottingham Justices regarding the number of appeals.

Mark awarded:
AO1 – 11
AO3 – 1
Total = 12 out of 14 (86%)

This is a good sound answer that deals with both police bail and court bail, citing specific relevant and correct legal authority. Wide range of relevant issues discussed that shows a sound understanding of bail and when it can be granted. Though lacking a conclusion and seeming a little rushed towards the end, it is a sound answer. See comments for ways to gain full marks in this question.

b) Discuss the role of the Crown Prosecution Service within the English and Welsh legal system. *(11 marks)*

Tom's answer: Grade C

① The Crown Prosecution Service (CPS) is the name for the system in place in Britain to prosecute defendants.

② There are different levels of courts for different circumstances, also whether a matter is civil or criminal affects whether they are tried in civil or criminal court.

③ The role of the CPS is to determine whether or not a person should be prosecuted for the crime they have done. Prior to the Crown Prosecution Service, the police would decide whether or not to follow up a case and whether or not to take the accused to court. This was a concern as the police were too concerned with winning or losing a case and not discovering the truth. The CPS was set up to work independently from the police.

④ The CPS and police did not work together; however, the police were unhappy with the amount of cases the CPS dropped because the case didn't pass the evidential or public interest tests. The evidential tests looks to see if there is enough evidence for them to win the case and the public interest test sees if a case is in the public interest. A case must pass both tests and stops court time being wasted.

⑤ The CPS was then reformed by Glidewell and it was agreed that the CPS lawyers should work in police stations in criminal justice units and more CPS offices should be set up to match up to the number of police forces.

⑥ The CPS and police now work together better and deal with cases more effectively.

Examiner commentary

① A weak opening statement that merely outlines the role of the CPS in prosecuting offenders.

② This paragraph is wholly irrelevant to the question as the CPS are involved in criminal cases.

③ Good to see some background here from Tom on why the CPS was set up. This is important though needs further development. He should have drawn in the JUSTICE report and the RCCP report that led to the establishment of the CPS. In addition, he could have cited the Prosecution of Offences Act 1985 that set up the CPS.

④ Some good evaluation, though unsophisticated, regarding the fact the police were unhappy with the number of discontinued cases. Tom has then progressed to discuss the two tests that determine if a case should go ahead for prosecution. This is important for focus on the question posed. Tom needed to cite the Full Code Test in s.10 Prosecution of Offences Act 1985 to give some legal authority and depth to his answer.

⑤ Though it is good to see mention of the key Glidewell report, this point is not developed and there is a lot more depth needed on his main findings and how these changes were put into effect. Tom has done well to also discuss the criminal justice units but needs to evaluate why these will improve the working relationship of the police and CPS. He should also be more specific by stating that the CPS has been restructured into 42 areas to correspond with the 42 police force areas and the impact of this.

⑥ A weak conclusion here that does not sum up the main body nor focus on the question posed.

Mark awarded:
AO2 – 6
AO3 – 1
Total = 7 out of 11 (64%) Grade C

This answer is just within the adequate boundary. Another examiner might have put it as a limited answer (1 mark less). Tom's answer lacks specificity and only mentions one report – Glidewell. The stronger parts of his answer were relating to the evidential and public interest test, though these needed further development and evaluation to show more than a superficial understanding.

Seren's answer

① The Crown Prosecution Service is headed by the Director of Public Prosecutions, Alison Saunders, who is answerable to the Attorney General. It has had a turbulent history, coming under fire firstly from the Phillips Commission and the Justice Report. The Justice report said that the police should not be responsible for the two tasks of investigation and prosecution and the Phillips Commission said that there was a lack of consistent prosecution policies amongst the police forces. As a result, the CPS was set up with the Prosecution of Offences Act 1985.

② The CPS decide whether or not to prosecute defendants charged with offences. Since the Criminal Justice Act 2003, they now also decide the charge, using the threshold test where they see if there is a realistic prospect of conviction.

③ Before a case goes to court, the CPS must ensure that it passes the Code for Crown Prosecutors contained in s.10 of the Prosecution of Offences Act 1985. There are two tests – evidential and public interest. First, the evidential test is that the CPS believe that due to the charges being brought and available evidence, the court is more likely than not to convict. This is to stop wasting court time with cases that may fail. If it doesn't pass the evidential test, it doesn't go any further. If it does, it then goes through the public interest test. It looks at whether or not the case is in the public interest or against the public interest to proceed. The Code for Crown Prosecutors 2013 sets out questions which will identify and determine the relevant public interest factors tending for and against prosecution. They consider issues such as how culpable the defendant is, whether a weapon was used, the circumstances of and the harm caused to the victim and the impact on the community. When they have balanced all of the factors they decide whether the case should proceed to trial

④ In 1998, the Glidewell report by Sir Ian Glidewell reported that a huge overhaul was needed of the CPS. Glidewell found the acquittal rate was too high and the relationship between the police and CPS was not strong or efficient enough and mainly that the CPS was too centralised and bureaucratic with just 13 areas.

⑤ Glidewell rearranged the CPS into 42 CPS offices, one for each police force to make the relationship stronger between the police and CPS. The Narey report recommended the CPS work in police stations to overcome such issues. As a result, Criminal Justice Units were established. These work directly in police stations and have improved relations. There are also admin case workers who can prosecute guilty pleas in the Magistrates' Court saving time for the barristers in the Crown Court. The close working of the police and CPS led to the successful prosecution of Ian Huntley and Maxine Carr in just 6 weeks.

⑥ Since Glidewell reorganised the CPS into 42 areas, which meant that there was one CPS office for each police force area, there has been another reform in April 2011 that restructured the CPS once again into 13 geographical areas. Each area is headed by a Chief Crown Prosecutor.

⑦ The role of the CPS is to ensure the correct charges are brought against the defendant and to prosecute in court, bringing together the evidence collected by the police. They are now working better with the police and their success is improving.

Examiner commentary

① Seren has given a very good opening statement paragraph here. She has brought in two key reports that led to the establishment of the CPS. She has also discussed the key personnel responsible for the CPS and brought in the Act that set up the CPS – the Prosecution of Offences Act 1985. A logical introduction that starts at the beginning of the history of the CPS.

② Seren has done well here to discuss the decision to charge made under the CJA 2003. This is an important development and she has done well to bring in key terminology such as the 'threshold' test and 'realistic prospect' along with backing up with reference to the correct statute.

③ This is a strong paragraph where she is focusing on one of the main roles of the CPS. It is to be commended that she has cited s.10 Prosecution of Offences Act specifically and she has shown a sound understanding of how the two tests within the full code test operate. The fact that she mentions factors for and against the public interest enhances her answer.

④ Logical progression here onto the Glidewell report. This is a key development in the CPS. Good discussion of the main findings and Seren has given the correct figures.

⑤ Another sound paragraph where Seren has evaluated the impact of the Glidewell report (important for part b questions) and also brought in the Narey report. A good end sentence where Seren has linked the developments to the successful prosecution of the Ian Huntley case.

⑥ Good evaluation here assessing the impact of the restructuring following the Glidewell report. Seren has also done well to discuss the personnel now involved for extra depth.

⑦ Good to see a conclusion here that focuses on the question posed (the role of the CPS) but that also brings in factors that affect their role such as the working relationship with the police.

Mark awarded:
AO2 – 9
AO3 – 2
Total = 11 out of 11 (100%)

This is a sound answer that moves logically from the establishment of the CPS to the Glidewell reforms. Good focus in the middle on their role in the decision to charge and prosecute with very good reference to the correct and specific legal authority. Importantly for this part b question, Seren has evaluated the impact of the reforms and how they have helped to improve the CPS. Well-structured answer with a clear introduction and conclusion. Though not perfect, it still achieved full marks.

5. Criminal Procedure: CCRC

a) Outline the role of the Crown Court in hearing criminal cases.
(14 marks)

Tom's answer

① The Crown Court is for the most serious cases, like murder and rape where the Magistrates do not have enough power to deal with them. If you are not happy with the decision in the Crown Court, you can appeal to the Court of Appeal.

② In the Crown Court, a jury is used to decide whether the defendant is guilty or not guilty. They retire to a secret room to decide the verdict and the judge will then decide a sentence. A jury is made up of 12 people randomly selected from the electoral register; they must not have any serious criminal convictions and must not have any mental disorders. A trial by jury is a right laid down by the Magna Carta which stated that everyone should have the right to be 'tried by their peers'. Therefore in the Crown Court, the role of the judge is not very big and it is mainly down to the jury to decide guilt or innocence.

③ The Crown Court can also hear appeals from the Magistrates' Court where the defendant appeals against his conviction for a minor offence. A jury is not always used for this type of case, and the Crown Court has the power to change this conviction and maybe let the defendant walk free. The judge in the Crown Court can sentence a person to life, or give any other sentence that he feels appropriate. There are also times when a Crown Court will hear a triable either way offence; these are cases that are mid-range, and the defendant can choose whether he wants a trial by jury or not, so long as he pleads not guilty.

④ Overall, the Crown Court is one of the most important courts in the English and Welsh legal system and is the court that most people think of when they think of the criminal law and trials.

Examiner commentary

① A limited outline of the role of the Crown Court, but there is a distinct lack of legal authority, and legal substance to this answer.

② This is not strictly true and Tom seems to be a little unsure of the role of the jury and thus his knowledge is a little limited in terms of the Crown Court.

③ This is a good outline of a key role of the Crown Court, though an obvious omission is the lack of detail and the lack of legal authority to support the answer and take it beyond 'limited'.

④ Again, another important role of the Crown Court outlined in basic terms. A little expansion would have made this paragraph a little more convincing and legally substantive.

Mark awarded:
AO1 – 6
AO3 – 1
Total = 7 out of 14 (50%)

Despite having many of the important roles of a Crown Court, this answer is lacking legal substance and is rather brief in places. Tom needs to expand on all the points he made, and give the examiner more in terms of detail about the trial procedure and legal authority or even examples of recent cases that have been heard in a Crown Court. There needs to be less vagueness about the appeal routes, and more explanations as to the routes of and grounds for appeal.

Seren's answer

① The Crown Court has a massive role when dealing with criminal cases. Criminal offences can be divided into three categories known as summary offences, triable either way offences or indictable offences. Summary offences are when minor crimes have been committed and you would usually have to be tried in a Magistrates' Court. Either way offences are when you can request for a jury in a Crown Court or be tried in a Magistrates' Court. The seriousness of this offence includes theft, burglary or in some cases actual bodily harm. Indictable offences are the most serious and they will have a judge and maybe a jury and they will be tried in the Crown Court. The type of offences that would be deemed to be indictable are murder, manslaughter and rape. All cases start in the Magistrates' Court but due to s51 Crime and Disorder Act 1998 as amended by the Criminal Justice Act 2003 the defendants will get transferred to the Crown Court.

② During trial procedures in the Crown Court, the jury is sworn in and the facts of the case are outlined by the prosecution. The prosecution will then call some witnesses to support their case and will be examined in chief, there will then be a cross examination of those witnesses by the defence counsel. When the prosecution has finished their case, the defendants may submit no case to answer and if the judge agrees that there is not enough evidence then the jury may be directed to enter a not guilty verdict. The defence would then get their turn and they will start by calling their witnesses and examining them in chief. They will then be cross examined by the prosecution counsel and then both sides must make closing speeches to the jury whilst the defence always goes last. The judge will then sum up all the facts

of the case before the jury retires to come to a unanimous decision although majority verdicts are accepted too. Finally, if the jury finds that the defendant is not guilty then they will be acquitted and released from court, but if they are found guilty then it will be up to the judge to deliver a sentence.

③ If a defendant is unhappy with the outcome of a trial in the Crown Court then they can appeal to the Court of Appeal about a certain point of law. If the Court of Appeal considers the conviction unsafe they will allow an appeal, or they may order a retrial or they will dismiss the appeal. The prosecution cannot normally appeal against an acquittal although the Criminal Justice Act 2003 allows the prosecution to seek to quash an acquittal so that a re-trial is ordered and this under the reforms of double jeopardy rule. There was a case called Thompson & Venables v UK (1999), where the European Court of Human Rights upheld complaints about the boys who were convicted of murdering James Bulger in an adult Crown Court. They believed that the trial was a breach of Article 6 ECHR because they were intimidated by the wigs, and it is now the case that youths are not tried in the Crown Court, but in a special Youth Court where wigs and gowns are not worn and the defendant is permitted to sit with his family.

④ The main type of offence that will be heard in the Crown Court is indictable offences – however, there will be a preliminary hearing at the Magistrates' Court to decide legal aid and bail. The Crown Court is also used for sentencing defendants who have committed either way offences where the Magistrates feel that their sentencing powers are inadequate. The Crown Court will also hear appeals on summary offences from the Magistrates' Court.

Examiner commentary

① Good illustration of the three categories of offence, with examples. This is important because it signposts the rest of the answer and allows Seren to progress and talk about these in more detail later on. Establishment of the Crown Court came under the Supreme Court Act 1981 – this would have been a useful piece of legal authority to introduce the role of the Crown Court.

② This is quite a detailed paragraph on the actual procedure in the Crown Court, and shows a sound knowledge of trial procedure – Seren needs to make sure that exam time is not wasted on copious detail to the detriment of including important points.

A common mistake for candidates is to turn this type of question into just juries – beware of falling into this trap Juries

should only be mentioned in terms of their role in an indictable trial. Remember they are used in only around 1% of criminal cases.

③ Excellent use of legal authority here talking about appeals in the Crown Court which is a key piece of knowledge central to this answer. Legal authority is always impressive and shows the examiner that you can write cohesively and have more than an adequate understanding of the topic.

④ Further expansion on the use of the Crown Court for other types of offences, which is excellent. It would also be appropriate to talk about the sentencing powers of the Crown Court – this is maximum life imprisonment and/or an unlimited fine.

Mark awarded:
AO1 – 11
AO3 – 1
Total = 12 out of 14 (86%)

Overall, this is an excellent answer which covers all the main roles and functions of the Crown Court – it is well written, logically structured and has a good balance of legal authority and examples. Seren has produced a coherent answer which shows a 'sound' knowledge of the topic. More time needs to be allocated to the various roles of the Crown Court; rather than a big chunk on the trial procedure itself, which is relevant, but only a small part. There is articulate use of legal terminology throughout.

b) Discuss the impact of the Criminal Cases Review Commission.
(11 marks)

Tom's answer

① The CCRC was set up to deal with miscarriages of justice and allow people who have been convicted of a crime to walk free from prison. The CCRC was set up in 1997, and has helped high profile people such as Sally Clark and Ryan James seek justice as they were imprisoned for crimes they did not commit. Sally Clark was imprisoned for supposedly murdering her babies, but it turned out they had both died of cot death. Ryan James was a case where a man was accused of murdering his wife and he was sent to prison, but it was later discovered that his wife had committed suicide. These cases were only resolved when the CCRC investigated the case and found there to have been missing or flawed evidence. One of the first cases the CCRC investigated was Derek Bentley. He was accused of murder but after the CCRC investigated, it was found that it was actually the other man in the case that fired the fatal shot.

② The CCRC cannot release a defendant; they can only ask that the case be sent back to the Court of Appeal for another trial. This is no guarantee that the result will be any different though, but for some people it is the only hope that they will prove their innocence.

③ Overall, the CCRC has a limited role as it does not suit everyone's case, but for some people it can be very useful to avoid a miscarriage of justice.

Examiner commentary

① A good introduction with excellent explanation of some high profile cases that have involved the CCRC. Common mistakes surrounding this question are candidates getting it mixed up with CPS or IPCC – be careful to avoid making this very simple mistake.

② Very brief outline of the actual role of the CCRC; more time needs to be spent talking about the evaluative aspects of the question. This paragraph needs to be much more detailed.

③ Good conclusion but lacking legal substance, as the rest of the answer has no logical progression to sum up.

Mark awarded:
AO2 – 5
AO3 – 1
Total = 6 out of 11 (55%)

This is a very poor answer with little in the way of detailed evaluative content. As a result, it should gain no more than 'limited' marks. The question is requiring very specific evaluation points which look at the success of the CCRC, and any negativity that may surround its operation. Therefore, a balanced argument is required with appropriate and relevant use of authority. There is some excellent use of legal authority in terms of examples in the first paragraph, but sadly the arguments are unsubstantiated from there on.

Seren's answer

① The Criminal Cases Review Commission (CCRC) was set up in 1997 to investigate possible miscarriages of justice because of cases where people had been imprisoned for crimes they did not commit; for example the Birmingham Six and the Guildford Four. For some people who have not been able to appeal, it is the only place where they can get their case re-investigated and allow innocent people to be set free. For example, Sion Jenkins, a convicted murderer was investigated by the CCRC and he was later released from jail. The CCRC do not have the power to overturn a conviction; they can only send it back to the Court of Appeal or demand that it is reinvestigated by the police. It is an independent body and cannot be influenced by any part of the criminal justice system. One of the earliest cases it investigated concerned that of Derek Bentley, but unfortunately Bentley had already been hanged for his crimes so he could not receive justice.

② The CCRC has been quite successful because they have quashed over 300 cases, so these people may have served prison sentences for crimes they did not commit. Although a disadvantage would be that it is not actually an appeal court, so the defendant is not guaranteed to be released, and a big problem that is found is that the police re-investigate the crime and they are often the reason why there was a miscarriage of justice in the first place, because they tamper with evidence and force defendants to confess.

③ Anyone can complain to the CCRC; including the defendant or their family. This means that there is a good chance that the case will be taken on; a disadvantage would be that there are a lot of cases that are waiting to be heard and it may take years for the case to be investigated. Another disadvantage is that the way the CCRC calculates its statistics is that a 'successful' case can be any case where there has been a positive outcome; this could include having the sentence reduced.

④ There will always be miscarriages of justice, and the CCRC will only be successful if the reasons why miscarriages of justice happen are investigated. The CCRC has been very successful and in some cases such as Derek Bentley, Ryan James and Sally Clark, they have helped release innocent people from prison.

Examiner commentary

① This is an excellent introduction, with appropriate and relevant examples cited. It gives a good background to the role and history of the CCRC without being too copious so as to impede on the evaluation of the CCRC.
Remember it is a question asking you to EVALUATE not DESCRIBE, so it is important that you spend the majority of the essay EVALUATING.

② A balanced argument here – Seren shows evidence of knowledge of both advantages and disadvantages, and these are convincing, sound arguments which

are based on verifiable research and statistics.

③ Again, further points of evaluation are made in a balanced, logical way.

④ Excellent use of examples, though it would have been pleasing to see these in appropriate places throughout the answer, rather than rushed in at the end. A little explanation as to their relevance and why they are so important would also have been appropriate. Credit should be given though as there is evidence of knowledge of recent cases.

Mark awarded:
AO2 – 8
AO3 – 2
Total = 10 out of 11 (91%)

Overall, this is an excellent answer which has a good degree of evaluation throughout. The biggest criticism is the lack of expansion on the cases, but this is not a major flaw – evidence of the cases is creditworthy. Seren provides a balanced argument with a good mix of positive and negative evaluation points demonstrating a 'sound' evaluation of the CCRC.

6. Civil Procedure

a) Outline the major reforms introduced to the Civil Justice System in 1999.

(14 marks)

Tom's answer

① The introduction of the Civil Procedure Rules came about after a report in 1999 in which Lord Woolf stated that a civil justice system should be quick, be just in the results it delivers, and all parties should be treated fairly. He said that costs were too high and it could often take the County Court three years for a trial to start and five years in the High Court.

② The overriding objective stated that simpler language is to be used instead of a writ or summons, you now use a claim form, and instead of a plaintiff you are now known as the claimant.

Rule I.I stated that it should have allocated timetables and the judge plays a more active role in the proceedings. ADR is also to be recommended instead of resorting to trial proceedings.

③ Fast track cases from £10,000 to £25,000 are dealt with in the County Court with very strict timetables. Multi-track cases are for cases between £25,000 and £50,000; this is for more expensive matters and is heard in the County Court or the High Court for more intrinsic matters.

④ In conclusion, the Civil Procedure Rules introduced simpler language, quicker consideration of cases through the track system and strict rules and timetables to follow.

Examiner commentary

① A good introduction, which puts the topic into context and demonstrates an understanding of the reasons behind the implementation of the Woolf Reforms.

② This is an excellent paragraph, and had Tom continued the whole answer in this fashion, he would have scored much more highly. There is an understanding of key terminology contained in the report, and an overall summary of the key

provisions. What he needed to do was now take each of these provisions and talk about them in a lot more detail.

③ Accurate description of two of the tracks, but Tom has failed to discuss the small claims track, and indeed his description of the two tracks is limited and lacking in detail.

Mark awarded:
AO1 – 7
AO3 – 1
Total = 8 out of 14 (57%)

There is a definite knowledge here, but it is far from detailed enough to warrant a higher level. Tom clearly understands the main provisions of the Civil Procedure Rules but he has not alluded to all of the key features, and has not dealt with the ones he has mentioned in sufficient detail.

Seren's answer

① In 1996, Lord Woolf reported that any successful civil justice system should have the following aims; to be just in the results it obtains, to be fair in the treatment of litigants, to be understandable to those who use the system, and also to conduct the appropriate procedures at appropriate prices. He believed that they system should deal with cases at a reasonable speed and ensure efficiency, relevant resources

and organisation. Woolf concluded that the current system lacked these ideal qualities and put forward 303 recommendations which he felt should be considered. He felt the current system was costly, complex and ordinary people may not understand it, making it inefficient.

② Following his aims, Woolf reformed the civil justice system with the introduction of the Civil Procedure Rules 1998, which were enacted in 1999. The system became simplified in many ways, including the language used. For example, the 'plaintiff' became the 'claimant', and the 'writ' or 'summons' became the 'claim form'. The most outstanding rule of them all would be Part 1 of the Civil Procedure Rules, which summarises the 'overriding objective'. It states that 'the court must deal with all cases justly' which includes dealing with them in proportion to the costs involved, the importance and complexity of the case and the financial position of both parties. The Civil Procedure Rules also included many other changes, such as the introduction of pre-action protocols which are designed to increase communication within the process and encourage pre-action exchange of information to 'front load' cases, which may reduce delay. Also, Lord Woolf introduced active case management where judges became 'case managers', and took an active role in the proceedings in terms of setting strict timetables, restricting witnesses and adopting a much more inquisitorial approach to settling disputes.

③ Also the reformed rules included the encouragement of Alternative Dispute Resolution; judges should encourage the use of ADR where appropriate but cannot force claimants into attempting an alternative to the courts. It also allowed the judge to 'stay' proceedings until the case had been tried. Another reform that helped make the system simpler was the allocation of the tracks, where disputes would be put into different categories. Disputes concerning amounts up to £10,000 would be placed in the small claims track. The small claims track is the cheapest and simplest of procedures. It is informal in terms of rules, and legal aid cannot be provided in order to discourage lawyers. Limitations of this are that businesses use this to collect debts and the defendant usually has representation, which puts them at an unfair advantage. Disputes between £10,000 and £25,000 are placed in the fast track. This method uses a strict timetable and is thought to have lessened waiting time, although the wait is still currently 74 weeks which is a long time. Disputes between £25,000 and £50,000 enter the multi-track which involves the case being managed by the courts.

Examiner commentary

① Excellent introduction, putting the question into context; and explaining why the reforms were necessary. Using the terminology from the report is impressive and shows a sound understanding immediately.

② The pre-action stage of the case is the most significant of the reforms because a huge emphasis is placed on the pre-trial stages of the process. It would therefore be appropriate to talk about the flowchart procedure, particularly in relation to the role of the defence issuing their claim and what the options are for the defence, and maybe giving some examples of pre-action protocols.
All the major reforms are covered here.

It is useful to revise them in four broad areas:
- Encouragement of ADR
- Judicial case management
- Simplification of procedures
- Pre-action protocols

And then to discuss them in as much detail as possible, again taking care to use accurate legal terminology where possible.

③ A good outline of the three tracks, but it would also be appropriate to talk about the differences in personal injury values for each of the tracks. Also, each track has particular features in terms of legal representation, and the timetables which could also have been mentioned.

Mark awarded:
AO1 – 11
AO3 – 1
Total = 12 out of 14 (86%)

This is the higher end of 'adequate' in terms of knowledge because it is clear, well-structured and there is evidently a knowledge of the Woolf Reforms shown, supported with accurate use of terminology from the report. However, there is detail missing in places, which has prevented this answer from being 'sound'.

b) Discuss the impact on the Civil Justice System of these reforms.
(11 marks)

Tom's answer: Grade C

① Regarding the impact of the reforms on the civil justice system, there have been many opinions. Two of these are Suzanne Burns and Lawrence West QC.

② Suzanne Burns reported that it is difficult to isolate the impact of the reforms as many problems that happened before such as disqualification of cases still take place. On the other hand, Lawrence West QC described the reforms as an 'abject failure'. He believed that they were failing the civil justice system in ways such as cases being turned away and previous problems not being fixed.

③ The overall advantages of the Woolf Reforms are that the introduction of pre-action protocols has encouraged cooperation and made the system less adversarial. The encouragement of ADR has led to an increase in 'stayed' cases which is cost effective and overall more efficient for the parties themselves. Also the idea of case management allows issues to be identified straight away and prevent unnecessary time being wasted.

④ However, there are also disadvantages of the Woolf Reforms. The pre-action protocols are expensive, and the management of cases by the court has led to the overuse of judges, which increases court fees. The simplicity of the rules has gradually become more and more complex again because there have been more than fifty amendments resulting in the current Civil Procedure Rules running into thousands of pages.

⑤ Overall, I think the reforms have improved civil procedure a great deal. The majority of issues are addressed correctly, but the overriding problem is the upkeep of these rules.

Examiner commentary

① This candidate has used these two academic's opinions – you should refer to the academics that you have studied. What is important in this question is that you provide a balanced argument and make points showing both effectiveness and ineffectiveness.
Refer to p37–38 for the opinions of Prof Michael Zander and Tony Allen QC

③ A classic mistake is being made here because the candidate is not referring these points back to the authority. Try and attach every point to a piece of legal authority, or in this case, the opinion of an academic.

④ There is a lack of detail here, and there are not enough evaluative points made to credit anything more than a bottom of Level 3.

Mark awarded:
AO2 – 6
AO3 – 1
Total = 7 out of 11 (64%) Grade C

This student has just made it into 'adequate' in terms of skills because it is clearly lacking substance and detail. There are some good arguments made but Tom has not shown how these arguments are supported by the academics. It is crucial, particularly in a part b question that you support every argument you make with relevant legal authority.

Seren's answer

① The Woolf Reforms were introduced to reform, update and modernise the English and Welsh legal system. Since the introduction of these reforms, the success of them has been much debated as a result of the many advantages, disadvantages and the need for further reform.

② The Woolf Reforms have had much criticism and much praise. The main advantages of the reforms are the low costs of claims under £1,000 – it is free and the fact that the claimants and the defendants can represent themselves makes the process much cheaper and easier. There are claims that the encouragement of ADR seems to be working as many cases are now settled out of court, which saves the parties money and the hassle of having to go through court.

③ However, there are disadvantages of the reforms too, such as the judges not supporting unrepresented clients, the front loading of costs has been criticised by Prof Michael Zander. Also, the National Audit Office claims that only 54% of successful claimants receive all their money. There is also the unfair advantage that big businesses have when they have access to experienced and expensive legal representation.

④ The success of the reforms has been debated among many legal professionals; Zander has stated that despite the reforms, some of the same problems are still around, such as delays in some cases, high costs, judges not acting as case managers and legal experts not working effectively. Also Richard Burns argues that the courts need to be modernised in order for the reforms to work to their potential. He says that a lack of resources like time and money are causing the reforms to have a negative effect, as the strict timetables are putting solicitors and barristers under pressure and prices are rising for legal representation.

⑤ It has been argued by Peter Thompson QC that under the old rules there were 391 pages of procedure, and under the new rules there are 2,301 pages with 53 updates. This is certainly not achieving Lord Woolf's aim of making the system simpler and more user friendly. Despite this criticism, the majority of legal professionals argue that the reforms have been a success despite not having the huge impact that was expected, they are slowly improving the civil justice system.

Examiner commentary

① A good introduction that puts the question into context. However, a common mistake among students is to make their introduction a little 'waffly'. Seren should take care to define any key terms in the introduction and allow for maximum impact straight away.

② Good discussion of some of the key advantages. However, more detail is required here to create a truly balanced answer, and there needs to be more use made of legal authority.
Other positives could include the emphasis on pre-exchange of information, the success of pre-action protocols and the inquisitorial method used by the judges.

③ Excellent use of legal authority here, and now we are seeing more use of the evaluation and analysis skills that are required of a higher level answer.

④ Again, Seren has given a clear statement of the flaws within the reforms with some good use of academic opinion to support her points.

⑤ Good conclusion by Seren here bringing the whole topic back into context and summing up the evaluative points.

Mark awarded:
AO2 – 8
AO3 – 2
Total = 10 out of 11 (91%)

Seren has produced by no means a perfect answer, and there is a lot of detail missing. However, in terms of using skills of evaluation and analysis, she has shown that she has a good knowledge of the topic, and can provide arguments for and against the implementation of the reforms, with some good use of legal authority.

7. Alternative Dispute Resolution; Tribunals

a) Outline the different forms of Alternative Dispute Resolution.
(14 marks)

Tom's answer

① ADR is a method of resolving a dispute in a place outside of the court. It is encouraged by the Civil Procedure Rules 1998.

② There are several different types of ADR. These are Negotiation, Mediation, Conciliation, Arbitration and Tribunals. The general positives of using ADR are that they are cheaper, less stressful, quicker and they free up court congestion.

③ One method of ADR is Negotiation. This is the cheapest and quickest method of solving a dispute. It allows the two parties to talk to each other and try and solve it themselves. The parties can instruct a solicitor to draw up a settlement; obviously, the more a solicitor is used, the more it will cost.

④ Another method of ADR is Mediation. This is where a neutral third party acts as a 'referee' or 'go between' for the two parties. The idea of mediation is to encourage the parties to talk and settle their dispute. This is what the mediator aims to do.

⑤ A third method of ADR is Conciliation. This is in some ways very similar to Mediation in the fact that there is a third party involved. However, the main difference is that the conciliator takes a more active role in the settlement and will actually suggest ways that a settlement can be achieved.

⑥ The final method of ADR is Arbitration. This is where you pay for a party to represent your case. This is still done outside of the court, but is similar to court proceedings. The parties must come together to decide how many arbitrators they are going to use and they can also supply trained or professional arbitrators if they cannot decide how many arbitrators are to be used.

Examiner commentary

①–② A good start with reference to Tom's plan for the rest of the answer, putting the question into context.

④–⑤ Accurate definitions of both Mediation and Conciliation, but Tom is really missing examples and a more convincing detailed description of the methods.

⑥ What is immediately apparent is that although Tom provides an adequate description of the different forms of ADR, he does not progress with his explanations, and this makes the knowledge little more than adequate. He needs to provide detailed explanations and cite legal authority where relevant, particularly in relation to Arbitration, where the Arbitration Act 1996 is a vital inclusion.

Mark awarded:
AO1 – 7
AO3 – 1
Total = 8 out of 14 (57%)

This answer is just in the 'adequate' level of Knowledge and Understanding, because there is no more than a general understanding of the law. It would seem that Tom has little or no awareness of current debate and criticism, which means that he cannot be credited with marks that are at the top of the level.

Seren's answer

① Alternative Dispute Resolution (ADR) is a means of settling disputes and claims outside of court and is encouraged by the Civil Procedure Rules 1998. Often it is better to resolve certain issues outside of the court as it saves money, time, and stress and can also avoid the deterioration of relationships. Such forms of ADR include Negotiation, Mediation, Conciliation, Arbitration and Tribunals.

② Negotiation is the largest form of ADR, involving two parties discussing their problem with each other in order to find a suitable solution. It is probably the cheapest and least formal method, avoiding stress and hassle. It can involve solicitors acting on behalf of their clients but there is no third party involved. Negotiation happens in ordinary lives such as when faulty goods are exchanged.

③ Mediation involves a third party, the mediator, who will act as a 'referee', or 'go between' passing information between both parties. The Family Law Act 1996 actively encourages divorcing couples to use mediation services before going to the courts to settle matters. This form of ADR can thus only work if there is some hope of cooperation between the parties. Recent government proposals mean that from April 2011, all divorcing couples will have to attend mediation before settling their divorce in court. This could potentially lead to an infringement of the Human Rights Act 1998. As mediation is growing, more and more commercial services have been set up such as the Centre for Dispute Resolution and numerous services online.

④ Conciliation is a third form of ADR, very similar to Mediation but the third party will take a more active role, suggesting grounds for compromise or the basis for a settlement. Again, this requires a degree of cooperation from both parties and it avoids the stress and cost of courts if successful. Often used in industrial disputes, a particular example of an organisation that offers such services is ACAS, which also aims to prevent industrial disputes.

⑤ Arbitration is arguably one of the more formal forms of ADR. It involves a third party, the Arbitrator, making a judgement and then a decision on how to settle the dispute and both parties are then bound by it. The decision can also be enforced by the courts if necessary. However, the Arbitration Act 1996 stipulates that the procedure must be very flexible for both parties involved. Also, s15 of the Act allows the parties to decide who and how many arbitrators they may have – either a single one or a panel of two or three. They may choose a lawyer to be an arbitrator or an expert in the relevant field. The Institute of Arbitrators offers training for arbitrators involved in disputes. Scott v Avery clauses are often used in contracts that mean any dispute that arises within the contract must be settled via arbitration. Due to the decision being binding, there is little room for appeal.

⑥ Tribunals are another form of ADR, despite being regarded as specialist courts. They were set up to give the public a means of resolving disputes regarding their social rights and various other areas such as employment law. Therefore it can be said that there are numerous forms of ADR that encourage people to avoid the courts and thus relieve congestion.

Examiner commentary

① This is an excellent introduction, putting the question into context and immediately showing knowledge of the different types of ADR and what she is planning to discuss in the rest of the answer. Seren has used legal authority straight away, immediately showing the examiner that there is deep background knowledge.

② An immediately well-structured answer with each form of ADR clearly discussed. This paragraph on Negotiation is thorough and shows a sound knowledge of the use of negotiation. Further discussion of the availability of online services and DIY divorces, etc., would have further enhanced an already in-depth knowledge.

③ Excellent use of legal authority here; Seren has shown how mediation has developed and has impressively shown an awareness of current reforms in the area. This paragraph could also have included the case of Dunnett v Railtrack to truly trace the history of compulsory mediation.

④ Good description of Conciliation; but could be further enhanced with an example of where ACAS has been involved recently.

⑤ Some excellent use of legal authority here deserving of a high level. Seren has alluded to major sections of the Arbitration Act 1996 and provided detailed explanations about arbitration procedures.

⑥ It is always recommended to discuss Tribunals as a form of ADR, even if only briefly, and Seren has done this confidently and accurately, finishing off with a rounded conclusion which highlights the need for ADR.

Mark awarded:
AO1 – 13
AO3 – 1
Total = 14 out of 14 (100%)

An excellent answer, which confidently and accurately answers the question. It demonstrates a convincingly 'sound' knowledge of the different forms of ADR with an appropriate use of legal authority and examples throughout.

b) Evaluate the role of tribunals in England and Wales. *(11 marks)*

Tom's answer

① Tribunals are known as specialist courts or often as another form of ADR. There are many advantages and disadvantages to tribunals.

② Firstly, tribunals do not cost a lot for the parties taking part. This is important as cases often involve a big company taking on a single person. Also, tribunal procedures are a lot faster than that of court. Thirdly, the informality of tribunals often means a person is far more relaxed than they would be had they gone to court. Furthermore, each tribunal case will involve professional experts in the area that is concerned, which means that they are more likely to understand the situation and a more reliable decision will be made. Finally, tribunals involve a lot of independence and so the party is not overwhelmed by legal professionals.

③ However, there are many disadvantages that come with the use of tribunals. Firstly, there is a lack of funding. Legal funding is not always available and so when a smaller party, often consisting of one person, comes up against a large company, there is a disadvantage to the single person as the company can afford legal expertise. Secondly, intimidation plays a big factor in people. Tribunals encourage people not to have a legal representative which can often scare and intimidate people as they do not have the expertise to fall back on.

④ Furthermore, tribunals lack the use of precedent, and so when it comes to making a decision, there is nothing to go by. Overall, I feel that tribunals have been a good addition as they decrease court congestion and often have the same outcome.

Examiner commentary

② There is some insight into relevant advantages here, but they are very generic and limited in nature. The lack of legal authority will immediately affect Tom's marks, since there is little more than a limited selection of authorities and application.

③–④ All the points made in these paragraphs are accurate and relevant, but once again they are very generic and could apply to any form of ADR; the lack of legal authorities means that this answer cannot be credited with any more marks than the 'limited' level allows.

Mark awarded:
AO2 – 5
AO3 – 1
Total = 6 out of 11 (55%)

Tom has only demonstrated a 'limited' evaluation here because there is no reference to current issues surrounding the Tribunal system. In order to increase his marks he needs to link the advantages and disadvantages with knowledge of the current system, because as it stands these evaluative points are very generic and could apply to any form of ADR.

Seren's answer

① Tribunals are an important part of our legal system and despite being a specialised court, they are considered a form of Alternative Dispute Resolution. A tribunal will involve a legally qualified chairperson and two lay persons. They were originally set up to give the public a means of settling disputes regarding their social rights. Currently, there are three types – administrative (involving social and welfare rights), domestic (settling disputes within a private body, e.g. Law Society) and employment tribunals, which deal with disputes between employers and employees. In the case of Peach Grey & Co v Sommers, the High Court held that tribunals were inferior to the courts.

② After a report by Sir Andrew Leggatt (Tribunals for Users: One System, One Service), several recommendations were made and implemented in the Tribunals, Courts and Enforcement Act 2007. This was a large reform to the tribunal system which prior to the Act had been really complicated with over 70 different tribunals, all with different procedures. Now the system is much more organised, similar tribunals are grouped together and a two-tier approach has been adopted under one Tribunal Service.

③ There are numerous advantages with tribunals – most notably the cost, which is significantly less than a court battle, as parties are encouraged not to use legal representation. Also, there is an element of expertise as the judge will have a great deal of knowledge in the relevant area. The procedures are considerably more flexible, which is much more informal and relaxed than a full court battle. Speed is significant too, with tribunal judges taking an active role in case management, in line with the Civil Procedure Rules 1998 and keeping to a strict timetable as cases are often heard within a day. They are much more independent too, as the Tribunal judge will have been appointed by the Judicial Appointments Commission.

④ There are several disadvantages, however, notably a lack of funding. Often parties will be unable to find decent representation against large companies that can afford the best legal representation. This leads to a certain degree of intimidation where parties find it daunting to put forward their case in court. Also, sometimes there can be delay in waiting for the case to be settled.

⑤ To conclude, it can be said that the new Tribunal Service offers an important role in our legal system, acting as a form of ADR and easing congestion from the courts. The Administrative Justice and Tribunals Council has been set up to monitor progress of the Tribunal Service and report to the government.

Examiner commentary

① A detailed introduction which again puts the answer into context, and shows the examiner that she knows the different types of tribunal. It is good exam practice to start an answer by defining the key terms in the wording of the question.

② Seren is showing here that she has a sound understanding of the legislative background to the tribunal system, and can therefore go on to evaluate it with confidence. These are two key pieces of legal authority in any tribunals answer.

③ A good paragraph on the advantages of tribunals with particular attention paid to appropriate legal terminology, such as case management, strict timetables, Judicial Appointments Commission, etc.

④ A slightly smaller paragraph on the disadvantages, but still showing good evaluative skills, and sound points of analysis.

⑤ A well-rounded conclusion, still consistently showing an awareness of recent reforms in the area. Students often make the mistake of making their conclusion quite vague; Seren does not do this, she continues to demonstrate 'sound evaluation' skills.

Mark awarded:
AO2 – 9
AO3 – 2
Total = 11 out of 11 (100%)

This is a sound answer with a well-substantiated application of the law and thorough use of legal authority. Seren has clearly shown that she has excellent background knowledge to the Tribunal system and has taken the time to understand current reforms in the area.

8. European Union: Institutions

a) What is the role of the Court of Justice of the European Union?
(14 marks)

Tom's answer

① The Court of Justice of the European Union (CJEU) has a huge role in the development of European law. It has two main roles – a judicial one and a supervisory one. Its judicial role is to hear cases against Member States or other EU institutions and its supervisory role is to hear cases from other Member States on a point of law. This is a quite clear role in developing European law as it doesn't bind itself but binds everyone else. It is at the top of our court hierarchy, above the Supreme Court. As times change, the CJEU can update its previous decisions. This has no regard for parliamentary sovereignty in the UK which is undermined by the CJEU as it is supreme (as is EU law).

② The decisions of the CJEU must be followed in all Member States and this ensures uniformity and efficiency in the various legal systems. An example of this is the Tachograph case where it was decided that the UK had not fulfilled its EU obligations by not making it compulsory for lorry drivers to have tachographs fitted.

③ The supervisory role helps develop the law further still. Courts can refer to the CJEU for help on a point of law. This is a way for the CJEU to update its decisions if they feel the previous one isn't right. This guidance should be followed.

④ So, it can be seen the CJEU play a huge role in developing EU law and making sure that all of the Member States are following the same law. It also creates precedent for all of these countries too.

Examiner commentary

① There is a lot of information contained in this opening paragraph. Tom has done well to identify the two roles of the CJEU and has generally explained them correctly. He has also done well to comment on the position of EU law as supreme to domestic law and the position of the CJEU at the top of the hierarchy. Lots of good information. Each of these points requires further development and substantiation to gain the higher mark boundaries.

② An important case to illustrate the judicial role of the CJEU. Tom has used this case in the context of precedent, which isn't incorrect but isn't the focus of this case. As per my comment above, each of the points mentioned in paragraph 1 needed further development.

③ Good to see the supervisory role expanded here. Tom is correct in saying that courts can refer for guidance but should refer to art. 267 of the Treaty on the Functioning of the European Union which gives them this right to refer. To achieve higher marks, he needs to further expand this point, commenting on the Bulmer guidelines and the Marshall case to illustrate the supervisory role in action.

④ Good to see a conclusion but as the main body lacks depth and authority, so too does the conclusion.

Mark awarded:
AO1 – 7
AO3 – 1
Total = 8 out of 14 (57%)

This is a 'just' adequate answer at the lower end of the band. There are some errors of expression and Tom doesn't always convey his points clearly or sophisticatedly. There is a general lack of legal authority with only one case mentioned. He does highlight that there are two roles of the CJEU but does not develop these points. In addition, if compared with Seren's answer below, the lack of depth is evident. He gains credit for discussing the two roles, appreciating the role of the CJEU in precedent and the court hierarchy and the importance of developing law consistently throughout the EU, but there is a lack of sophistication in his answer that means he can't achieve more than 7 out of 13 for AO1.

Seren's answer

① The Court of Justice of the European Union sits in Luxembourg. This court is completely separate to the European Court of Human Rights. Its overall role is to supervise the European Union law throughout Member States. It is a body which helps sorting out disputes in the European Union and also aids with ensuring laws are applied and upheld correctly.

② The CJEU consists of judges and Advocates-General who produce opinions on issues raised, and suggest conclusions to resolve these issues. There are 28 judges and some Advocates-General who are chosen from the top judge posts in Member States.

③ Most cases brought to the CJEU are disputes concerned with Member States or international companies, and consequently it is very rare that cases are brought by individuals. The CJEU has two major roles: a judicial role, concerned with settling disputes; and a supervisory role, concerned with answering questions courts may have, and advising.

④ The judicial role is to adjudicate and decide cases. An example of such a case as Re Tachographs: EC Commission v UK. The CJEU was resolving a complaint about the use of tachographs (devices used to measure speed and distance travelled) in lorries, as the UK had not ensured all lorry drivers fitted these devices, and just suggested they should. This was brought to the Commission before it was brought to the CJEU. Many cases are brought before the Commission and the Member State is given the opportunity to put things right before bringing the case to the CJEU. Such decisions made by the CJEU cannot be questioned in UK courts.

⑤ The supervisory role of the CJEU is usually the referral of questions to the court under Article 267 of the Treaty on the Functioning of

the European Union. This treaty states that any court in a Member State may ask the CJEU for guidance on EU law, if it considers that 'a decision on that question is necessary to enable it to give judgment', though normally only the top court like the Supreme Court will refer for help. The purpose of this is to ensure a uniform law is implemented in the same way throughout Europe.

⑥ An important case using the supervisory role is Bulmer v Bollinger. The Court of Appeal was asked to review a judge's exercise of discretion to refer a question. Lord Denning created a set of guidelines to be followed before a case should be referred. He stated no reference could be made:
– Where it would not be conclusive of the case and other matters were to be decided.
– Where there had been a previous ruling on the same point.
– Where the court considers that point to be reasonably clear and free from doubt.
– Where the facts of the case had not yet been decided.

⑦ An example of the use of Article 234 is Marshall v Southampton and South West Hampshire Area Health Authority, in which Miss Marshall was asked to retire at 62. The state retirement age was 60; however, this rule had been waived for two years by the Authority. Miss Marshall claimed that this was discrimination against women by adopting a policy which forced women to retire before men. This policy was legal under UK law but went against the equal treatment of men and women. The national court therefore made a reference to the CJEU asking for advice and they decided Miss Marshall should be allowed to continue working. The UK eventually changed its law as a result of this decision.

Examiner commentary

① A good opening statement where Seren has given some background on the location and role of the CJEU.

② The composition of the CJEU is considered here. This is an important aspect of the question. She could also comment on the way they make decisions such as in plenary or all sitting at once.

③ Good identification here of the two main roles of the CJEU. These can then be expanded below.

④ Very good discussion of this important case that shows the judicial function of the CJEU. Seren has done well to present some of the facts of the case and to show how the CJEU intervened.

⑤ This is an excellent paragraph that starts well by citing art. 267 as giving the right to refer for guidance. Seren has done very well to recognise the importance of EU law being applied uniformly throughout the Member States.

⑥ This is a very important case and demonstrates a sound knowledge and understanding on Seren's part. She has done excellently to refer correctly to the four guidelines.

⑦ Seren has further developed the supervisory role here by considering a case in which art. 234 was used. Again she has presented the correct facts of the case and the impact of the CJEU guidance. Seren's work is lacking a conclusion here. It would benefit from a paragraph summing up the main body and the role of the CJEU, 'answering' the question posed.

Mark awarded:
AO1 – 11
AO3 – 1
Total = 12 out of 14 (86%)

This is a good sound answer that deals with the dual role of the CJEU. A good understanding demonstrated through key legal authority and accurate explanation of some difficult points such as the Bulmer guidelines. Seren has also included some detail about the composition of the CJEU. As commented above, it would have been preferable to include a conclusion summing up the essay, but this is a minor point.

b) Discuss the powers and decision-making procedures of the Council, Commission and European Parliament. *(11 marks)*

Tom's answer

① The Council of the European Union makes the law in the European Union. The Parliament is not the body responsible for making law despite the term 'parliament'.
The Commission is like the civil service of the European Union.

② In the Council sit Council Ministers and they vary according to the topic they are discussing on that occasion. They are the body that makes the law in the EU and have the final say.

③ The parliament despite the word 'parliament' doesn't make law but does give an opinion. We elect our parliament members in our country but they sit in the EU.

④ The commission is like the civil service of the EU and makes sure it all runs smoothly. They put forward ideas for the laws of the EU but it is the Council who decides if they become actual laws.

Examiner commentary

① This is a very brief introduction to the role of each of the institutions. Tom has only merely indicated the law making power of the Council and likened the Commission to the 'civil service' of the EU. Much more depth was needed to fully explain the law making procedure between the institutions.

② This is correct and a fair point. Tom needed further expansion on the composition of the Council and the fact the membership changes according to the topic under discussion.

③ Again this point is lacking in depth on both the composition and selection of the MEPs and the role of the Parliament in the law making procedure.

④ Here Tom has identified the role of the Commission. More again needed on the composition and Tom has barely mentioned the role of the Commission in law making which should be the focus of this question.

Mark awarded:
AO2 – 5
AO3 – 1
Total = 6 out of 11 (55%)

This is a limited answer. Tom has demonstrated a superficial understanding of the role of each institution and his answer is both colloquial and lacking in detail. He fails to develop the points he starts to make about the role of each of the institutions and doesn't comment on the composition of the institutions. He does, however, correctly touch upon the law-making role of each body. These points, however, require much greater expansion.

Seren's answer

① The European Union is currently made up of 28 countries called 'Member States'. Just like any country, it has to have bodies that are responsible for passing the laws that govern it and ensure it is run smoothly. I am going to look at the Council of the European Union, Commission and European Parliament.

② The Council of the European Union is the primary decision-making body of the European Union. It is made up of one representative from each country, each a specialist in the particular topic under discussion. The membership of the Council therefore changes each meeting. It makes decisions on European legislation regarding any topic. This legislation will have been proposed and drafted by the Commission.

③ The Commission members, of which there are 28, are independent from their Member State and represent the EU overall. Their role is to propose ideas for European legislation. They also make sure that Member States uphold their EU obligations and if not they can take them to court (called the CJEU).

④ The European Parliament consists of MEPs democratically elected in their own countries for 5-year periods. These MEPs will pass new European legislation by voting on it like any other parliament but it doesn't have the final say. This is for the Council of the European Union. The number of MEPs per country is proportionate to the size of the country's population. They will debate any legislation drafted by the commission.

⑤ It is important for the EU and how large it is with so many different countries to have institutions governing it. We have already seen that EU law is supreme to Member States' law. It is the job of the institutions to make sure that the law is appropriate to all the Member States but to take them to court if they are not upholding this.

Examiner commentary

① Seren has given a clear introduction here putting her answer in context. She has highlighted the position of the institutions and their importance.

② Good understanding demonstrated on the role and composition of the Council of the European Union. She has done well to comment on the changing membership of the Council and their role as the primary decision makers. They are the main legislative body of the EU.

③ Again, Seren has done well to consider the composition of the Commission and

how this contrasts with the Council of the European Union. She has also included detail on their role as proposers of EU law.

④ Logical progression onto the European parliament here. She has understood the election procedure for the MEPs and their role in passing EU law, correctly recognising the Council of the European Union as the final decision makers.

⑤ Good to see a conclusion. Seren has produced an 'adequate' answer and conclusion.

Mark awarded:
AO2 – 7
AO3 – 2
Total = 9 out of 11 (81%)

Seren has correctly identified the composition and role of each of the required institutions. She has discussed their role in law making. In order to achieve marks in the 'sound' boundary, she should have also considered the law-making procedures of: Co-decision, Consultation, Co-operation and assent and generally given some further depth on the decision making of each institution.

9. The Supreme Court; Judicial Precedent

Study the text and answer the questions based on it.

The Supreme Court

'The Constitutional Reform Act 2005 made provision for the creation of a new Supreme Court for the United Kingdom. There have, in recent years, been mounting calls for the creation of a new free standing Supreme Court separating the highest appeal court from the second house of Parliament, and removing the Lords of Appeal in Ordinary from the legislature.'

Source: Ministry of Justice Website

(a) Explain the role of the Supreme Court. *(14 marks)*

Tom's answer

① The House of Lords changed its name from the House of Lords to the Supreme Court in 2009. The Supreme Court is the final court in the UK, it is an appeal court and only cases that are very important go to this court, you also need permission to take your case to the Supreme Court.

② The Supreme Court now has its own building, the old House of Lords used to be in the Houses of Parliament, this was very confusing as there is also a chamber in Parliament called the House of Lords, and this led to many people being confused, so

in 2009 the court was moved from Parliament and now has its own building.

③ However, the Supreme Court does not have the power to strike out laws passed by Parliament; this is because Parliament is supreme. So the role of the court is limited here. The Supreme Court has 12 full-time judges and they have a huge role to play in developing precedent. As they are the highest court, they do not have to follow any other court decisions and since 1966 they do not have to follow their own decisions they can change them when they like.

Examiner commentary

① Limited opening paragraph, Tom has mentioned when the Supreme Court was established and that it is the final appeal court, but no mention of the Constitutional Reform Act 2005 which established the Supreme Court.

② Tom is attempting in this paragraph to discuss the issue of separation of powers. Tom needed to develop this further and state that removing the House of Lords from Parliament also removed the judges from the law-making chamber, which offended against the doctrine of separation of powers.

③ Limited attempt to answer the question, very limited discussion of precedent and the supremacy of Parliament.

Mark awarded:
AO1 – 6
AO3 – 1
Total = 7 out of 14 (50%)

This is a limited answer, showing limited understanding of the role of the Supreme Court. Some good points made, but the answer is far too brief, each of the points made should have been developed further. No supporting statutes or case law.

Seren's answer

① The Supreme Court was established in 2009 by the Constitutional Reform Act, changing the name of the House of Lords; one of the main reasons for the establishment of the Supreme Court separating it from Parliament was to ensure that the doctrine of the separation of powers was upheld. It is the highest court within the English legal system for all matters that are not EU related. In this essay I shall explain the many powers and roles of this highly important court.

② The Supreme Court is an appellate court. It deals with high profile cases of the utmost importance, not just for the parties involved but often matters that affect the public as well. Due to the fact that it is the last court of appeal, any decision made by the Supreme Court is final.

③ Members of the Supreme Court arguably have the most creativity. With regards to precedent the Supreme Court is not bound by the decisions of any other court, except the CJEU on EU matters. All courts below the Supreme Court must follow the decisions of the Supreme Court, the Supreme Court is also free to depart from their own decisions, this has been the case since 1966, therefore within their role as the final appellate court they have a great deal of scope to develop precedents and overrule those from lower courts.

④ However, the Supreme Court, or the old House of Lords as it was then called, has not always had this much freedom. Before 1966 they could only depart from their own decisions if they had been made per incuriam, by mistake. In London Street Tramways v London County Council (1898), this was a pivotal time in the development of the House of Lords. This case declared that certainty in the law was much more important than judicial creativity, and so judges were no longer allowed to ignore their own previous precedents. However, the Practice Statement of 1966 changed this decision. This stated that judges in the House of Lords can depart from previous decisions, not just if made by mistake but if it was right to do so. This power to depart was used tentatively at first, case examples where they have overruled their own previous decisions can be seen in R v Shivpuri and Anderton v Ryan; Hemingway v BRB and Addie v Dumbreck.

⑤ The role of the Supreme Court is perhaps even more important today, the new Supreme Court is a body legally separate from the English and Welsh Courts, since it is also the Supreme Court of both Scotland and Northern Ireland.

⑥ The Supreme Court's role in reversing precedent is vital. In the cases of R v R (1991) the House of Lords was bound by a precedent that had stood for hundreds of years concerning the issue of rape within marriage. In R v R the House of Lords overruled their previous precedent and set a new precedent that this would now be an offence.

⑦ The Supreme Court has a very big role to play in the development of the law in the future, Now that they are separate from Parliament they can exercise their independence more transparently and the decisions they make affect the lives of us all. Under the Human Rights Act they have a big role in developing human rights and they have the power to issue declarations of incompatibility to force changes in laws that are incompatible with human rights. I believe that this role will increase even more in the future as the judges establish themselves in the new Supreme Court.

Examiner commentary

① Good opening paragraph stating when the court was set up and also reasons for it, i.e. separation of powers. Seren should have gone on to describe how this doctrine works and why the old House of Lords was seen to be at odds with the doctrine.

② Seren has done well to state that the decisions of the Supreme Court affect not only the litigants involved in the cases but the general public as the court deals with such high profile cases.

③ Seren is answering the question by bringing in the role of the court in developing precedent. It is extremely important that the Practice Statement is explained in a precedent or Supreme Court answer.

④ Very good use of case law to illustrate when the House of Lords depart from previous decisions.

⑤ Excellent point to mention the role of the Court within Scotland and Northern Ireland.

⑥ Perhaps this paragraph should have come directly after the cases of R v Shivpuri, etc., as it deals with the House of Lords overruling their own previous decisions and the structure of the essay would have been better if it had come directly after that paragraph.

⑦ Good closing paragraph, very good to mention the role of the Court in developing human rights.

Mark awarded:
AO1 – 11
AO3 – 1
Total = 12 out of 14 (86%)

This is a very good answer. Seren really attempted to answer the question and looked at the role of the Supreme Court. There is a danger with a question like this that the student turns it into a general answer on precedent or just gives a general description of the Supreme Court without looking at their role. Good use of supporting case law.

b) Read the following and consider the application of the doctrine of precedent in this case. *(11 marks)*

On 18 May 2010 an emergency application was made to a family division judge by a hospital in respect of a refusal of treatment by an adult woman. The adult woman had been in labour for more than two days with her third child. The pregnancy was at full term. Labour was obstructed and the lives of the mother and child were at risk. There was evidence that in order to save both lives an emergency operation had to be performed on the mother. Both she and her husband refused consent to the operation on religious grounds. The hospital was seeking a declaration that the operation could be performed lawfully been without the mother's consent. The issue of the mother's consent to an operation on her own body was left open in a previous case called Re – X (Adult: Refusal of Treatment) and there is no English authority which is directly in point. There are, however, some American and Europeans authorities which suggest that if the case was being heard in American courts or in some European jurisdictions, the answer would be likely to be in favour of granting a declaration in these circumstances.

Tom's answer

① The doctrine of precedent in this case is persuasive. This is because it says in the application that the issue of the mother's consent to an operation on her own body was left open in a previous case. However, there was no English authority directly in point. This means that it is not binding because judges must use a previous case for this, we also do not know which court the previous case was heard in, as this is very important if from a higher court.

② However, judges are not meant to make law like Parliament does, but the issue as to whether judges have too much creativity in terms of law making remains controversial. Cases such as R v R and original precedents demonstrate how creative judges can be in terms of law making. This is also demonstrated in cases such as Donoghue v Stevenson.

③ Judges have four options available to them, they can follow previous decisions, or they can distinguish, overrule or reverse. There are many advantages with precedent, consistency, certainty, fairness, precise, flexible and time saving. These, however, have to be weighed up against the disadvantages which are unpredictability, rigidity, complex rules, illogical distinctions, slowness of growth and the undemocratic nature.

Examiner commentary

① Weak opening paragraph, Tom is correct identifying the persuasive value of the precedent but the rest of the paragraph mainly repeats the question.

② Tom has correctly identified cases where judges have been seen to make law, but has failed to link this to the scenario at all.

③ Again Tom has clearly identified the options available to judges to avoid awkward precedent, but this has not been developed and linked to the scenario. Including advantages and disadvantages of precedent is not needed here unless Tom can apply them to the scenario.

Mark awarded:
AO2 – 5
AO3 – 1
Total = 6 out of 11 (55%) Grade D

This answer shows limited understanding of the application of precedent to the scenario. Some good points made, but the answer is not linked to the scenario and is a general limited answer on precedent.

Seren's answer Grade A

① This case is riddled with controversial and ethical issues. This essay will look at the different aspects of precedent to determine how the family division judge will make a ruling in this case. An emergency application is not used often in law, this is used when there is little time and a decision needs to be made fast.

② The previous case law Re-X left no clear ruling as to what decision should be made, it is also not clear which court Re-X was heard in, as this may affect the persuasive value of the decision. If Re-X had set a precedent then the family division judge should look at the option of overruling, this depends again on which court it was decided in, as if in the Supreme Court then the family division of the High Court would be bound by the decision and would have to follow it. The part of the judgement they would have to follow would be the ratio decidendi; this is the part that binds all other judges depending on their position in the court hierarchy.

③ In the event that the past precedent is from a lower court in the hierarchy, the precedent can be overruled, though this is usually left to judges in the higher courts. If this case was being heard in the Supreme Court and the ruling in Re-X was from the Supreme Court/ House of Lords, then since the 1966 Practice Statement they can depart from their previous decisions if right to do so, an example of this is Rondel v Worsley and Simons and R v R.

④ The family division judge does have another option, the judge could distinguish, and this allows the judge to distinguish the facts of the two cases and therefore if different does not have to follow the precedent. Case examples where distinguishing has happened include Balfour and Meritt.

⑤ The judge in the family division, however, does have the option of following the reasoning in Re-X, particularly in the light of no direct precedent, for example the judge would reason by analogy.

⑥ The family division judge should also consider the significance of precedents on this matter from other common law jurisdictions. Here there are decisions from both America and Europe that would allow the operation to go ahead if followed. Whilst these decisions are not binding on the family division judge, they can be persuasive precedent, especially if there is an English reference. If the judge does use these as persuasive precedent then the treatment will go ahead. This could be seen as a controversial decision by some who on religious grounds may argue that the mother's rights should be respected and she should be able to refuse the treatment, but the court has a balancing act and also has to consider the rights of the unborn child as well and using the persuasive precedents the treatment would go ahead.

Examiner commentary

① Good to see an introduction that puts the answer in context

② Good application of the doctrine of precedent to the question. This is a difficult question in that Re-X left no direct precedent so Seren has done well to discuss which court the case may have been heard in and also the persuasive value of judgements. Good to see the use of correct legal terminology, e.g. *ratio decidendi*.

③ Good recognition of the Practice Statement and the role of the Supreme Court in departing from previous decisions. Seren has done well to include examples here.

④ Good to see that Seren is aware how precedents can be avoided, e.g. distinguishing, and she has mentioned overruling as well. She could have also discussed reversing, though she probably felt this was not relevant due to the emergency nature of the case.

⑤ Excellent to see that Seren has considered that in the light of no direct precedent from Re-X the judge can reason by analogy.

⑥ Very important to consider the persuasive value of precedents from other countries. Good application by Seren of this in this paragraph.

Mark awarded:
AO2 – 8
AO3 – 2
Total = 10 out of 11 (91%)

Overall this is a very good answer. There is a danger with questions that have moral and controversial issues that students answer them purely from a moral viewpoint. Seren has applied the doctrine of precedent well to the scenario and this is key to answering these scenario type questions. The law must be applied to the scenario; it is not acceptable to just write everything you know about the topic.

10. Human Rights Act 1998

Part a) Study the text and answer the questions based on it.

'The year saw the first occasion since the coming into force of the Human Rights Act 1998 in 2000 when a decision of the House of Lords on the interpretation of the European Convention on Human Rights was overturned by the European Court of Human Rights. In S and Marper v UK (decision of 4 December 2008) the Strasbourg court disapproved of the House's decision in R (S) and Marper v Chief Constable of the South Yorkshire Police (2004) UKHL39 and held that the English law's blanket policy of retaining fingerprints and DNA samples taken from persons who were not later convicted of the offence being investigated was a breach of the right to a private life guaranteed by Art. 8 of the European Convention.'

Source: Dickson, New Law Journal 23 January 2009

a) Explain the effect of the Human Rights Act 1998 on English and Welsh law. *(14 marks)*

Tom's answer

① The Human Rights Act has had a big effect on English and Welsh Law. Before the Act was passed we used to have to take our case on human rights to the European Court of Human Rights, this would sometimes take 6 years to do, also British judges were never really bothered with human rights before the HRA, so the Act has made a big change.

② There are sections in the Act that have made more changes than others. For example, judges can now send a note to parliament if they don't like laws, laws they think go against our human rights. I think this is good as judges can force parliament to change the law; however, parliament can ignore the note and refuse to change the law, but this would not look good if they did this. Public bodies must also make decisions that do not go against human rights.

③ The HRA is good for many reasons, it should mean that cases will be much quicker, and we now know everything about our human rights, that we did not know before it came in. However, there are also some bad things, judges cannot get rid of laws they don't like, and the rights in it are very old. Overall though it is better now we have the HRA than before.

Examiner commentary

① Tom's opening paragraph does include a brief explanation of the system pre HRA, but the grammar is not good and explanation lacking in any detail.

② Tom is attempting to refer to sections 4 and 6 in this paragraph; the answer would have improved greatly if he had included the sections numbers and relevant cases to support.

③ Tom has discussed, briefly, advantages and disadvantages in the final paragraph, not entirely relevant for this question, unless related to the question.

Mark awarded:
AO1 – 6
AO3 – 1
Total = 7 out of 14 (50%)

This is a limited answer, showing limited understanding of the effect of the HRA. Tom did make some good points, but is lacking in any legal authority, and detail. No section numbers or cases included, you must include sections and cases for this topic.

Seren's answer

① Before the Human Rights Act came into force in 2000, the nature of human rights in English and Welsh law was very different. Prior to the Act, the UK had signed the European Convention on Human Rights in 1951; however, this did not put the rights in the Convention into our law, therefore the rights were not directly applicable in UK courts, therefore to assert these rights UK citizens had to take a case to the European Court of Human Rights, this was a very slow process, and UK citizens were only granted this right in 1966 – the right of individual petition.

② The passing of the Human Rights Act has altered the way in which rights are treated in the UK, and had a huge effect on English and Welsh Law. Under section 7 of the HRA – the rights in the Convention are now in our law; this means that they are directly applicable in our domestic courts so a UK citizen can argue breaches of the rights in their own courts. This is a huge change of the position before.

③ Other sections of the Act have also had a big effect. Under section 2 domestic judges must take into account all relevant Strasbourg jurisprudence, this means that when deciding human rights cases our judges must look at case law from the European Court of Human Rights but they don't have to follow them; the cases are there for guidance. This is a good thing as the European Court has been deciding cases for over 60 years and is very experienced in these matters.

④ Another section that has had a big effect is section 3 – this states that judges must interpret all laws to be compatible with human rights if possible to do so. If judges find laws to be incompatible with human rights then under section 4 they can issue a declaration of incompatibility, this section has probably had the biggest effect on English and Welsh law. Under this section judges can inform Parliament if they believe that laws are incompatible; however, there is no obligation on Parliament to change the law and judges cannot strike out laws; cases where they have issued declarations include A & Others; Wilson and Brown.

⑤ Finally section 6 has also had a huge effect on our law. Under section 6 public bodies must act in a way which is compatible with human rights, this places a big burden on public bodies. Under the Act 'public body' has also included a private body performing a public function, e.g. Poplar Housing case.

⑥ In conclusion, the Human Rights Act has had a big effect on English and Welsh Law, it has created a new regime for human rights and ensured better protection of our human rights than under the old system.

Examiner commentary

① Good opening paragraph, summarising the background to the Human Rights Act, this is good to do and it shows more clearly the effect that the HRA has had by comparing it to the position pre HRA.

② Seren has really answered the question here, by citing section 7 she has shown the first major change to the way rights are now protected.

③ Again Seren is explaining all the correct sections and how they have affected our law. Excellent explanation of section 2. Section 2 is a key section which must be discussed.

④ An excellent paragraph, clear explanation of the effects of sections 3 and 4 using relevant legal authority to support.

⑤ Seren has done well to also include section 6 and the Poplar Housing case, as section 6 has had a big effect on our law in the way that public bodies must now act in accordance with human rights.

⑥ Brief conclusion, but it does sum up the essay. Good to see a conclusion being used.

Mark awarded:
AO1 – 13
AO3 – 1
Total = 14 out of 14 (100%)

This is an excellent answer. Seren has been awarded top marks for answering the question throughout, using correct legal authority; excellent structure to the essay throughout.

b) Evaluate the role of the European Court of Human Rights in English and Welsh law. *(11 marks)*

Tom's answer

① The European Court of Human Rights was set up to make sure that human rights are being followed. In section 4 it says that there must be a declaration of incompatibility if human rights do not comply with the act set out by Parliament. However, judges can try and make it comply, but they must not go beyond the powers of the British law.

② When passing a new law, parliament now has to declare it incompatible or compatible with human rights, this is in section 19. The European Court of Human Rights is situated in Strasbourg, this is the appeal court for when someone believes their human rights have been breached, they will go here and the court will have the final say. This court has heard many cases brought to from people who live in the UK claiming that their rights have been breached, Diane Pretty is one of them, she wanted the right to end her life, but the court said no, and that the UK was not breaching her human rights; however, in other cases the court has said that the UK has breached human rights, in Malone.

③ Parliamentary sovereignty has been limited by having to apply with human rights.

Examiner commentary

① The opening paragraph has too many different points within it, Tom should have begun by stating when the court was set up, and the reasons for it, and the role that it carries out. He has included section 4 here; he could have discussed this later if relevant to the role of the European court, but not here, a confusing opening paragraph.

② This paragraph does attempt to discuss the role of the European Court, but again it is not structured well, no evaluation of the role, this is vital to be awarded marks for AO2.

③ No conclusion offered and poor structure throughout.

Mark awarded:
AO2 – 5
AO3 – 1
Total = 6 out of 11 (55%)

This is a limited answer, showing limited understanding of the role of the European Court. Tom has made a vague attempt to answer the question, but the information discussed is too brief and with little use of case law.

Seren's answer

① The European Court of Human Rights and the Grand Chamber was set up in the early 1950s to handle claims made by one state against another and by individuals against a state. The European Court of Human Rights can only hear individual claims where the state has recognised the right of individuals to bring a case to it, this is called the right of individual petition, and we were given this right in the UK in 1966.

② The UK did not incorporate the European Convention into our domestic law until the Human Rights Act 1998, therefore before this, UK citizens could not bring their claim through domestic courts and had to go to the European Court, since the passing of the HRA the European Court still has a very important role to play in human rights but UK citizens can now directly apply on the rights in the convention in our domestic courts.

③ Before the passing of the HRA the European court had a very big part in shaping human rights, to take a case to the court a claimant must have exhausted all domestic remedies first, then file case within six months of final domestic decision. The process was slow, expensive, and remedies from the court were often inadequate. Since the HRA our courts now play a more active role and going to the European court in Strasbourg should only be as a last resort.

④ The European Court is in Strasbourg and has heard many cases brought against the UK, D v UK; Pretty v UK; Evans v UK. Before the Human Rights Act, taking a case to Strasbourg could take up to 6 years. This has greatly improved since the convention has been incorporated into our law.

⑤ Section 2 of the HRA brings in the role of the European Court for our judges, our judiciary must take into account any relevant cases from the European Court of Human Rights, but they are not bound by them, this ensures that the Court that has had over 50 years' experience in deciding human rights cases, their decisions are used as persuasive precedents for our judges.

⑥ In conclusion, the European Court has played a huge role in protecting human rights over the last 60 years, that role has now been extended to our domestic courts by the HRA, but the Court is still the final appeal court and will therefore have the final say.

Examiner commentary

① Good opening paragraph establishing when the court was set up and its overall role.

② In this paragraph Seren is attempting to discuss the role by stating that the European Court was the main court protecting human rights until the HRA in 1998.

③ Attempt at evaluating the role by discussing the process of taking a case to Europe.

④ Good use of case law, though Seren could have included more up-to-date cases.

⑤ Good use of section 2 in evaluating the role of the Court.

⑥ Good conclusion bringing together the main strands of the essay.

Mark awarded:
AO2 – 7
AO3 – 2
Total = 9 out of 11 (81%)

Overall this is a good answer. Good evaluation of the role of the court, though Seren could have included more up-to-date cases. Students tend to find this a difficult topic at AS, but it is a very important topic, that they must have detailed knowledge of as human rights pervades all other topics.

11. Judiciary

Study the table below and answer questions a) and b):

Judicial Annual Diversity Statistics – as at 1 April 2008

Post	Total	Female No.	Female %	Of Ethnic Minority Origin No.	Of Ethnic Minority Origin %
Lords of Appeal in Ordinary	12	1	8.33%	0	0.00%
Heads of Division	5	0	0.0%	0	0.00%
Lord Justices of Appeal	37	3	8.1%	0	0.00%
High Court Judges	110	11	10%	3	2.72%
Circuit Judges	653	87	13.32%	20	3.06%
Recorders	1305	194	14.86%	61	4.67%
Judge Advocates	9	0	0.00%	0	0.00%
Deputy Judge Advocates	12	1	8.33%	0	0.00%
District Judges	438	98	22.37%	20	4.56%
Deputy District Judges	773	211	27.29%	31	4.01%
District Judges (MC)	136	31	22.79%	3	2.2%
Deputy District Judges (MC)	167	40	23.95%	12	7.18%
Masters, Registrars, Costs Judges and DJ (PRFD)	48	11	22.91%	1	2.08%
Deputy Masters, Registrars, Deputy Costs Judges and DJ (PRFD)	115	39	33.91%	5	4.34%
Total	3820	727	19.03%	156	4.08%

Source: Ministry of Justice

a) Explain the way in which judges are appointed. *(14 marks)*

Tom's answer

① Before 2005, the appointments process was much different yet the Constitutional Reform Act 2005 dramatically changed this. There were several problems before this Act including the fact that only barristers could become judges, the system was dominated by politicians all with similar views, it was a secretive due to being based on secret soundings which isn't an open process, it was discriminatory process as it favoured people with a good network of contacts and additionally, those who fitted the general trend of judges (old, middle to upper class, etc.) rather than those with a strong ability to sit as a judge.

② The new appointments process is much different. The Judicial Appointments Commission has been set up to assess judges for appointment. This is a much fairer process as it gives everyone chance and reduces the danger of subjective or discriminative judgements in secret soundings. This is better than the old system as the wide range of commission members select judges on the basis of merit and good character rather than their stereotype.

③ These alterations stress the openness of the new process and the wide range of applicants they will take on. They stress they don't select on 'ethnic origin' or 'gender'. Candidates will also be selected if they have a high level of understanding of law and lots of experience. More women should be appointed as a result of the reforms.

Examiner commentary

① A logical place to start though there is a lot of information contained in this introductory paragraph. Tom has done well to mention the key Constitutional Reform Act 2005 which reformed the appointments procedure. He has also mentioned some of the main criticisms of the old system of appointments. It is a common examination error when discussing the appointment process to only discuss the old procedure, it is vital that students can fully discuss both the old and new procedure and that they can evaluate the new procedure. Tom here needs to explain the old appointments procedure and then compare it with the new procedure.

② Tom has done well here to discuss the new Judicial Appointments Commission and the fact that they are judging candidates on merit and experience. He needed to give some further depth demonstrating an awareness of the hierarchy of the judiciary, particularly as the Commission is not responsible for appointments to the Supreme Court.

③ This is correct and more women should be appointed but this is in part due to the changes made by the Tribunals, Courts and Enforcement Act 2007 which has opened up judicial appointments to legal executives. This is an important Act that Tom should have mentioned. His answer also stops quite abruptly and lacks a clear conclusion.

Mark awarded:
AO1 – 7
AO3 – 1
Total = 8 out of 14 (57%)

This is a barely adequate answer as Tom has not developed his points, despite showing an awareness of the key changes made as a result of the Constitutional Reform Act 2005. He has done well to mention some of the reasons why the system needed to be reformed (e.g. secret soundings) but gives limited depth on the reforms and crucially, doesn't mention the Tribunals, Courts and Enforcement Act 2007. He does well to comment on the Judicial Appointments Commission and links in some reasons why the establishment of this will overcome some of the old procedure's problems; however, he needed to previously state what the old appointments procedure was.

Seren's answer

① Before the 2005 act, the Lord Chancellor played a vital role in the process of appointing judges. The Lord Chancellor advised the Prime Minister on who he thought should be appointed as The Lord of Appeal in Ordinary and the Lord Justice of Appeal. The Prime Minister then advised the Queen, then she was the one who made the final decision. When it came to the High Court Judges, the circuit judges and the recorders, they were appointed by the Queen based on advice from the Lord Chancellor. This means that in both scenarios, the Lord Chancellor's opinions were heard first, meaning that it is very likely the decision made by the Queen was inevitably based on the advice from the Lord Chancellor. This went against the separation of powers.

② The process for appointing High Court judges involved the old department for constitutional affairs gathering information from other judges over a long period of time. These were called secret soundings. Sir Leonard Peach released a report in 1999 stating three main criticisms.

③ One issue, as I mentioned earlier, was that it was secretive and involved secret soundings. They would seek advice and consult with other judges and senior barristers on what a candidate would be like as a judge. The process was considered unfair because it didn't really rely on the skills and qualities of the individual, but rather the contacts. Because, if the civil servants had two candidates, and one candidate knew many judges and had many contacts, when it comes to the group consulting judges and barristers, they are likely to hear more about that candidate rather than one with very few contacts, meaning that they are relying on contacts to hear about prospective candidates. There could also be discrimination against women and ethnic minorities.

④ The second issue was that politics was too heavily involved in the process. The Lord Chancellor and Prime Minister played central roles in the appointment of judges.

⑤ The third issue was that it was discriminatory. Judges had a strong tendency to suggest judges from their own chambers. They also saw that there were a particular handful of chambers that the candidates came from. This is a very negative thing as it means that depending on what chamber you attend, you may or may not move up in your career. This meant women and ethnic minorities did not progress as well.

⑥ The Constitutional Reform Act 2005 created a new organisation that was entrusted with the responsibility of handling the appointment of judges procedure. This is called the Judicial Appointments Commission. This Commission has 14 members. These members are appointed by the Queen on recommendation of the Lord Chancellor.

⑦ Now to be eligible to be a judge, it is no longer judged on how many years they have had rights of audience, but now it is judged on the number of years of experience after they have qualified. This is contained in the Tribunals, Courts and Enforcement Act 2007. This Act has also allowed legal executives to be eligible to become a judge after enough experience. This should overcome the issue of women not progressing as well as men, as more than 60% of legal execs are female.

⑧ The Constitutional Reform Act 2005 has radically changed the appointment of judges and removed the Lord Chancellor from the process. This should overcome some of the problems Sir Leonard Peach identified and make the system fairer, allowing for a wider range of people to be appointed as judges.

Examiner commentary

① An effective opening paragraph here with good focus on the question posed. Seren has focused on the main issue – the appointment of judges and she has done well to recognise that to fully answer this, she needs to compare the old system with the recent changes to judicial appointment. She has done well to bring in the role of the Lord Chancellor and how his previous role breached the separation of powers. Good use of key terms relating to this topic.

② Good mention of Sir Leonard Peach's report and that he found three main criticisms of the old appointments procedure.

③ Seren has displayed good knowledge and understanding here of the process of secret soundings and discussed the main criticisms of this process. Ideally candidates should not write in the first or second person as this is not good academic practice but the content of Seren's answer is very good thus far.

④ Seren has also done well in these two paragraphs to explain the other two criticisms. A key criticism is that women and ethnic minorities do not progress as well through the judiciary as their male counterparts and Seren has done well to bring this in.

⑤ A key mention here of this important change in the law and the establishment of the Judicial Appointments Commission. Correct use of legal authority and key terms.

⑥ Very good discussion of this further development to the judicial appointment system. Another key piece of legal authority cited and a good knowledge and understanding demonstrated. Seren has made a good link to an earlier criticism of women being overlooked and how the recent reforms may help overcome this.

⑦ A solid conclusion that ties together nicely the main strands of Seren's answer. It focuses on the question and cites earlier mentioned legal authority.

Mark awarded:
AO1 – 11
AO2 – 1
Total = 12 out of 14 (86%)

This is a sound answer that demonstrates a very good knowledge and understanding of the judicial appointments procedure. Seren did well to compare the old system of appointment with the new system, examining some of the main criticisms that led to the reforms. A sound answer with a good range of legal authority. Seren should avoid using the first or second person in an academic answer and instead should write more formally in the third person.

b) To what extent are judges representative of society?

(11 marks)

Tom's answer: Grade C

① The table shows that judges are not representative of women and ethnic minorities. 19% of all judges are women and 4.08% are ethnic minority. The table also tells us that in the top courts, there are no people from ethnic minorities and only one woman. There are no women Heads of Division and only three women Lord Justices of Appeal and no ethnic minority Lords Justices of Appeal. The most women are: Deputy Masters, Registrars, Deputy Costs Judges and DJ (PRFD). The most ethnic minorities are: Deputy District Judges (MC). This tells us that women and ethnic minorities are not represented as judges despite there being a lot of women and ethnic minorities.

② If we think about what a judge looks like it will be a man, white, old, gone to Oxford or Cambridge and stuffy. It has been said judges do not know what young people are interested in and can be old fashioned. One judge did not know who the band Oasis is.

③ Judges should be well educated and intelligent but it is also important that they understand what is going on in society and shouldn't discriminate against women and ethnic minorities.

④ One reason women don't progress as far as a man is that once they have babies, they don't come back to work full time and give their time to their children. This is not true of all women but a more committed man may be the better person for the job.

⑤ The table has shown that judges are not representative.

Examiner commentary

① Though lacking a clear introduction, Tom has done well to correctly interpret the table above and select the main statistics that demonstrate that women and ethnic minorities are not represented in the judiciary.

② Good mention of the stereotypical judge here. There are other factors to consider such as judges political leanings. The example about a judge not knowing who Oasis is one that is mentioned a lot!

③ Tom attempts some evaluation here highlighting that judges need to be well educated and trained but they should do this without discrimination.

④ Tom has again provided some further evaluation though it comes across as one-sided. He should explore other reasons why women (and ethnic minorities) do not progress as far. In addition, he could consider some wider issues such as disability and language. Crucially he could evaluate how further reforms could help women and ethnic minorities progress to the higher levels of the judiciary bringing in some legal authority such as the Courts and Legal Services Act 1990 and the Tribunals Courts and Enforcement Act 2007.

⑤ This is not really adequate as a conclusion. A common mistake with questions that ask candidates to refer to a table is that the candidates feel they only need to repeat what is written in the table and not provide any deeper evaluation or explanation.

Mark awarded:
AO2 – 6
AO3 – 1
Total = 7 out of 11 (64%) Grade C

A 'just' adequate answer. The main positive about Tom's answer is the fact he has correctly interpreted the statistics presented in the above table. He has identified that judges are not representative and taken the main courts discussing the relevant statistics. He has made a superficial conclusion that this shows that judges are not representative of society. Later in his essay he tries to explain some of the main reasons for this but his answer lacks balance and deeper evaluation.

Seren's answer

① Judges are generally looked upon as a bad representation of modern-day society. The general stereotype for a judge is now pictured to be a white (British) man, relatively old, middle to upper class and of right-wing bias. Their backgrounds are also rather similar, with 80% being educated at a public school and 80% studying at Oxford and Cambridge. This narrow background has led to them being rather 'out of sync' with modern-day society. For example, judges would have to deal with cases involving people of all classes, ethnicities, ages and from all ranks of life and education yet such a lack of variation in the judges characteristics could and most likely will lead to cases being judged unfairly and inefficiently, due to the judges not understanding the situations and the lives of the people bringing forth a case. Furthermore, their political bias could seriously interfere with cases involving political issues.

② This stereotype given to judges isn't just a generalisation either; there are many facts to support it given in the table above. According to the table, there is only one female judge in the Supreme Court and no ethnic minorities. Out of 37 judges in the Court of Appeal, only three are female and again none are from ethnic minorities. 10% of High Court judges are women whereas 2.72% of High Court judges are ethnic minorities which is not representative of society as approximately 50% are women and 8% are ethnic minorities. However, lower down the courts, women are better represented though only to a maximum of 33.91%. Ethnic minorities remain low in all courts but more so in the top three courts where there are none.

③ Judges are selected from existing solicitors and barristers. According to statistics, the majority of these still tend to be relatively old, middle to upper class, white, British men. This would consequently continue the unrepresentative nature of the judiciary and the accusation that it doesn't truly represent society would remain standing. On the other hand, men and women now have equal rights in terms of education and so they would both have the same opportunities to study as barristers and solicitors.

④ The Courts and Legal Services Act 1990 allowed solicitors to become solicitor advocates and this gave them right of audience in all of the courts and this hence widened the entry to the judiciary. The Tribunals, Courts and Enforcement Act 2007 now also allows legal executives to become judges and as 60% of these are women, this should eventually filter through to the judiciary but it may take some time. Women tend to take time out to have children and this can affect their career prospects. They would struggle to commit to the long hours as it simply wouldn't fit around a young family, and no matter of law and logistics could alter that simple fact of life!

⑤ As well as gender and background, ethnicity and disability are also an issue. Ethnic minorities may have a language barrier and this could likely pose as a problem serving as a judge as they may not be aware of every single word in the English language, making judging less efficient and slower, possibly inaccurate.

⑥ In conclusion, who the judge is as a person can't determine how well they do their job. The judge appointed has passed tests, gained a degree, worked hard and had lots of relative experience to work their way into that position. Therefore, whether they're an old middle-aged British man from Oxbridge or a young, mother of three from Leeds, each has earned the right to be there and is qualified to serve in that position and so we should trust and respect their title and honour that they are there for our benefit.

Examiner commentary

① A strong introduction putting the answer in context. Seren has logically started with a discussion of the stereotypical judge and why this may affect their ability to judge a case impartially. She has also touched upon the key point that it may mean judges are 'out of touch' with reality.

② Seren has identified the correct statistics from the table and also provided some evaluation with a link to whether these statistics are representative of society. As this is an LA2 stimulus response style question, reference to the source is crucially important. The source is there to aid the candidate and, though candidates should not merely repeat what is in the source, they should be advised to use the information to help structure and guide their answer. Seren has done this and presented the main statistics that support the conclusion that judges are not representative and explained how they are better represented in the lower

courts. Good skills demonstrated here.

③ Good evaluation here linking to the above statistics but also explaining that it can't simply be down to education.

④ A sound paragraph touching upon a key reason why women fail to progress as quickly and far as their male counterparts. Seren has done well to cite two main Acts here as legal authority and to evaluate what is being done to try and overcome this.

⑤ Seren has brought in some wider issues here that are not mentioned in the source material. This is important for a sound answer and will make the difference between an 'adequate' and a 'sound' answer.

⑥ A good conclusion here where Seren has summed up that though judges are not representative, this may not affect how well they do their job. A nice end to a very good answer.

Mark awarded:
AO2 – 8
AO3 – 2
Total = 10 out of 11 (91%)

A sound answer that discusses many of the main issues relating to how representative the judiciary is. Seren did particularly well to consider some wider issues not mentioned in the table such as disability and language but she has also used the table to guide her answer and correctly highlighted the main statistics relevant to the question posed. Good reference to key legal terms and authority.

12. Law Reform

Study the text below and answer the questions based on it.

Pressure groups are an important element in promoting the reform of English and Welsh law. They are organisations of people who all believe in the same cause. Whether it is a sectional group, campaigning for personal gain, or a cause working towards a specific cause, they all possess strongly held views and wish to influence some aspect of society. They use many methods to influence including the use of traditional media such as newspapers but more commonly nowadays through the use of electronic media such as the Internet. Other than these, the most common methods they tend to use involve carrying out petitions, distributing leaflets whilst some pressure groups employ professional lobbyists to speak to MPs on the group's behalf.

Source: unattributed

a) Explain, with examples, the role of pressure groups in promoting law reform.

(14 marks)

Tom's answer

① Pressure groups are groups of people who are interest in particular subjects in Law reform and use different tactics to make the Parliament listen to the changes they think should happen. They can be extremely persuasive and the area they are fighting for is normally something the pressure groups are passionate about, so their tactics they use can be very extreme.

② Pressure groups try to influence a change in the law by using some illegal methods. A prime example of this is fathers for justice. They have dressed up as batman and Spiderman and climbed up the Buckingham palace. This gained attention for the fact they wanted to see their children but wasn't legal and so it probably wasn't the best tactic to use to convince a court to allow them to see their children!

③ Other examples of pressure groups are Greenpeace who have also used some illegal methods such as stopping whaling and breaking onto boats in the arctic. They are trying to pressurise the government into changing the law. There are also trade unions that are legally recognised bodies. They try to pressurise the government into changing the law but can also use techniques such as striking.

④ These are just some of the examples that pressure groups use. Other methods that they use include speaking to their MP to see if they have any influence in parliament or doing petitions and getting people to sign it as a way of supporting them. These tactics are not guaranteed to work, especially not the illegal ones.

Examiner commentary

① A limited opening statement merely indicating the role of pressure groups. A brief mention of the fact they can use extreme tactics to persuade parliament to change the law. This point about using methods to influence parliament and law reform is important and needs to be expanded later on.

② A good point made about the Fathers4Justice example. This is a relevant example and Tom has done well to highlight some of the illegal methods they used.

③ Another two good examples of Greenpeace and trade unions. Though these examples are good, it would have been preferable to not answer the question entirely through examples. He needed to give some background information on pressure groups and the methods they use along with their relationship with parliament.

④ Good mention here of some other methods used and an important point discussed about their relationship with parliament.

Mark awarded:
AO1 – 7
AO3 – 1
Total = 8 out of 14 (57%)

This is a 'just' adequate answer at the lower end of the band. There are some errors of expression and Tom doesn't always convey his points clearly or sophisticatedly. He has answered the question mainly through examples and it lacks depth. His answer would have benefited from looking at some areas that pressure groups have successfully influenced. He also needed to examine other methods used to exert pressure.

Seren's answer

① It is essential that domestic law does not stand still and evolve and adapt to be accessible and appropriate for contemporary society. Huge reforms have taken place over the past 100 years especially with regard to:
  – Employment legislation – changes to laws regarding dismissal and equal pay.
  – Social and welfare rights – legal rights of citizens have grown massively since WW2.
  – The equality of women both in marriage and in the workplace. Until 1991 rape was not considered an offence within marriage.

Undoubtedly pressure groups have had a bearing on how laws such as these have evolved.

② There are many and varied pressure groups, they may be multi-caused such as union bodies or professional bodies, and they may be single caused, such as 'Save the Whale', but all use similar processes in an attempt to influence the political process. Examples of pressure groups are:
  – British Medical Association
  – Royal College of Nursing
  – Unions such as Unite
  – Charitable organisations, e.g. Scope, Age Concern
  – Greenpeace and other environmental groups.

③ Pressure groups attempt to influence legislation by lobbying ministers and members of parliament to campaign their cause. Members of groups do not usually seek political office themselves. They may influence by:
– Writing to ministers/mop
– Meeting with ministers/mops
– Sending petition to Downing St
– Attracting media attention
– Sponsoring electoral campaigns
– Block voting as often seen with unions
– Draft proposals for government ministers to view and debate.
The key challenge for pressure groups is to get a minister involved in their cause. Mary Whitehouse championed changes to the pornography industry and censorship with regard especially to young people/children and this eventually led to the Children Act (1977).

④ Once a minister is involved the likelihood of the law evolving is greater through great debate in parliament and public awareness.

⑤ Public awareness of the need for changing or adapting legislation is also a key challenge. The media take up causes and can be very influential on parliament. The media intervention in the Stephen Lawrence case led to reinvestigation of the case and similarly the case of the Birmingham Six, a miscarriage of justice was also led by media because the Home Secretary and the Court of Appeal felt that by reinvestigating the case it may lead to a loss of confidence in the public and the justice system.

⑥ We also see the case of Greenpeace whose battle over GM crops was very visible. The case in question helped ensure parliamentary thinking and legislation about GM crops in the UK. The case was also significant in that although Greenpeace were clearly guilty of the offence, they were acquitted by the jury. This case illustrates how pressure groups such as Greenpeace reflect the public view and help pressurise the government into accepting that law.

⑦ Pressure groups are an influence on parliament. They cannot compel parliament to change the law but they can exert pressure on them to reconsider. They use the media and a variety of other methods (such as Fathers4Justice climbing up Buckingham Palace) to highlight their cause.

Examiner commentary

① A good introduction here by Seren putting her answer in context and highlighting why law reform is needed. It is always advisable to avoid lists in an academic answer, though as will be seen this does not affect Seren's mark greatly due to the high standard of the content. Some good examples given here of where changes have been made as a result of law reform.

② Seren has identified the key word in the question here – pressure groups – and moved her discussion onto these. Good identification of pressure groups as influencing the political process. Like lists, bullet points should also be avoided and continuous prose with paragraphing used. However, some good examples of pressure groups given here.

③ Good identification of some of the techniques used by pressure groups. This answer is unconventional in the style it is written but still has very good content and range. However, it would still be advisable for AO3 to write in continuous prose to allow the 'argument' to flow.

④ Good progression here and relevant legal authority cited.

⑤ Seren has done well here to recognise the importance of getting the public on side and the important role of the media. Two good examples given of where the media have contributed to law reform.

⑥ Another relevant example. Key to this question is being able to cite a range of groups that participate in law reform and demonstrating the changes they have effected. Seren's answer is enhanced by the range of examples she has given and how they have contributed to changing the law.

⑦ This conclusion rounds off Seren's answer nicely. She has focused on the question posed and summarised the main strands of her essay.

Mark awarded:
AO1 – 11
AO3 – 1
Total = 12 out of 14 (86%)

This is a good sound answer that deals with the role of pressure groups and their various tactics to effect law reform. Good understanding demonstrated that pressure groups are influential on parliament and court the media but cannot compel parliament to change the law. Seren did particularly well to give a good range of examples and legal authority to substantiate her answer. As stated in the comments, it would be preferable to avoid using bullets and lists but this does not affect Seren's marks greatly.

b) Evaluate the role of the Law Commission in the law reform process in England and Wales. *(11 marks)*

Tom's answer: Grade C

① The law commission was set up to look at the law as it currently is and make changes as needed. It was set up in 1965 and suggests new laws for the government to make along with getting rid of old and out of date laws. It has some main tasks of passing new laws, getting rid of old laws, consolidating laws, codifying laws and amending existing laws. It has tried to codify the criminal law but hasn't had any success.

② Codifying is where the laws on a topic are put in one place called a code. This is different from our common law system but codes are used in European countries. It doesn't suit our law making style and this is one of the reasons why the commission has not codified the law successfully. Also, the criminal law is such a huge area of law that is was too big a task.

③ The law commission consists of judges, experts and lawyers so they have the subject knowledge to reform areas of law. They either decide on projects that they want to work on or are told by parliament and the Lord Chancellor. They research the area of law and may even write the new law. They sometimes see how a foreign country deals with the same law. When they pass it to parliament they don't always change the law like the commission has suggested. They usually say no and keep the law as it is. The law commission has only led to a few major changes such as the Family Law Act. They haven't had much luck otherwise.

Examiner commentary

① An adequate opening statement where Tom has identified the role of the law commission and some of its main tasks such as proposing new law, amending law and codifying. He has also done well to recognise that they have attempted and failed to codify the criminal law. Tom should ideally have mentioned the Law Commission Act 1965 here and considered its composition (which he does later on).

② He has provided a definition of codification here which is good and draws a comparison with common law countries. This has the potential to be very good but he doesn't develop this point. He could have gone on to explain why it is not suited to our law-making system and some of the main differences between common law systems and codes.

③ This final paragraph is both a conclusion and contains information on the composition of the law commission. It would have been preferable to include detail on the composition at the start. That being said, he has discussed how they undertake a project, albeit in a superficial way. It lacks depth and progression. One relevant example cited of the Family Law Act 1996. He ideally needed several further examples to bring his answer safely into the adequate boundary and push for the sound boundary of marks.

Mark awarded:
AO2 – 6
AO3 – 1
Total = 7 out of 11 (64%) Grade C

This answer is just within the adequate boundary. Tom has demonstrated a superficial understanding of the role of the law commission but has failed to be precise or detailed enough to achieve any higher. The above comments highlight where he needed extra depth and specificity. He also needed a wider range of legal authority to illustrate the success/ failure of the law commission.

Seren's answer

① As mentioned in part (a) it is essential that the Law does not stand still but evolves in a way that makes it accessible and manageable for the modern day.

② In the UK (England and Wales) parliament is able to make whatever laws it chooses under the principle of the supremacy of parliament. Dicey calls this 'parliamentary sovereignty' and is where:
– Parliament can make laws on whatever it wishes
– Judges are expected to accept that law as valid
– Although government cannot bind itself and its successors.

③ Therefore successive governments are constantly creating, amending and repealing legislation. The law therefore becomes messy, confused and liable to misunderstanding and misinterpretation.

④ Thus the Law Commission (LC) was established in 1965 under the Law Commission Act specifically to simplify and modernise the law to make it more accessible and manageable. Their key role is:
– Codify the law
– Consolidate the law
– Remove and repeal obsolete laws
– Simplify the law
– Propose new legislation.

⑤ The LC consists of judges, researchers, civil servants and administration staff.
– They look at a particular area of law they require amending.
– They research that area with experts in the field (e.g. technical experts, BMA, unions).
– They research that area with those the law in that area will affect, e.g. nurses, teachers.
– They then publish a consultation document and include the comments from appropriate bodies.
– They then construct a draft proposal.
– The draft proposal is then sent to parliament for discussion.
– The parliament accepts the new piece of legislation then it is approved.

⑥ However there has been mixed success on terms of the LC function:
– In the first 10 years of its existence, 85% of its proposals were accepted by parliament.
– In the second 10 years only 50% of its proposals were accepted by parliament.
– In 1990, none of its proposals were accepted.

⑦ Parliament's response was that there was not enough time but essentially parliament showed little interest in the proposals.

⑧ The Law Commission sought the help from the Lord Chancellor and some progress was made where:
– Parliament agreed to make a first response within 6 months.
– Parliament agreed to make a final response in 12 months.
– The Jellicoe process aimed to speed up non-confrontational areas of the law.
– The Law Commission agreed that it would at the outset work more collaboratively with ministers.

⑨ However, although this has improved areas, more confrontational areas have been ignored.

⑩ One key area that the LC attempted to change was criminal law from codification. It was a very ambitious project, and indeed many projects have been and therefore its lack of success may not be surprising. Parliament showed little interest in the way the LC attempted to codify all criminal law into one statute.

⑪ The problem with modernising the law is not the case of just bringing the law up to date. 'Modernising Justice', the white paper that established the LC has two meanings. Modernisation also means streamlining or 'leaning' the process. Law is a very complex area and streamlining legislation, producing rigid definitions and commonally may not fit the way in which the justice system works. The judiciary and lawyers need to interpret the law in a flexible manner and not be constrained. The law should remain purposive and making legislation too rigid and streamlined may make a literal approach more common where judges are unable to use wider interpretation.

⑫ So what of the future of the Law Commission? It seems that the majority of 'catch up' work for the LC has been achieved and this I am sure has been of benefit to the justice system. It may be that the LC now reduces its overheads and just concentrates on areas of law that need amending such as where domestic law breaches the European Convention on Human Rights, rather than attempt to simplify the complex.

Examiner commentary

① A brief introduction but still succeeds to put the answer in context. The paragraph below also looks to be part of the introduction.

② Correct discussion of the very important doctrine of parliamentary sovereignty. This links to law reform and the position of the law commission in relation to Parliament.

③ Good focus on the question here. The essay is progressing logically and Seren is making the link between parliamentary sovereignty and law reform.

④ Good mention of this key Act here. And a good summary here incorporating key terms and demonstrating knowledge of the role of the law commission.

⑤ A clear summary of the ways the law commission research an area of law for reform. Here though it would have been preferable to write this in continuous prose and not bullet points. This helps with assessment objective 3 (language and argument) and is good practice for essay writing.

⑥ Good to see some evaluation here on the success/failure of the law commission.

⑦ Another important observation. The law commission plays an advisory role and cannot compel Parliament to change the law, just point it in the right direction.

⑧ Some very good evaluation here especially the point about the Jellicoe process aimed at fast tracking certain Bills. Seren has demonstrated a sound understanding and analysis and focused well on the question posed.

⑩ Seren has done well here to identify the role of the law commission in codifying the law and the limited success it has had in this area.

⑪ A really interesting paragraph where Seren has demonstrated her rounded knowledge referring to concepts within other topics and how they relate to the question in hand. Good opinion presented appropriately. Excellent use of key terms.

⑫ A sound conclusion here with very good focus on the question posed and an offering of substantiated opinion.

Mark awarded:
AO2 – 9
AO3 – 2
Total = 11 out of 11 (100%)

A top sound answer that is an impressive response to the question. A wide, rounded knowledge presented with several wider concepts included. Sound evaluation backed up with reference to legal authority and an excellent range and depth.
Seren has appreciated the need to more than describe but, rather, evaluate the effectiveness of the law commission and its role with Parliament.

13. Statutory Interpretation

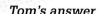

Study the text below and answer the questions based on it.

'... reference to Parliamentary material should be permitted as an aid to the construction of legislation which is ambiguous or obscure or the literal meaning of which leads to an absurdity.'

Lord Browne-Wilkinson in Pepper v Hart (1992)

a) Explain the role of Hansard in the interpretation of statutes.

(14 marks)

Tom's answer

① Hansard is a written document recording everything that is said in Parliament and it is an extrinsic aid to statutory interpretation. It is used to show that not only do the private members agree on the Bill but also Parliament.

② The use of Hansard is shown in the famous case of Pepper v Hart (1992). This shows that you should use Hansard when constructing legislation, as it allows you to get the full meaning of the Bill and avoids absurdity and obscurity. It also allows you to back your evidence on why the Bill went through as Hansard shows Parliament's discussions, which is the authority.

③ Hansard has not always been allowed to be used, because it can take up too much time to refer to it, and there may be parts that the legal professionals cannot understand which will make the result for the defendant unfair. Judges do now use it, though, to find out what Parliament's thoughts were when they were debating the Bill.

Examiner commentary

① There is an understanding of what Hansard is and when it is used, and a hint that it is used to determine Parliament's intention, but there is not enough detail, and no more than a limited knowledge.

② Good use of legal authority; but there is no progression with it; no explanation as to its relevance to the topic or any further explanation of the rules of statutory interpretation that may use Hansard. It is quite obvious that this answer is not long enough to warrant a great deal of marks, though there is some insight into a knowledge of Hansard.

③ There is a hint here that Tom knows Hansard is used with the Mischief Rule/Purposive Approach but there is no direct reference. Had he identified the link, he would have significantly increased his mark.

Mark awarded:
AO1 – 7
AO3 – 1
Total = 8 out of 14 (57%)

Tom clearly lacks the in-depth knowledge of Hansard that is required for this question. He shows a general awareness but by no means understands enough about in its use and the implications of its use.

Seren's answer

① The role of Hansard in the interpretation of statutes is to discover Parliament's intentions and the mischief Parliament was trying to prevent. It is used in conjunction with the Purposive Approach as opposed to the Literal approach which is more concerned with the words of the Act rather than Parliament's intention when passing the Act.

② Hansard is the official record of what was said when the Bill was going through the legislative process and how it was being debated. Hansard contains the underlying reasons why an old Act was not working and the problems with it which led to the creation of the new Act of Parliament. This helps discover Parliament's intention in passing the Act and the mischief it was trying to prevent. Judges interpret statutes where they are not clear and explicit. However, up until 1992 judges were not allowed to access Hansard as an aid to interpretation. It was argued that most often Hansard reported the petty, political squabbles of the Bill being debated and it was unnecessary and a waste of time and would just lead judges to confusion rather than clarity. It was also argued that although Hansard reported the debating of the Bill it would still not effectively and accurately record what was being said and that a point of law could be misunderstood which would lead to absurd and unfair results in the cases the judges were dealing with.

③ However, in the case of Pepper v Hart (1992), it was held that judges could have access to Hansard in the following imposed conditions: judges were looking for statements made by the government minister which enabled them to structure understanding of the Act. Also, judges would only have access to Hansard if they could realistically prevent further confusion in understanding the mischief Parliament was trying to remedy. They could also have access to Hansard when it regarded the Court of Justice of the European Union and the interpreting of a piece of EU Law. Hansard has also been talked about in the case of Wilson v Secretary of State for Trade and Industry (2003) where its use was limited: statements made by a Minister can be used; other statements must be ignored.

④ Hansard is a form of extrinsic aid, with the Purposive Approach and it is criticised for being likely to lead to judicial law making and this does not uphold the constitutional roles of judges as they are only required to apply laws. Also, the use of Hansard can also lead to unreliable and unfair results. On the other hand, it gives judges more discretion and acts as a wider approach to the interpretation of statutes. This opposes the Literal approach and intrinsic aids where it is a popular belief that judges give effect to the words of Parliament rather than promoting the fundamentals of the mischief trying to be prevented by Parliament. However, the Literal Approach is criticised for taking the words of an Act of Parliament too literally and this can lead to harsh results, such as in the case of Railway v Berriman. Overall, European countries prefer the Purposive Approach and this is adapted in their cases.

Examiner commentary

① Immediately, the question is being addressed, with a sentence that shows the examiner Seren knows what she is talking about.

② This is an excellent paragraph which talks about what Hansard is, and importantly why it is criticised and why there is controversy surrounding its use in the interpretation of statutes.

③ This is a key case in the use of Hansard and it is thoroughly explained with the guidance on the use of Hansard detailed. This balances the argument with what was said above. Other cases that have subsequently used Hansard could also have been mentioned, such as Pickstone v Freemans (1988), Davis v Johnson (1979). Also, a little mention

of Lord Denning's relentless arguments for why Hansard should be used..... '... [not to use Hansard] would be to grope around in the dark for the meaning of an Act without switching the light on'. At the end there is an impressive use of the most recent controversy surrounding Hansard; which truly tells the story of the progress surrounding the use of Hansard in court.

④ Here, the candidate is showing that she has a knowledge of the fact that Hansard is commonly used with the Purposive Approach, and why it would not be used with the Literal Approach. This clearly demonstrates a sound knowledge of statutory interpretation and convinces the examiner that she not only has a knowledge but an understanding of the more evaluative elements.

Mark awarded:
AO1 – 13
AO3 – 1
Total = 14 out of 14 (100%)

This is a difficult question and Seren has done well to highlight all the key points relevant to the use of Hansard. She has identified where Hansard is used as an aid and why it is so necessary. More importantly, she has traced the history of the use of Hansard with supporting legal authority.

> ## b) Using your knowledge of statutory interpretation, consider whether an offence has been committed in the situation set out below.
> *(11 marks)*
>
> Great concern was expressed in 2008 about the depletion of fish stocks particularly by ocean going trawlers. As a result Parliament passed the Coastal Waters (Prevention of Fishing) Fictitious Act 2009.
>
> ### Coastal Waters (Prevention of Fishing) Fictitious Act 2009
> Section 1 Any fishing boat under 100 tons which fishes within 5 miles of the coast will require a licence.
> Section 2 Any fishing in coastal waters undertaken in the course of a business and conducted without a licence constitutes a criminal offence.
>
> Walter, who operates a 1000-ton ocean going trawler and is therefore ineligible to hold a licence pays Alison, who holds a licence in respect of a small fishing boat, £10,000, on the understanding that Alison would give him first refusal on all her catches. Alison has returned from a fishing trip with a full catch and offered them to Walter, whereupon he was arrested and charged under the Act. Advise Walter.

Tom's answer

① Statutory Interpretation means the methods which judges use to interpret statutes and make sense of the words of an Act of Parliament.

② Under the Literal Rule, Walter would be not guilty, as taking the literal words of the Act means that Walter has not actually taken part in any fishing. There would be no charge brought under the Golden Rule, as charging Walter under the Act would create an absurdity. Alison should be to blame, licence or no licence as she caught the fish on her boat and sold them, indicating the course of a business.

③ Under the Mischief rule, however, as there is ambiguity, Parliament was trying to limit fishing close to the coast, so a licence was required and if in coastal waters in a business, a licence is required. The overall aim is to prevent over fishing, therefore with Alison accepting a large sum of money in exchange for her catches, this indicates a business and therefore Alison should be charged.

④ The rules of language ejusdem generis, expressio unius est alterius and noscitur a sociss are irrelevant here.

Examiner commentary

③ Even though all rules are confidently applied here Tom has made the classic mistake of not explaining the rules and using case law to support his application. This question is always marked in a strictly mathematical way; and marks are given according to how many rules are convincingly applied, and how many cases are cited to support the application. Tom has not done this, so has immediately denied himself marks.

Mark awarded:
AO2 – 5
AO3 – 1
Total = 6 out of 11 (55%)

Here, Tom would have only been credited with marks for his application of three rules; where he has lost marks is in the explanation of the rules and the supporting case law. It is good exam practice for this topic to use supporting cases as a matter

of course when outlining a rule, even if you feel like you are repeating yourself. The AO2 component tests your application as well as your use of authorities, so it is critical that a detailed critique is provided. Remember this will be one of the most popular questions on the paper; make it your chance to shine!

Seren's answer

① When in court, judges can follow three rules: the Literal Rule, the Golden Rule and the Mischief Rule as well as the Purposive Approach. These rules help judges interpret the law that Parliament passed in order to try and establish and solve the problem that Parliament was aiming to rectify.

② The Coastal Waters (Fictitious) Act 2009 was put into place [2a] to stop people and boats going into coastal waters and fishing for business reasons. If judges applied the Literal Rule, which is when judges follow the exact wording in the Act as seen in the case of Whiteley v Chappel (1968), Walter would be found not guilty as by applying the literal rule, Walter was not actually fishing in the water as s2 states 'any fishing in coastal waters' and Alison holds a licence which does not breach s1. The Literal Rule is useful because it means judges cannot abuse their powers of interpretation. [2b]

③ The judges could also apply the Golden Rule; this is where the judges will apply the Literal Rule, but where that leads to an absurd result, the judge can 'bend' the law to offer a more sensible interpretation,

as seen in the case of Adler v George (1964) where a defendant who had committed an offence under the Official Secrets Act 1981 could have escaped prosecution if the judge had used the Literal Rule. In the present case, Walter can state that he has not committed an offence under the Act as he did not need to own a licence and was not actually fishing himself; however, his intentions were to sell the fish on for his business.

④ The Purposive Approach can also be followed by judges; this is where they look at the Act and decide what Parliament intended. This is an advantage as it does not result in injustice and means that errors in old law can be changed. The disadvantage is that judges are effectively making the law, which is not democratically acceptable as judges are not elected. This rule was used in the case of Magor & St Mellons Rural District Council v Newport Corporation (1950). In the case of Walter, he should be found guilty using this rule as his intentions were wrong even though he did not literally catch the fish in the water, Walter paid Alison to do his work and then his business benefited. The Purposive Approach is the best way to interpret the law as it lets judges apply what Parliament wanted from the Act.

Examiner commentary

② a) It is always good practice to try and identify what you think the intention of Parliament was when they passed the Act. You will not be marked down for getting it wrong, you will be credited for attempting to find the intention

b) This is excellent application of the law to the scenario. Again, your conclusion is not important; what matters is that you show the examiner that you can apply the rule to the scenario. So for every rule, you should:
- Give a definition of the rule
- Cite a supporting case for that rule
- Apply the rule to the scenario –

i.e. would the defendant be guilty or not guilty if the judge applied that rule?

③ Supporting rules with relevant cases is absolutely crucial, and Seren has done well here to do that whilst applying the rule to the scenario.

④ It would be favourable for Seren to apply the Mischief Rule too; and students often make the mistake of thinking the Purposive Approach is the same as the Mischief Rule, and although there are similarities, both rules need to be mentioned in order that the examiner can see a knowledge of all approaches to statutory interpretation.

Mark awarded:
AO2 – 8
AO3 – 2
Total = 10 out of 11 (91%)

This is an excellent answer, with all the key features that examiners are looking for in this type of question:
1. Explanation of the rules
2. Supporting cases
3. Application to the scenario.
Examiners will mark you down if you do not discuss ALL of the rules, and do not use supporting cases when you are applying the law. The fact that Seren has not discussed the Mischief Rule in addition to the other three will have affected her mark slightly. Remember it is not necessarily about ACCURATE application, but evidence that you can apply the rule and come to a sensible conclusion.

14. Statutory Interpretation

Study the text below and answer the questions based on it.

When Parliament has passed an Act, the words of the Act are authoritative as words. In ordinary life, if someone says something that you do not understand, you ask for a fuller explanation. This is impossible with the interpretation of statutes because only the words of the Act have passed through the legal machinery of law making and individual Members of Parliament cannot be put into the witness-box to supplement or interpret what has been formally enacted.

Source: Glanville Williams: Learning the Law (13th ed; A.T.H. Smith)

a) Outline the ways in which the courts have interpreted statutes.

(14 marks)

Tom's answer

① Ways in which the courts have to interpret statutes are through the literal rule, golden rule and mischief rule.

② The literal rule states that you have to use the literal and natural meaning of the words given in the statute. So a court has to follow this rule and use the correct meaning of the words in a case.

③ The golden rule is if the literal gives an absurd result they can then take it through this rule to give a better meaning and result. They are looking for a reasonable result.

④ The mischief rule was set out in Heydon's case and there are 3 parts:
 – What the statute is trying to solve,
 – What mischief it is trying to overcome and
 – What remedy it wants to put in place.

⑤ An advantage of the literal rule is that it provides parliamentary sovereignty. A disadvantage is that it can give absurd results. A case to illustrate the literal rule is Whiteley v Chappel where a man pretended to be a dead person. The Act said it was an offence to pretend to someone else when voting but the defendant had pretended to be a dead person and a dead person is not entitled to vote so he hadn't done anything wrong.

⑥ An advantage of the golden rule is that it stops absurdity but a disadvantage is that the judges are the ones to decide if it is absurd or not. An advantage of the mischief rule is that it looks for the intention of parliament but a disadvantage is that it again leaves flexibility to judges and not parliament.

⑦ The judge can also use internal aids such as headings and titles and external aids. These include things like Hansard, textbooks and precedent. The judge can also use rules of language like ejusdem generis.

Examiner commentary

① A brief introduction here. Tom would have done better if he had given a concise introduction outlining some of the reasons why judges need to interpret statues. This would have put his answer in context. However, he has done well to identify the three rules available, though as will be seen, this is not all that is needed for this question. It is a common error to leave out the purposive approach as the fourth rule but this is required to gain all of the available marks.

② Good to see an explanation of the literal rule. This is broadly correct though the final sentence implies a judge has to use this rule which isn't correct.

③ Good explanation of the golden rule and how it relates to the literal rule.

④ Not quite correct but Tom has got the general gist of the rule.

⑤ Tom has done well to include a case here to demonstrate the use of the literal rule. He has given the correct and full case title and the correct facts, though not always well expressed. It is important to include a case for each of the four rules of interpretation for a statutory interpretation question. Tom has also provided an advantage and a disadvantage of the literal rule here. This is again good practice and should be provided for each of the four rules.

⑥ Good discussion of some advantages and disadvantages of the golden and mischief rules here but Tom has not included a case for each of these rules. It is essential to include a case for each rule. If a student cannot remember the case title, they should include the facts of the case and how it demonstrates use of the rule of interpretation. This will still gain most of the available credit.

⑦ Tom has done well to identify some of the other aids available but has not expanded on them. It is important, with a statutory interpretation question, to identify what the question is asking. This question is asking very generally for the 'ways' that judges interpret statutes. This requires a student to discuss:
 ▪ The four rules of interpretation (literal, golden, mischief, purposive, with a case for each).
 ▪ The internal aids.
 ▪ The external aids (particularly Hansard).
 ▪ Three rules of language.
 ▪ Presumptions.

Other questions may only require students to discuss one or two of the above aspects so be careful to read the question carefully.

Mark awarded:
AO1 – 7
AO3 – 1
Total = 8 out of 14 (57%)

Tom's answer is in the lower end of 'adequate'. It covers the 3 rules of interpretation and though giving a superficial explanation, does so correctly. He does well to provide one case example for the literal rule but needs a case for the golden and mischief too. It is a common error to leave out a discussion of the purposive approach. This would be required to gain all of the marks available. Tom has briefly mentioned the other aids available (such as internal, external, etc.) but only does so briefly with little explanation and no examples. It is important with questions that ask about all of the aids judges can use, to fully address these other aids explaining and giving examples.

Seren's answer

① When an Act is passed, the statute uses particular words that sometimes have to be interpreted by judges. This may be because the wording is unclear or inadequate or because a vague term is used like vehicles. A few decades ago, statutes were mainly interpreted through the literal rule which establishes what Parliament were saying through their literal words used, but now judges have a wider range of approaches.

② First, they have the literal rule which takes the words literally, grammatically, their plain meaning. A case to illustrate this is Fisher and Bell. This was a case that is most intriguing and emphasises the faults that the literal rule can sometimes have. After several knife attacks with flick knives, the Restriction of Offensive Weapons Act was amended to state that it was an offence to 'sell or offer for sale' flick knives. Fisher owned a shop and in the shop window was a flick knife. The court established that the literal of 'offer for sale' should be used. The court said that Fisher was merely giving an 'invitation to treat' and not an 'offer to sell' in the contract law sense and therefore no offence had been committed. Absurdity is the key of this case. The literal meaning can sometimes cause an absurd result and an unjust conclusion. The advantage is that it is respecting the words of parliament as in Whiteley v Chappel and parliament is sovereign.

③ When the literal rule does produce an absurdity, the judge can turn to the golden rule. This allows him to look at a reasonable meaning instead of the absurd one. A case to show this is Adler v George. The Official Secrets Act stated that it was an offence to cause a nuisance 'in the vicinity of an army base'. In this case, the man was inside the army base. The literal meaning of 'in the vicinity of' is around and not inside and so if the judge used the literal rule, he would have got away with it. But the judge decided to take a reasonable meaning and decided this was not what Parliament had meant using the golden rule to decide that the statute included around and inside. The golden rule promotes just results and represents a reasonable meaning, but does give the judge the power to decide what is absurd and not.

④ The mischief rule looks deeper into the reasons for passing the statute to begin with. It was laid down in Heydon's case and looks for the intention of parliament and the 'mischief' that parliament was intending to overcome by passing the Act. This can be seen in the case of Smith v Hughes where a prostitute was tapping on her first floor bedroom window trying to attract men on the street. The Act said that it was an offence to 'solicit' people 'on the street'. She wasn't on the street as she was in her bedroom on the first floor. The judge decided that the Act was passed to stop people being bothered as they walked down the street and she was convicted. The advantage of this rule is that it looks for parliament's intention but gives lots of power to the judge.

⑤ The purposive approach has increased since we joined the European Union as it is more suited to EU style laws. It is very similar to the mischief rule and looks for the 'purpose' of the Act.

⑥ The judge also has internal aids to help him which are found in the Queen's Printers copy of the Act. They include headings, preamble, schedules, etc.

⑦ The judge can also use external aids. These are outside the Act. They include Hansard which is a daily record of Parliamentary debate. This has not always been allowed. It was not until the case of Pepper v Hart that judges were finally allowed to use Hansard. Other external aids are dictionaries, articles, human rights and textbooks.

⑧ Judges also have rules of language to help them interpret some words in the Act. One is called, ejusdem generis and this means general words which follow specific ones mean the same kind of thing. Another rule of language is expression unius which means if one thing is mentioned in an Act, everything else is excluded. The last rule of language is the noscitur rule where words draw meaning from the other words around. All of the above aids can be used by a judge and he has the choice over the ones he wants to use.

⑨ There are also presumptions such as the statutes do not affect the Queen.

Examiner commentary

① Seren has given an introduction here to put her answer in context. She has identified some of the reasons why judges may need to interpret statutes, which is good. There have been questions previously based entirely on the reasons why judges need to interpret statutes.

② This is a very good explanation of the literal rule. Seren has clearly explained the rule and incorporated a case as an example. This is a good approach with questions such as this and a case is needed for each of the four rules. Seren has provided some wider detail by including an advantage and a disadvantage of the rule.

③ Good progression onto the golden rule. A logical structure and a sound understanding demonstrated. Seren has given a good explanation of the case and how it demonstrates use of the golden rule.

④ Another sound explanation and case identified. Seren is thus far, providing a balanced answer.

⑤ I am pleased to see Seren has included the purposive approach here as all four rules are required to gain all of the marks available. Ideally she would have included a case for the purposive but due to the range of other material she has included and the fact she has a case for the other three rules, she will not lose too much credit for this.

⑥ Good identification here of some internal aids and where they are found. It is important, due to the wording of this question, to include all the aids available to judges, not just the rules of interpretation.

⑦ A good paragraph considering the time constraints. Seren has done well to discuss Hansard and include the point about it not being permitted until Pepper v Hart. There have been questions in the exam that focus entirely on Hansard for a 14-mark question, so bear this in mind. This would require a much more detailed discussion of Hansard and the progression of its permitted use.

⑧ Seren has provided a really good range in question 1 and she has understood that there is a time limit to the question, skimming over some points but still demonstrating range and spending longer on more important points such as the rules of interpretation. This is inevitable due to the volume of information required for questions of this nature. However, the marks are easily achievable with the correct formula:

- Four rules plus case plus advantages/ disadvantages for each.
- Rules of language (Latin terms plus explanation).
- Internal aids with examples.
- External aids (particularly Hansard with at least case of Pepper v Hart) plus other examples of external aids.
- Presumptions explanation with examples.

⑨ An afterthought but still important and would gain credit.

Mark awarded:
AO1 – 13
AO3 – 1
Total = 14 out of 14 (100%)

This is a top sound answer that deals with all of the aids available to judges to help them interpret statutes. Though not perfect, Seren has been able to gain all the marks available due to the range contained in her answer and the array of legal authority to substantiate.

---

b) Using your knowledge of statutory interpretation, consider whether an offence has been committed in the situation set out below. *(11 marks)*

The Prevention of Unwanted Parties (Fictitious) Act (2009)

Section 1(1) – This Act applies to a gathering on land for a social purpose in which it is likely that alcohol will be consumed and more than 100 people will attend.

Section 1(2) – Subject to Section 1(3), it is a criminal offence to organise such a gathering without the permission of a local magistrate unless the organiser is an exempt person.

Section 1(3) – For this purpose, an exempt person means the occupier, any member of his family or his employee or agent of his.

Emma's best friend Lucy is abroad on holiday. Emma emailed a few friends to attend her 18th birthday party in a disused barn on Lucy's parents' farm land. Emma expected 20 people to attend. However, the email invitation was copied and 1,000 people arrive in a large crowd. Emma has now been arrested for breach of the Act. Advise Emma.

Tom's answer

① Under the literal rule Emma may be charged as in section 1(1) it states that it is a criminal offence to organise such a gathering without the permission of a local magistrate or the family. Under s.1(3) she is not an exempt person either as she isn't the occupier of the land or family. She is just a friend.

② Under the golden rule she may not be charged as she actually personally only invited 20 people and she didn't know that more people would come. But she was still using land she didn't have permission to use.

③ Under the mischief rule she may be charged as she organised the party for 20 but more turned up. But what is the aim of the Act? It may be to stop large parties without the land owner's permission. If Emma is convicted it may make people more careful about who they invite. There have been cases where people have arranged a party on Facebook and thousands of people have turned up. It may make people more careful.

④ I think Emma could probably get away with this as she had only intended to invite 20 people even though more turned up. She didn't actually know everyone else. But she could still be charged as she was using somebody else's land even if she did know the daughter.

Examiner commentary

① Tom has done well here to identify the relevant parts of the statute that may apply here. He has also done well to identify and apply the literal rule, though he needed further depth on the explanation of this rule and how it applies. Cases are important in this part, too, and therefore despite maybe including them in part a) above, they should be mentioned again here.

② Good identification of the golden rule but limited explanation on how it applies and why a judge might progress from the literal to the golden. As with the point above, no case law cited.

③ A good comparison with the unlawful 'Facebook' parties. Tom has done well to identify the mischief rule as it is important to define and apply all four rules (Tom, however, only applies three). He needs to explain more about how this rule would apply to the facts and again he needs some legal authority. Tom should then progress to apply the purposive approach as application of all four rules is required to achieve the 'sound' boundary.

④ Tom has provided a conclusion here but hasn't concluded on which rule of interpretation would be likely to give this conclusion. It is important not to give a 'common sense' answer but a legal one by referring to legal concepts.

Mark awarded:
AO2 – 5
AO3 – 1
Total = 6 out of 11 (55%)

This answer is the top end of limited boundary. Though Tom has done well to identify the three rules of interpretation, he has not demonstrated an adequate understanding of how they apply. His conclusion is confused. He successfully identified the correct parts of the given statute but has not logically worked through the rule to reach a conclusion on each one. In addition he has not substantiated with reference to any legal authority nor discussed the purposive approach.

Seren's answer

① The Prevention of Unwanted Parties Act 2009 was established to stop parties getting out of hand. The literal interpretation which takes words literally, would find Emma being guilty. This approach was used in Whiteley v Chapell. This can be seen through section 1 as she has more than 100 people attending her party and it can be assumed that there will be alcohol as it is her 18th birthday party and it is a 'social gathering'. Also, section 1(2) she did not get the permission of local magistrates. But, if you applied the literal meaning to section 1(3) she may be able to get away with it as she could be classed as an 'exempt person'. However, it is not clear if Emma would be excluded as the Act says 'the occupier, any member of the occupier's family or his employee or agent of his'. As Emma is Lucy's (who if the occupier's daughter) best friend, she is not excluded. So, under the literal rule, Emma would probably be found guilty.

② But is this absurd? It seems to be a mistake and Emma did not mean for so many people to attend. But she is still likely to be found guilty under the golden rule as none of the other sections seem to offer her a way out and so the judge can't take a wider 'reasonable' meaning of the statute as a whole as in the case of Maddox v Storer.

③ The mischief rule may provide some more flexibility as this looks for the mischief the Act was intending to overcome as in the case of Smith v Hughes. In this case, the Act wants to stop large parties with alcohol and nuisances without magistrate's permission. If this is the aim of the Act, she may still be found guilty. However, they may take into account the fact she didn't want to do anything wrong and it is a mistake. There is a presumption that you always need mens rea (guilty mind) and she hasn't intended to do anything wrong so she may get away with it under the mischief rule. The same would be applied under the purposive approach as this is not the purpose of the Act to convict people of mistakes. But we don't know which rule the judge will use.

Examiner commentary

① The key approach with questions such as this (known as 'application of the law' or 'legal scenario' questions) is to apply a range of aids available. It is never clear (unless bound by precedent) which rule a judge will follow, therefore students need to explore all options before concluding on the most sensible approach. This normally involves a student working through each of the four rules from literal to golden, to mischief and purposive, drawing in any other aids as needed and discussing what the conclusion should be under each rule.

Logical application of the literal rule here. Seren has taken each section under which Emma could be charged and applied the literal rule reaching a conclusion. She has identified the key points of her not being included within s.1(3) as an exempt person. There are also some facts that we are unsure of, such as whether alcohol was consumed. It is ok to make assumptions based on the facts or also it is ok to state that more information would be needed in order to give a full answer. The key trick to tackling these scenarios is for each rule/aid:

1. Define rule/aid
2. give a case to illustrate
3. apply to facts
4. conclude

② Seren has done well here to progress through the literal onto the golden rule. She has recognised that the literal result may be absurd but that the golden rule may not be able to substitute a reasonable meaning. In fact, it could be argued the literal is not absurd but the outcome of the student's interpretation is not as crucial to get correct as it is to apply and evaluate the application of the four rules. It is important to show an understanding of how the rules may apply, backing up with case law for each of the rules/aids if applicable.

③ Good application of these other two rules. Well worked through and applied to the facts. A good approach and level of discussion for this case. Seren could have also applied the expressio rule of language as Emma is not expressly mentioned as an excluded person.

Mark awarded:
AO2 – 8
AO3 – 2
Total = 10 out of 11 (91%)

This is a good sound answer that applies all four rules of interpretation. This is key for the problem scenario part b) questions on LA2 for statutory interpretation. Seren has applied all four and given authority to support for three of them. This is sufficient to achieve a mark in the 'sound' band. She could also have brought in the expressio rule of language as Emma is not mentioned as an excluded person. Had she done this, she could have achieved full marks.

15. European Union: Sources of Law

Study the text and answer the questions based on it.

House of Commons Written Answer June 2010

Lisa Nandy: To ask the Secretary of State for Business, Innovation and Skills whether he plans to seek any amendment to the EU Agency Workers Directive. [1659]

Mr Davey: The Agency Workers Directive was proposed by the European Commission in 2002, it was finally adopted by the European Council of Ministers in June 2008 and by the European Parliament in October 2008.

The final version of the Directive was published in December 2008 and has to be implemented by all Member States into national law by December 2011. Therefore we do not intend to seek any amendment as the Directive has already been finalised.

The Directive does foresee a review by the European Commission in December 2013 in consultation with Member States and social partners at European level to review the application of the Directive. This may result in proposals for amendments. This is normal practice for similar Directives.

Source: Parliament website (June 14 2010)

a) Explain the role of European Directives in English and Welsh law. *(14 marks)*

Tom's answer

① The role of European Directives in English and Welsh law is to fulfil the wishes of the EU. The Directive set out by the EU will all be expected to be set out within a time limit and an eventual date in the Member State, they are not primary but secondary as they are done second hand. They can be used to update the law in a little way but not a major way like treaties which I will discuss in the second part.

② Directives are instructions to Member States to do something in a certain time limit. Member States have to do this because it is part of being a Member State of the EU. A case that shows this is the Tachographs case where lorry drivers in the UK should have had tachograph machines which record how fast they have gone and for how long. They are to make roads safer. However the UK didn't force lorry drivers to have tachographs as the Directive said so they were fined.

③ Member States have to listen to the EU. Their law has become second to it. I don't think this is right as we are all individual countries, though we don't have the euro. European law has to all be the same in 28 different countries which can be difficult to do as this countries may be very different.

Examiner commentary

① Tom has demonstrated a limited understanding here. He has recognised that Directives are secondary and time-bound but has not expressed himself clearly and has jumbled some of his explanation.

② Tom has made several points in this paragraph but each lacks clear explanation. He has done well to refer to a relevant case and has indicated he has an understanding of the requirements of Member States to implement Directives.

He doesn't, however, include key concepts such as direct effect and any case law in relation to this.

③ Tom has begun to consider the position of EU law as supreme over domestic law, which is important, but his answer lacks specificity and legal authority. He also makes the mistake of giving personal opinion rather than focusing on the question posed.

Mark awarded:
AO1 – 6
AO3 – 1
Total = 7 out of 14 (50%)

This is a 'limited' answer. There are some errors of expression and Tom doesn't convey his points clearly or sophisticatedly. There is a general lack of legal authority with only one case mentioned. He does highlight the position of Directives as a source of EU law and does show he has an understanding of the general, basic principles but that is it.

Seren's answer

① Directives are a form of secondary EU legislation. They are not directly applicable and require implementation by the Member State. In the UK, this can be done either by passing an Act of Parliament or a piece of delegated legislation like a statutory instrument. Member States usually have a time limit in which to pass Directives, but the Directive must be clear and precise and leave no room for discretion.

② A case that demonstrates this is Re: Tachographs v UK. In this case, a Directive made it compulsory for Member States to require their lorry drivers to install tachograph machines in their lorries. These record the speed and distance travelled with the aim of improving road safety. The UK had failed to implement the Directive and they were fined.

③ Directives are only binding on who they are addressed to and so they only have vertical direct effect as they need to be implemented by the Member State government. Only they have control over their implementation. The case that decided this was Van Duyn. It would be unfair for a Directive to have horizontal direct effect as ordinary people or companies can't control whether they are passed or not.

④ Vertical direct effect is where the rights given in the law are enforceable against government (the state) but horizontal direct effect is where they are enforceable against other people and companies.

⑤ Another case that demonstrated that Directives can only have vertical effect is Marshall v Southampton Health Authority. In this case, Mrs Marshall wanted to continue to work until she was 65 but was made to retire at 62. This discriminated against women. She was able to continue to work until 65 as she could rely on her rights in a Directive to treat men and women equally. The NHS is the 'state' and so Directives which have vertical direct effect can be enforced against them.

Examiner commentary

① A good opening paragraph demonstrating the position of Directives as secondary legislation. Seren has done well to state that they require further implementation and also that they can be implemented in the UK by either statute or statutory instrument. She also begins to consider direct effect.

② Seren has used a good case here to demonstrate the impact of not implementing a Directive.

③ Seren has provided some good explanation and analysis here and has understood a difficult concept of Directives only having vertical direct effect. She has also cited, though not expanded the relevant case of Van Duyn.

④ Seren has done well here to provide some extra explanation of vertical and horizontal direct effect. Not a brilliant explanation but generally correct.

⑤ Another good use of a key case to demonstrate the vertical effect of Directives. She has understood the facts and linked them to the principle of direct effect.

Mark awarded:
AO1 – 11
AO2 – 1
Total = 12 out of 14 (86%)

This is a sound answer that demonstrates a very good knowledge and understanding of Directives and their effect. Seren has demonstrated a good understanding of the key concepts of vertical and horizontal direct effect and substantiated with a good range of legal authority. Some points could have been more fully explained hence the award of 11 and not 13 for this question.

b) Evaluate the primary and secondary sources of EU law.
(11 marks)

Tom's answer

① As I have said above Directives are a secondary type of EU law. They are instructions to Member States to do something in a time limit.

② There are also other sources of EU law. First there are Treaties like the Treaty of Rome. These are the highest laws and are primary too. They are signed by all the heads of government in the EU. They apply in all Member States and people can rely upon them as they are part of our law. A law example is that you can't discriminate between men and women.

③ The European Union was set up originally to stop another world war and to improve relationships between the countries in Europe.

④ The next source of regulations and these are also primary. These are like our acts of parliament and they apply to all Member States, if there is a UK law that says one thing and an EU law that says another, we have to follow the EU law. A regulation example is that we can rely on rights given in Directives automatically. There are also decisions as a source of law.

⑤ Directives are secondary as I have considered above. There are a range of cases that show that EU law is dominant over Acts of Parliament. One case is about the Spanish fishermen who came to the UK to steal our fish as they had fished all of their fish for the year. They were banned but then won a case and allowed to fish in the UK. This case shows that EU law is dominant over UK law.

Examiner commentary

① This is a common mistake where students refer back to something they discussed in the other 'part' of the answer. There is no 'cross credit' available so, students should discuss in both parts if required by the demands of the question. This question is asking about primary and secondary sources of law and therefore Directives need to be included.

② Tom has identified Treaties as a source of law and has also understood how they come about (at a basic level). He has suggested an area of law they have impacted upon but has failed to expand on this and provide any legal authority. There are a range of cases to demonstrate that 'you can't discriminate between men and women' and Tom needed to substantiate his answer with reference to legal authority.

③ A bit of a random sentence. This is not relevant to the question posed.

④ Tom has identified another two sources of EU law in the form of regulations and decisions. He has also correctly considered that they take precedence over domestic law if there is a conflict. In the final sentence, he seems to be suggesting that regulations have direct effect but doesn't do this explicitly, nor make his understanding clear. This would require much further expansion to achieve more marks.

⑤ Tom is referring in a rather confused way to the Factortame case. He is not incorrect in including this case but has not demonstrated his understanding very well. His expression is limited and confused.

Mark awarded:
AO2 – 5
AO3 – 1
Total = 6 out of 11 (55%)

Tom's answer is again 'limited'. He has not developed his points and, though he has done well to consider the main sources of EU law. His answer seems to suggest that he understands the supremacy of EU law but is not substantiated with reference to any legal authority other than a mention of the Factortame. This is an important case but it needs to be better explained.

Seren's answer

① In the UK, primary sources of law are Acts of Parliament. Secondary laws are statutory instruments and bye laws. The EU has a similar system. Primary laws are Treaties and Regulations and secondary sources are Directives and Decisions. In this essay, I am going to look at the effect of these sources of law.

② Treaties are the highest source of EU law. They are directly applicable, meaning they become part of the law of the Member State as soon as they are passed with Member States not needing to do anything else. An example of a Treaty is the Treaty of Rome or the recent Treaty on the Functioning of the European Union. Treaties have both vertical and horizontal direct effect, meaning that the laws in the Treaties can be enforced against the state and against other individuals or companies. A case that shows this is Mcarthys v Smith. Mrs Mcarthy was being paid less than the man who had her job before. This was clear discrimination against women. She therefore asked for equal pay. The Treaty of Rome says men and women should be treated equally for doing the same work. Even though there was no UK law protecting her, she could still get the Treaty right.

③ Regulations are the next source of law. They are like Acts of Parliament. If there is a conflict, Regulations are supreme. They have limited the parliamentary sovereignty of each Member State. They have both vertical and horizontal direct effect. A case that shows this is the Italian farmer.

④ Directives, as discussed above, only have vertical effect as decided in the Van Duyn case. They have to be implemented by Member States so it would be unfair for them to be enforceable against other people or companies. This is also demonstrated in the Marshall v Southampton case where she was allowed to continue to work until she was 65.

⑤ Lord Denning described the way EU law was affecting UK law as like an 'incoming tide'. He said this because EU law now applies directly in the UK without the government needing to do anything. S.2(1) of the European Communities Act 1972 says that EU law is supreme. A key case to show this in the UK is the Factortame case. This case was about Spanish fishermen who appealed against the Merchant Shipping Act preventing them from setting up business in the UK. In the case, it was the first time a UK Act of Parliament had been set aside in favour of the EU competition policy.

⑥ It can be seen that EU law has a great impact on the law of the Member States of the EU. There are primary and secondary sources but either way, they are supreme over the law of that country. Lots of people don't agree with this.

Examiner commentary

① A good opening paragraph here where she has set out the position of the different sources of EU law. She has also compared with UK sources to draw comparisons.

② A very good paragraph where Seren has shown an understanding about Treaties. She has included key terms such as direct applicability, vertical and horizontal direct effect. She has also done well to provide two examples of Treaties and a correct, well-explained case.

③ Seren doesn't seem to remember the Leonesio case here. She has used a good tactic here of mentioning a case where she can't remember the name. Students should be encouraged to do this when they cannot remember the case name.

She could have explained this case further though.

④ Though Seren has referred to work she discussed in part a), she has repeated the main points here. This is important as there is no 'cross credit' available.

⑤ A very good paragraph incorporating a good deal of relevant information. This is good within the time limit and conditions. She has done well to mention s.2(1) and also Lord Denning's comments. She also did well to cite the Factortame case as legal authority. This provides good focus on the question and has provided some good evaluation of the sources of EU law.

⑥ Good to see a conclusion as this is an essay question.

Mark awarded:
AO2 – 9
AO3 – 2
Total = 11 out of 11 (100%)

A sound answer that discusses many of the issues relating to the question. She has successfully considered each source of law and, though not a perfect answer, she has done enough to warrant full marks. Her answer has a good range and correct reference to key legal terms and authority that demonstrate a good underlying understanding of EU law and direct effect.

Index